The People's

Other titles by Polygon

Elegies for the Dead in Cyrenaica   Hamish Henderson

*Radical Renfrew: Poetry from the French Revolution
    to the First World War*   Tom Leonard (ed.)

*An Aghaidh na Siorraidheachd (In the Face of Eternity):
    Eight Gaelic Poets*   Christopher Whyte (ed.)

Salutations: Collected Poems 1960–89   Alan Jackson

St Nynia   John MacQueen

Scotland Before History   Stuart Piggott

*Kings, Queens and People's Palaces: An oral history
    of the Scottish Music Hall 1920–1970*   Vivien Devlin (ed.)

Voices from the Spanish Civil War   Ian MacDougall

Voices from the Hunger Marches   Ian MacDougall

Odyssey: The Second Collection   Billy Kay (ed.)

The Eclipse of Scottish Culture   Craig Beveridge and Ronald Turnbull

Towards Independence: Essays on Scotland   Paul Scott

A Claim of Right for Scotland   Owen Dudley Edwards et al.

Archaic Cosmos   Emily Lyle

The People's Past

Edited by Edward J. Cowan

Polygon
EDINBURGH

© Polygon, Edward J. Cowan and
individual contributors, 1980.

Prepared for publication by Bruce Young, Clare
McKeown, Jennifer McDowell and Robert Sutherland.

First published in 1980 by
EUSPB,
1 Buccleuch Place,
Edinburgh.

This edition published in 1991 by
Polygon, 22 George Square, Edinburgh.

Reprinted 1993.

Set in Palatino by Koinonia, Bury and
printed and bound Great Britain
by Bell and Bain Ltd, Glasgow.

ISBN 0 7486 6157 3

CONTENTS

LIST OF ILLUSTRATIONS

Neil Gow, by Raeburn, painted in 1806

Penny Wedding, by David Allan, painted in 1818

Children Drawing, by Geikie

Highland Piper, by Geikie

James Livingston (town piper in Haddington) with Andrew Simpson (drummer), c. 1770. An engraving by George Mabon of a painting by Robert Mabon, a local artist. From William Forbes Gray and James A. Jamieson: *A Short History of Haddington.* Edinburgh, 1944, p. 98. (By kind permission of the National Library of Scotland.)

Pig playing a bagpipe with a single drone, carved in stone; Melrose Abbey, 14th century. From John Graham Dalyell's *Musical Memories of Scotland,* Edinburgh, 1849, Plate XVI. (By kind permission of the National Library of Scotland.)

Engraving of *The Bagpiper,* a painting by Sir David Wilkie, R.A., painted in 1813.

Neil Gow and *Penny Wedding* reprinted by kind permission of the National Galleries of Scotland.

INTRODUCTION

At the close of Grassic Gibbon's *Sunset Song* the minister describes those who died during the Great War as 'the last of the Peasants, the last of the Old Scots Folk. A new generation comes up that will know them not, except as a memory in song. It was the old Scotland that perished then, and we may believe that never again will the old speech and the old songs, the old curses and the old benedictions, rise but with alien effort to our lips.' For well over two hundred years now the imminent demise of the Scottish Folk tradition has been confidently predicted. As a Gaelic prophecy has it, 'the feather of the goose would drive the memory from man'. Despite the pessimism Folk has survived, though it has been curiously ignored by Scottish historians.

The rot perhaps set in with that most influential, and somewhat overrated, of Enlightenment historians, William Robertson. He dismissed 'the fabulous tales of ignorant chroniclers' and actually advocated as desirable the total neglect of the first millenium of Scottish history, 'a region of pure fable and conjecture'. Even as he wrote, Dr John Gregory was discovering the wealth of the Scottish tradition. 'There are two different species of music with us,' he observed in 1763, 'one for the learned in the science, and one for the vulgar.' This latter – folk music – was 'perfectly well fitted to inspire that joyous mirth suited to dancing and a plaintive melancholy attendant on distress in love; both original in their kind, and different from every other in Europe'. The literary and historical richness of the vernacular tradition was widely recognised for the first time in the published collections of the period though the words were often unfortunately separated from the tunes. The growth of literacy, however, posed a further threat to the tradition. Robert Burns, who rescued much folk material for posterity, warned:

1

> A chiel's amang you takin notes
> An faith he'll prent it.

James Hogg's mother, in a deservedly oft-quoted passage, berated Sir Walter Scott for his effort to record the passing tradition.

> There war never ane o my sangs prentit till ye prentit them yoursel and ye hae spoilt them awthegither. They were made for singing an no for readin: but ye hae broken the charm noo, and they'll never be sung mair.

At the same time the near-superstitious reverence for print in nonliterate or semi-literate communities – 'if it's in a book it *must* be right' – almost ruined the custom of oral transmission. Yet in Scotland, with a few honourable exceptions, comparatively little attention has been paid to such problems.

At an early stage in the planning of the first Edinburgh Folk Festival the organisers invited representatives of Edinburgh University and the Workers' Educational Association to mount an 'academic fringe'. In response, staff of the School of Scottish Studies provided a series of daily seminars. The WEA and the University's Departments of Scottish History and Extra-Mural Studies organised a series of lunchtime talks on various aspects of Folk as well as a day conference on the subject of 'The People's Past', designed to investigate the place of Scottish Folk in Scottish History. To the knowledge of the organisers no such previous survey had been attempted. Their problems were compounded by the fact that many experts on folk are so thirled to the oral tradition as to be possessed of a certain antipathy towards the idea of communicating their knowledge through the medium of the written word. Over a period of weeks and months a programme was eventually hammered out over a few pints in such appropriate establishments as Sandy Bell's, which can claim to be one of the temples of the Scottish folk revival .

The contributors to this volume make no claims to be definitive or exhaustive in the treatment of their chosen topics. What they have in common is a love of folk and a willingness to carry out investigations in the context of their individual disciplines and specialisms. Editorial policy has been to preserve as far as possible the individual flavours, not to say the idiosyncrasies, of the papers now presented.

The editor compounded problems of publication by departing for Canada in the course of arranging the material. Special thanks are therefore tended to Bruce Young of EUSPB and to Bonnie Edwards for their much-valued help and forebearance in coping with the contingencies of transatlantic communication. Sincere gratitude is also owed to all who assisted with publicity and to the musicians who evocatively illustrated these papers when they were first delivered. Lastly, the greatest debt is due to the people who actually attended the talks, the seminars, the conference and the festival itself – the enduring folk without whose support no achievement is possible.

University of Guelph,
Ontario.   EDWARD J. COWAN

'It Was In You That It A' Began'

Some thoughts on the Folk Conference

HAMISH HENDERSON

Scotland, which with MacPherson's *Ossian*, Burns and the eighteenth and early nineteenth-century ballad collections, played a significant part in the growth of European Romanticism, has also in recent years served as a lively and populous cross-causeway for the modern 'folk' revival. The reasons are not far to seek. Unlike its larger neighbour, Scotland has never had the good fortune to develop a fairly unified homogeneous culture; it has always been an ethnic 'debatable land' in which different and sometimes mutually hostile traditions and languages have cohabited – at best in uneasy symbiosis, and at worst in a state of trigger-happy armed conflict. No wonder the political cause – Jacobitism – which served as a focus for the nation's aspirations and fantasies in the early eighteenth century was a mottled mixed-up affair in which the designs and motives of all parties seem as often as not highly ambiguous.

Anyone who reads the letter which 'Bobbing John', the Earl of Mar (who raised King James VIII's standard in 1715), sent from Invercauld to the bailie of Kildrummy in September of that year will catch a depressing glimpse of the drab reality behind the tuppence-coloured pageantry of the 'Chevalier's Muster-roll':

> Jocke,
> Ye was in the right not to come with the 100 men ye sent up to-night, when I expected four times the number. It is a pretty thing, when all the Highlands of Scotland are now rising up on their king and country's account, as I have accounts from them since they were with me, and the gentlemen of our neighbouring

Lowlands expecting us down to join them, that my men should be only refractory ... I have used gentle means too long, and so I shall be forced to put other orders I have in execution ... let my own tenants in Kildrummy know, that if they come not forth with their best arms, I will send a party immediately to burn what they shall miss taking from them; and they may believe this not only a threat, but, by all that's sacred, I'll put it in execution, let my loss be what it will, that it may be an example to others ... Your assured friend and servant,

MAR.

A letter from Rob Roy MacGregor to General Alexander Gordon (the Marquis of Huntly), written a month later, tells much the same story:

... He [Locheil] has met with such difficulties in raising his men in Morven, who are threatened by Argyle's friends to be used with utmost rigour, if they rise with their chief; he is so fatigued and angered with them, that he is rather to be pitied than quarrelled for his longsomeness ... His people in Lochaber are threatened after the same manner; he is to take other measures with them than he did at first with the Morven men ... I am, to the utmost of my power, honoured Sir, your most humble and obedient servant,

MACGREGOR .

These letters patently have more in common with the famous recruiting scene in *Henry IV* Pt. II, when Jack Falstaff is 'pricking' his likely lads ('Come, prick Bullcalf till he roar again') than with the perfervid martial world of Jacobite balladry. Yet over 250 songs in James Hogg's *Jacobite Relics* testify to the strength of popular feeling at the time – although it must be remembered that several of the songs were the editor's own composition – and the overwhelming impression that one gets from these songs is one of valour, devotion, heroism, chivalrous self-sacrifice. The contemporary accounts of the various risings cannot be said to give the songs the lie; indeed one can hardly cavil with Hogg's judgement when he asserts:

. . . the history of the adherents to the house of Stuart is one of unparalleled bravery, loyalty, misfortune, and suffering.

5

The Gaelic war-songs gathered by John Lorne Campbell in his *Highland Songs of the Forty-Five* convey the same feeling with even greater intensity, and one finds an echo of it in some of the work of modern Gaelic poets like George Campbell Hay. Jacobitism was one of the principal inspirations of the great folksong and folktale collector Calum I. Maclean (younger brother of the poet Sorley Maclean) who died in 1960. His book, *The Highlands* (recently reprinted by Mainstream Publishing, with an introduction by his brother), is very largely an eloquent evocation of the spirit which must have animated the committed Jacobites, and which in the person of a man like Calum himself can be perceived as a recognisable strand in the web of modern Scottish nationalism. In her fascinating book, *Essays in the Study of Folk-Songs* (first published in 1886), the Countess Martinengo-Cesaresco has a passage which is highly relevant in the present context:

> Popular poetry is the reflection of moments of strong collective or individual emotion. The springs of legend and poetry issue from the deepest wells of national life; the very heart of a people is laid bare in its sagas and songs: there have been times when a profound feeling of race or patriotism has sufficed to turn a whole nation into poets: this happened at the expulsion of the Moors from Spain, the struggle for the Stuarts in Scotland, for independence in Greece. It seems likely that all popular epics were born of some such concordant thrill of emotion. The saying of 'a very wise man' reported by Andrew Fletcher of Saltoun, to the effect that if one were permitted to make all the ballads of a nation, he need not care who made the laws, must be taken with this reservation: the ballad-maker only wields his power for as long as he is the true interpreter of the popular will. Laws may be imposed on the unwilling, but not songs.

(It is no accident that the famous aphorism put on record by – if not coined by – that choleric frustrate patriot Fletcher of Saltoun originated in Scotland, for this is pre-eminently the country which throughout its history has given much greater credence to its ballads than to its laws.)

Why have the Jacobite songs taken such firm root in the Scottish national consciousness, while songs which were the response to other political events have fallen away? Kenneth Logue remarks on the paucity of political songs reflecting the popular movements of a later period, and postulates the existence of songs which served their turn and were then forgotten. There are, in fact, in the Mitchell Library and elsewhere, caches of songs belonging to the period of the United Scotsmen, the militia riots etc., but these now seem the merest fossils – dusty museum pieces. Another passage in the book by the Countess Marinengo-Cesaresco, already quoted, provides evidence that even a song thrown up by such a famous event as the Garibaldi expedition of 1859, when all Italy thrilled to the exploits of the 'Thousand', fell almost into oblivion after reunification was successfully achieved:

> Proscription does not kill a song. What kills it sometimes, if it have a political sense, is the fulfilment of the hopes it expresses; then it may die a natural death. I hunted all over Naples for someone who could sing a song which every Neapolitan, man and boy, hummed through the year when the Redshirts brought freedom: *Camicia rossa, camicia ardente.* It seemed that there was not one who still knew it. Just as I was on the point of giving up the search, a blind man was produced out of a tavern at Posilippo; a poor creature in threadbare clothes, holding a wretched violin. He sang the words with spirit and pathos; he is old, however, and perhaps the knowledge of them will not survive him.

Camicia rossa, camicia ardente (red shirt, flaming shirt) was only slumbering in the earth, however; it burst into flower again later in the century when *Bandiera rossa (Avanti o popolo – è la riscossa)*, the anthem of the socialist movement in Italy, resounded under the balconies of the Italian bourgeoisie. It was this song which inspirited the workers in the heroic days of the fight against Fascism led by Giacomo Matteotti and Antonio Gramsci. In the same way, perhaps, one of the songs of the 1790s unearthed by Michael Donnelly in the Mitchell Library may in the future find its way into the hands of a ballad-maker who is looking for a theme and an inspiration in response to new political challenges and developments in Scotland. The moral is clearly that one must expect a partisan song to go under unless it contrives to give voice to an emotion which transcends the actual political moment. I would think, therefore, that Kenneth Logue is probably correct in surmising that there were songs in the period of the French Revolution that have completely disappeared.

Folk – the 'Folk' that matters – has always in fact something of the rebel underground about it; whether it be the love-songs which reject the values and prejudices of a money-minded bourgeois society, or a hypocritical puritan religious set-up; the bawdy songs which frankly rejoice in the fun and the comedy of sex; the 'Ding Dong Dollar' CND songs which pillory the antics of military bigwigs and the bonzes of imperialist power politics; the 'Sangs of the Stane' which send up the pretensions and absurdities of a stuffy royalist Establishment; the bothy songs which put on record the cheese-paring niggardliness of skinflint farmers – all share to a greater or lesser extent this rebel élan.

Readers of my own contribution later in the present symposium may well be surprised by the documentation contained in it of the vast 'primitive rebel' underground represented by the Horseman's Word. Yet the work of Eric Hobsbawm and others has shown how widespread the ramifications of such secret societies have been – and are. The kirk government against which Burns rebelled was an arid and oppressive theocratic straitjacket in which the more submissive of the population were held fast; folksongs collected by David Herd show how irksome the rule of the Calvinist mullahs must have been to the vast majority of people.

> As I came in by Fisherraw,
>   Musselburgh was near me;
> I threw aff my mussle pock,
>   I courted wi' my deary.
>
> Up stairs, down stairs,
>   Timber stairs fears me.
> I thought it lang to lye my lane,
>   When I'm sae near my dearie.
>
> O had her apron bidden down,
>   The kirk wad ne'er hae kend it;
> But since the word's gane thro' the town,
>   My dear I canna mend it.

> But ye maun mount the cutty-stool,
>   And I maun mount the pillar;
> And that's the way that poor folks do,
>   Because they hae nae siller.

Here again we will probably be on the right track if we assume the existence of other songs which explicitly attacked the *social* as well as the 'moral' domination which the Kirk exerted, but which have been lost for the same reason that the more overtly political songs have gone under. As it is, there are a number of fragments on record which tell us more than formal documentary evidence ever could:

> I am a poor silly auld man,
>   And hirpling o'er a tree;
> Yet fain, fain kiss wad I,
>   Gin the kirk wad let me be.

It should never be forgotten, when sizing up such wayward scantlings, that the survival of a song – at any rate, as far as the record is concerned – depends not only on the singer but also on the collector. The latter may, for any number of subjective reasons, impose a personal censorship on what he chooses to record. The great Greig-Duncan collection, gathered in Aberdeenshire in the early years of this century, is long on classic ballads and exquisite lyric love-songs but decidedly short on overtly political songs, or anything remotely resembling bawdry. The few exceptions to this general rule stand out, therefore, in bold relief. I am indebted to Dr Emily Lyle for supplying me with the text of an intriguing fragment collected by Gavin Greig from Bell Robertson, his principal informant. It is called *Vive la Republican*, and goes as follows:

> The second morning of January
>   The morning being fair and clear
> They cried to arms my clever fellows
>   The Russians are advancing near.
>
> *Vive la the new convention*
>   *Vive la Republican*
> *Vive la America*
>   *For it was in you that it a' began.*

> America's a lovely nation
> None on earth can equal her
> But they have spent their dear heart's blood
> To plant the tree of liberty.

This song is clearly something of a muddle – for Russians read Prussians? – but it does seem to reflect the republican sympathies shared (according to H. W. Meikle's *Scotland and the French Revolution*) by a large section of the Scottish population. Its nearest relative is a song, 'Rouse Hibernians', which was composed in 1798; this can be found in Georges-Denis Zimmermann's *Irish Political Street Ballads and Rebel Songs* (Geneva, 1966), Song 18. Here is a verse and the chorus:

> Erin's sons, be not faint-hearted,
> Welcome, sing then 'Ça ira'.
> From Killala they are marching
> To the tune of 'Vive la'.

> *Viva la, United heroes,*
> *Triumphant always may they be.*
> *Vive la, our gallant brethren*
> *That have come to set us free.*

Zimmermann's note points back to a Scottish connection:

> TUNE: Certainly 'Vive la! the French are coming', Stanford-Petrie, No. 996. This was in fact a Scottish tune 'Willie was a Wanton Wag', printed in William Thomson's *Orpheus Caledonius* in 1725. It was quoted under its Scottish title in *Paddy's Resource* [Belfast, 1795], p. 47, with the song 'The new Vive la'. This title might have something to do with the slogan 'Vive la Liberté'.

Later, Thomas Davis (1814-45), the poet of Young Ireland, wrote a stirring song, 'Clare's Dragoons', about the 'wild geese' who fought in the French service after the breaking of the Treaty of Limerick. He used virtually the same tune – which incidentally is now better known as 'Happy we've been a' thegither' – and wrote yet another 'Vive la' chorus to go with it. The process continued into this century,

10

as anyone who heard Brendan Behan in full voice in one or other Dublin pub can testify.

* * * * *

Readers who have accompanied me this far will not be astonished to learn that when Calum Maclean and I began working at the School of Scottish Studies in the early fifties, our activities were looked at askance by quite a number of characters, both inside and outside the University, and we rapidly came to realise that by embarking on the study and collection of folk material we were engaged willy-nilly in a political act. This meant that we encountered opposition from some expected and also from some less expected quarters. Lord Reith – whose posthumously published *Diaries* ingenuously reveal him as the very type-figure of a would-be theocratic dictator – learned that in 1947 I had (at the suggestion of Hugh MacDiarmid) published a small volume of soldiers' songs in various languages which I had collected in North Africa and Italy, under the title *Ballads of World War II*. (A fictitious *ad hoc* organisation called 'The Lili Marlene Club of Glasgow' was invented in order to facilitate the selling of it.) Reith got hold of a copy of this collection, and discovered that I had printed songs like 'The Ballad of King Farouk and Queen Farida' without doing them the discourtesy of bowdlerising them. He is reputed to have promptly issued a ukase forbidding the use of any of my work on the BBC-monopolised air.

(Reith was no longer at that time the boss of the BBC, but he continued to exert considerable influence as a sort of Black-Grey Eminence – particularly in the Scottish 'region ' – by virtue of his friendship with characters like the Rev. Dinwiddie.)

In 1957, Alan Lomax devised and introduced a series of folk programmes for the BBC entitled 'A Ballad-Hunter looks at Britain', and he invited me to co-operate with him on the two Scottish ones. These programmes were recorded in London, and the Scottish BBC did not at first accept them for broadcasting on its own wavelength; eventually, however, after a number of protests from people all over the country, the two Scottish programmes were actually broadcast here. A week or two later, Sasha Moorsom, the producer, showed me in London an incredible letter which she had received from two high-heid yins in the Scottish BBC. This more or less charged Lomax and myself with defaming Scotland by broadcasting scandalous material! The item referred to was 'A Blanket Sky for Me', recorded by Peter Kennedy in Orkney; this was a harmless jokey poem referring to the custom of 'bundling' – the so-called 'courting custom of cold climates' – which has been reported at various times and places from Scandinavia to Bavaria, and from Scotland to Canada and the United States. (In Lewis it was called *caithris na h-oidhche.*) According to the two gents who wrote the letter, this custom had never been known in Scotland; the whole thing was a 'sniggering' invention of Alan Lomax and myself. At Sasha Moorsom's request I supplied her with a list of some forty published references to send to this egregious couple of wowsers.

(Later I met one of their friends and cronies in the Abbotsford; he was very drunk, and eventually I had to get a taxi for him. As I was helping him out to the street and into the taxi – he was unable to walk unaided – he gave me the following just distinguishable farewell message: 'We have kept you off the air for ten years'.) I should add that the opposition to what I was trying to do did not by any means come exclusively from the Right. The Left could be every bit as blinkered, puritanical – and malevolent. When a proposal was made in the committee of the Edinburgh People's Festival – an account of this pioneer organisation will be found later in the book – to stage a production of Robert Burns's *The Jolly Beggars*, this was strongly opposed by one of the committee members on the grounds that in his cantata Burns was giving voice to the sentiments not of the Scottish working class but of the *Lumpenproletariat*. The idea that in this glorious, anarchic work Burns was talking revolutionary politics by presenting folk tradition to us live as something which is fundamentally 'anti' every kind of domination of people was firmly rejected as heretical by the lady concerned.

> A fig for those by law protected!
> Liberty's a glorious feast.
> Courts for cowards were erected,
> Churches built to please the priest!

* * * * *

I set down the foregoing anecdotes, at the risk of laying myself open to the charge of over-personalising the issue, because they seem to me to illustrate better than abstract theory could the sort of thing we were up against. The most galling handicap in the early days was the presence of a particularly unpleasant adversary, well entrenched on the inside of the Scottish School of Studies. It was a sair fecht! ... Although I never did a tithe of what Joe Orton did in his short life to outrage frowsty bourgeois susceptibilities, I have to admit it was with a pang of fellow-feeling that I later read the entry in Joe's diary dated 11 March 1967: 'It's no good making a show of affronting the middle classes, and then being surprised if your enemies retaliate in a nasty way. That's what enemies do.'

(It should be remarked, in passing, that some of the motifs in Joe Orton's plays – including the bawdy ones – are probably more immediately accessible to the folklorist than to the literary scholar. His letter and diaries show that he was quite aware of his classical sources – the Oedipus legend, Dionysus and Pentheus etc. – but he was possibly less conscious of the widespread ramifications of some of the others. The tenacity of oral tradition among the 'inarticulate' English working class is often underestimated. It's plain from John Lahr's *Prick Up Your Ears* that Joe's mother Elsie was a 'folk character' of large, indeed almost monstrous, proportions.)

As far as the theory – the whole 'idea' – of a folk revival was concerned, I was very much preoccupied with just this at the beginning of the fifties, partly because I had been working on a translation of the *Letters from Prison* and other writings of the great Italian Marxist philosopher Antonio Gramsci; these contained a number of illuminating passages on popular culture and the working-class movement. The following observation appears in *Letteratura e Vita Nazionale*, which is the sixth volume in the original series of Gramsci's works published by Einaudi between 1947 and 1951:

> That which distinguishes folksong in the framework of a nation and its culture is neither the artistic fact nor the historic origin; it is a separate and distinct way of perceiving life and the world, as opposed to that of 'official' society.

In one of the letters from prison, written to his sister-in-law

13

Tatiana on 19 March 1927, Gramsci speaks of his desire to 'do something *für ewig*' (for eternity) ... 'to occupy myself intensively and systematically with some subject which will absorb me, and provide a focus for my inner life'. He then lists four subjects: (1) research into the nature of the Italian intellectuals, their origins, groupings, etc.; (2) a study of comparative linguistics; (3) a study of Pirandello's theatre (Gramsci had been the first critic to 'discover' and popularise the plays of Pirandello); and (4) an essay on serial stories in the newspapers, and popular taste in literature.

Elaborating (4), he wrote:

> The idea came to me while I was reading the notice on the death of Serafino Renzi, leading actor in a company of barnstormers (the equivalent in the theatre of the serial stories), and remembering the pleasure I had every time I went to hear him. For in fact the performance was a combined effort; the anxiety of the public, the emotions let loose, the intervention in the play of the working-class audience was certainly not the least interesting performance of the two.
> ... At bottom, if you look carefully, there exists a certain homogeneity which binds these four subjects together: the creative spirit of the people, in its diverse phases and degrees of development, underpins each in equal measure.

(It is this same letter that Hugh MacDiarmid quotes in the opening section of *In Memoriam James Joyce.*)

Gramsci's insights, combined with the experience I had gained during fieldwork with Alan Lomax and his tape-recorder, suggested one urgent need: that of placing examples of authentic native singing-styles, and – wherever possible – actual performances of good traditional artists within the reach of the young apprentice singers of the Revival. Reactionary prejudices in the BBC and in the University proved a sorry hindrance in this respect; however, a lot of work did get done, thanks chiefly to the Edinburgh People's Festival and the earliest of the folk clubs; also to the efforts of school-teachers like Morris Blythman, Norman Buchan and Jack Stuart, sympathetic friends like Dougie and Queenie Moncrieff, and student enthusiasts like Stuart MacGregor, founder of the Edinburgh University Folksong Society. I conclude with another of Gramsci's prison letters, which I offer as food for thought to those Marxists – and there are some – who would dismiss minority languages and the whole question of folk culture as insignificant. This letter, which was written a week after the one already quoted, was first published in English in Ray Burnett's *Calgacus* (No. 2, Summer 1975). It is to Gramsci's sister, Teresina, and the Franco mentioned is Teresina's son:

> . . . Franco looks very lively and intelligent; I expect he's speaking well already. What language does he speak, though? I hope you will let him speak Sardinian, and not go on at him to speak 'properly'. I thought it was a big mistake not to let Edmea [his brother Genaro's daugher] speak Sardinian freely when she was a little girl. It damaged her intellectual development, and put a straitjacket on her imagination. You mustn't make the same mistake with your own children. Remember Sardinian isn't a dialect but a real language, although it can't boast of much of a literature. It's good that a child should learn more than one language, if that's possible. After all, the Italian you would teach him would be a poor crippled speech, consisting of nothing but those few words and phrases he got from you – a mere childish mixter-maxter. He wouldn't make contact with the world around him, and would finish up not with a language but with just a couple of jargons. An Italian jargon when he's 'talking proper' with you, and a Sardinian jargon, picked up in dribs and drabs, to use when talking to other children, or to people he meets on the square or in the street. I really do entreat you, from my heart, not to make the same mistake; allow your children to suck up all the 'sardism' they want, and let them develop spontaneously in the natural environment they were born into. I assure you this won't be a stumbling block for their future development – quite the reverse.

The Border Ballads

JAMES REED

The most important characteristics of Border Ballads, those which distinguish them from other kinds of folk-song, are locality and occasion; and one cannot involve these factors in anything without involving the folk themselves. Such a description, however, needs some minor qualification: Border Ballads are not worksongs, though these too usually incorporate locality and occasion; nor are they protest songs; they are not, in the generally accepted sense, patriotic; they do not exhort or moralise, like hymns, and unlike school songs and rugby songs, they are not the lyrics of a small, excitable group; they sing of love, but they are not love songs. Indeed, the conventions of these modes do not apply in any helpful or significant way to Border Ballads, because none of them finds its origin in a way of life in which history and locality play a continuing part.

One of Sir Walter Scott's firm beliefs, and the impulse behind his *Minstrelsy of the Scottish Border* (1802-3), was that the spontaneous poetry of a people mirrors its entire culture. It is this folk aspect of the ballads that this essay seeks to illustrate, taking as specific examples not the plots of the well-known narratives, but the incidentals on which those narratives depend for completeness; not what the sixteenth-century Borderers did, but what they felt: what were their attitudes towards authority; how did they cope with danger, with the approach of death, with bereavement and personal loss at a time when domestic comforts were slight and the consolations of religion rare?

In the Border Ballad at its best is found the richness of a simple but highly charged vocabulary used to record common, direct experience. However remote the origins of some of the songs: *Lord Randal* from Italy, for example, or the *Douglas Tragedy* from Denmark, those versions found in the Borders have thoroughly localised themes, specific in their application of family and place-names. They record with understandable elaboration and partisan feeling something of events that actually occurred, but of course they are not to be regarded as historical in any but the most generous sense; nor should their inaccuracies and embellishments be interpreted as errors of ignorance, or of deliberate propagandist deception (though both of these elements may be present). They are a commemoration, emotionally generated, of family and regional loyalties *within* the events the narratives portray. They look upon disaster and joy alike with the eye and mind of the participant, and though they are neither philosophical, nor religious, nor in any way didactic, their cumulative effect is one of the most remarkable in the history of British song or literature. They express with a simple elegance and a sensitive economy the patient endurance of suffering and violence, as well as the enduring commonplaces of life of a unique society. G. M. Trevelyan may sound sentimental, but he comes very close to the truth when he writes of the Borderers:

> Like the Homeric Greeks, they were cruel, coarse savages, slaying each other as the beasts of the forest; and yet they were also poets who could express in the grand style the inexorable fate of the individual man and woman, the infinite pity for all the cruel things which they none the less perpetually inflicted upon one another. It was not one ballad-maker alone but the whole cut-throat population who felt this magnanimous sorrow, and the consoling charm of the highest poetry.
> ... If the people had not loved the songs, many of the best would have perished. The Border Ballads, for good and for evil, express this society and its quality of mind.

It is in this expression of a society and its quality of mind that the truths of the ballads lie, not in their representation of history.

One ballad which frames the personal in the historical, involving as it does feuds and loyalties on both sides of the border is *The Death of Parcy Reed* (Child 193). [2] The folk interest in this is twofold: first that of the ballad narrative itself, and second, that of the man who gave it

17

to us; and whether to call him preserver, editor or writer is a matter not lightly decided.

Like Robert Burns and James Hogg, James Telfer was a man of the people, born in Roxburghshire in 1800, the son of a shepherd whose calling he followed as a young man. Gradually he educated himself, became a schoolmaster, and eventually settled in Liddesdale with his own tiny village school, where he remained in near penury for twenty-five years, until his death in 1862. For some years he corresponded with the ballad collector Robert White of Newcastle, and it was to him that he sent the manuscript of *The Death of Parcy Reed* for publication. In returning the galley proofs to White he added on the back what we now have as the first three stanzas of the tale, with the brief comment:

> If Mr White thinks proper he may prefix the above as the beginning of the ballad. The verses are not very good; they are written *currente calamo*.

No earlier version of this ballad exists, nor has it been possible to locate any documentary confirmation of the widespread assumption that Parcy Reed was a government official in Redesdale, or of the events of the ballad. Nevertheless, whatever the truth, Telfer in this piece of work seems, like Sir Walter Scott himself, to be totally absorbed into the spirit, and almost into the language and form of the ballad genre. These are his opening verses, with their clear echo of Sir Richard Maitland's *Complaynt Aganis the Thievis of Liddisdail:*[3]

> God send the land deliverance
>   Frae every reaving, riding Scot;
> We'll sune hae neither cow nor ewe,
>   We'll sune hae neither staig nor stot.
>
> The outlaws come frae Liddesdale,
>   They herry Redesdale far and near;
> The rich man's gelding it maun gang,
>   They canna pass the puir man's mear.
>
> Sure it were weel had ilka thief
>   Around his neck a halter strang;

> And curses heavy may they light
> On traitours vile oursels amang.

The tale is simple and bloody. Parcy Reed goes hunting in the Cheviots with his Redesdale neighbours, the Halls. (It was a Kitty Hall of Oxnam, just over the border from Redesdale, who supplied Telfer with the ballad.) Late in the day he takes his rest and falls asleep on the brae. The Crosiers of Liddesdale, a Scottish family in league with the English Halls, and at feud with Reed, ride up. Together with the Halls they disarm Parcy Reed and hack him to pieces:

> They fell upon him all at once,
> They mangled him most cruellie;
> The slightest wound might caused his deid,
> And they hae gien his thirty-three;
> They hacket aff his hands and feet,
> And left him lying on the lee.

The ballad ends with a typical 'Goodnight', the last words of the dying hero:

> A farewell to my wedded wife,
> A farewell to my brother John,
> Wha sits into the Troughend tower
> Wi heart as black as any stone.

> A farewell to my daughter Jean,
> A farewell to my young sons five;
> Had they been at their father's hand,
> I had this night been man alive.

> A farewell to my followers a',
> And a' my neighbours gude at need;
> Bid them think how the treacherous Ha's
> Betrayed the life o' Parcy Reed.

Whatever its provenance, *Parcy Reed* remains a striking example of those songs involving feuds of named, and regionally located, families, personal vengeance of the individual against another individual, or against lawful authority, and the frequent Border complexity of family alliance: one's nationality was often less important than one's surname.

And families had long memories for the wrongs they suffered, as we can see in another ballad, this time on a well-documented historical theme: *The Raid of the Reidswire*. (Child omitted this from his collection because he believed it employed 'a highly artificial stanza'; however, the earliest version, in the Bannadyne MS, is in ballad quadrams.) A stone commemorating this incident, the last significant frontier affray between England and Scotland on 7 July, 1575, stands on the site, just on the Scottish side of the border, east of the road that runs over Carter Bar. It took place, with a characteristic irony, on a Day of Truce, and though it almost led to an international conflict, it was essentially a domestic border affray, not a military affair.[4]

The meeting was one of those periodically called by the Wardens of the Marches on both sides of the border to hear complaints, administer justice and redress grievances. On this occasion, though the cases were of the usual kind, the violence with which the day ended was probably the result of a long-cherished desire for vengeance for blood that had been shed thirty years earlier. Coincidentally, the name of Crosier turns up again in the records, though not in the ballad.

At some time in the 1540s a party of Liddesdale Crosiers had slain a Northumbrian Fenwick, 'using', the account goes, 'much cruelty against him'. The feud thus begun continued for a generation, and flared up viciously three years before the Reidswire when a band of 'Phenicks' raided Liddesdale and murdered the Crosiers in their beds. It is at points like this that we remember the words of the English Warden answering a civil servant in London who had asked him what this word 'feud' meant, that occurred so frequently in his correspondence. 'Deadly foed, ' he replied, 'the word of enmitye in the Borders, implacable without the blood and whole family distroied.''[5] It was all stored in the long Border memory, and on 7 July, 1575 the Crosiers seized their chance of revenge. At least, this is the version given by John Forster, the wily old English Warden, in his report, though it was never proved.

The judicial proceedings that day began quietly, with the officers sitting at some distance from the crowd who had come not only to see justice done, but to have an enjoyable day out, to play games, drink, buy from the pedlars and packmen and perhaps, if the opportunity arose, settle an old score or two by sword, spear, shaft, hackbut or the strong arm, though theoretically the presence of armed men was forbidden on such occasions. Here is how the ballad describes the scene:

> Yett was our meeting meek enough,
>   Begun wi' merriment and mowes,
> And at the brae, aboon the heugh,
>   The clarke sate down to call the rowes.
> And some for kyne, and some for ewes,
> Called in of Dandrie, Hob, and Jock —
>   We saw, come marching ower the knows,
> Five hundred Fennicks in a flock.
>
> With jack and speir, and bows all bent,
>   And warlike weapons at their will:
> Although we were na well content,
>   Yet be my trouth, we feared no ill.
> Some gaed to drink, and some stude still,
> And some to cards and dice them sped;
>   Till on ane Farnstein they fyled a bill,
> And he was fugitive and fled.

In spite of the weaponry, however, justice took an orderly course as the wardens 'proceeded forwards and after did courteously drink together'.

It was after this interval of courteous drinking that the trouble began, when this man 'Farnstein' (really, Henry Robson of Falstone, in North Tynedale, Northumberland) failed to appear. The English Warden apologised, but high words grew between the leaders, and when these descended to personal abuse the crowd, tempted by the prospect of a fight, left the ale-booths and the packmen for better sport. Accounts of the first shot vary, each side accusing the other, but the brawl quickly became a battle in which the English, forcing a Scots retreat, began with premature confidence to loot the packmen's wares. Happily for the Scots, a chance reinforcement arrived from Jedburgh and the joint forces not only pursued the English back over the border, but took advantage of their visit to run a foray down Redesdale and drive off three hundred head of cattle.

The folk elements in this ballad are typical, and they appear in two forms. One has already been indicated: the social activities of eating and drinking, buying and selling, and playing games which traditionally grow round what are often ostensibly solemn occasions, a feature Robert Burns turned to satirical account in *The Holy Fair*, with its echoes of Fergusson's *Hallow Fair* and, even further back, of *Peblis to the Play* and *Christis Kirk on the Green*.

The second element lies in the character of the narrator, or minstrel, himself. His tone, from the beginning, is very close to that of the relaxed, speaking voice; a man telling his tale to neighbours by the fire:

> The seventh of July, the suith to say,
>   At the Reidswire the tryst was set;
> Our wardens they affixed the day,
>   And, as they promised, so they met.
>   Alas! that day I'll ne'er forget
> Was sure sae feard, and then sae faine —
>   They came theare justice for to gett,
> Will never green to come again.
>
> Carmichael was our warden then,
>   He caused the country to conveen;
> And the Laird's Wat, that worthie man,
>   Brought in that sirname weil beseen:
>   The Armestranges, that aye hae been
> A hardie house but not a hail,
>   The Elliot's honours to maintaine,
> Brought down the lave o' Liddesdale.

One can almost hear the interpolation after 'Carmichael was our warden then', the words, 'Ye mind, Wullie?'. Indeed, the word 'our' appears throughout the ballad as an intimate pronoun, not an objective, impersonal one; it refers to a small, definable, local community, not to a nation: 'our wardens', 'our warning', 'our folks', 'our meeting'. His presence as an eyewitness punctuates the narrative. For example, when he sees Carmichael's trousers pierced by an arrow,

'Into my stomack it struck a knell' he says. And finally, one finds a little hint of class-conscious moralising, typical of the dilemma of honour in which the little man, the powerless man of the people, finds himself:

> To deal with proud men is but pain
> For either must ye fight or flee.

This kind of quiet, wry humour is recurrent in the ballads, where we often find common man taking what delight he can from cocking a snook at authority. For instance, in *Dick o' the Cow* (Child, 185), a ballad of the West March, Dick gets twenty (or thirty) pounds and a milch cow from Lord Scroope, the Warden, and another twenty pounds and another cow from Scroope's brother – all in exchange for two horses out of three he has stolen from the Armstrongs who have persecuted him. The third, and best, he keeps for himself, and at the end of the song he gives loup for joy at his success. Since he has already escaped from his oppressors, the Armstrongs (who at the outset call him 'an innocent fule'), what we have here essentially is the old folk tale of the simple man outwitting both his foes and his betters. *The Lochmaben Harper* (Child, 192) has a similar outcome.

Much folk song, and especially worksongs, are directly concerned with, or reflect, some kind of class-struggle. Border Ballads are virtually classless in the sense in which we use the term now; master and man, laird and tenant, lord and tacksman, because they are bound by ties of family and community and not by labour relationships, do not have those antagonisms that were to develop so acutely in the industrial communities of the nineteenth century.

> Perhaps one ought to be actually a Scotchman to conceive how ardently, under all distinctions of rank and situation, they feel their mutual connection with each other as natives of the same country. There are, I believe, more associations common to the inhabitants of a rude and wild, than of a well-cultivated and fertile country; their ancestors have more seldom changed their place of residence; their mutual recollection of remarkable objects is more accurate; the high and the low are more interested in each other's welfare; the feelings of kindred and relationship

23

are more widely extended, and, in a word, the bonds of patriotic affection, always honourable even when a little too exclusively strained, have more influence on men's feelings and actions.[6]

One ballad, however, is exceptional. This is the tale of *Lamkin, or Long Lonkin* (Child, 93). It is the story of revenge for private grievance, and one in which we find clear indications not only of class resentment, but of the survival in class terms of ancient superstitions. The song is found in many parts of Scotland and in Northumberland; Child prints more than twenty versions of it, but it does not appear in Scott's *Minstrelsy*, though James Hogg provided him with a version.

Lamkin is a mason who, having built a tower for his lord, asks for payment in vain. When the master leaves to go on a journey, he warns his wife to beware of Lamkin, but the mason has an accomplice within the walls, a nurse who is resentful of the way her mistress has treated her, who admits him. Between them they kill both the lady and her baby, but in the end they are hanged (or, in some versions, burned, or boiled). Two important folk elements are present: the class consciousness of the servant, and the influence on the two murderers of ancient superstitions.

When Lamkin enters the tower, he stabs the baby to make it cry and so bring the lady, its mother, downstairs. Ballad literature contains fewer grimmer scenes than this, where Lamkin rocks the cradle as he injures the child, and the nurse sings, and the bonny babe's blood runs down on to the floor. Here is Hogg's version:

> 'How will we get her down the stair?'
>   Said cruel Lamkin;
> 'We'll stogg the baby i' the cradle,'
>   Said fause noorice then.
>
> He stoggit and she rockit,
>   Till a' the floor swam,
> An' a' the tors o' the cradle
>   Red wi' blude ran.

The lady tries to bribe Lamkin, but he will not listen and bids the nurse wash clean a basin in which to catch the blood of her mistress. In Hogg's version, among others, she does this willingly because she

24

hates the woman who has worked her so hard. It has been suggested that this precaution may be traceable to the blood-consciousness of a primitive past where the killer would not defile blood, the vehicle of the soul, by spilling it on the ground. However, in the Aberdeenshire version of this tale, by far the most complete, the nurse refuses bitterly:

> 'There need nae bason, Lamkin,
> lat il run through the floor;
> What better is the heart's blood
> o the rich than o the poor?'

Though such an attitude is unusual in the ballads, there is no means of telling whether or not it was present in the original version, or at what period it appeared; all the versions in Child's collection are as late as the nineteenth century.

It could be said that the ballads which have been examined so far and the well-known riding ballads reveal only what one would expect of the life of a remote, relatively isolated, relatively primitive community; they celebrate acts of violence, of treachery, killing stealing, battle and jailbreaking. What is less obvious is the way these same folk sang in a lower key the songs of that other life that goes on with, and is inseparable from the deeds of violent action and masculine glory. In this Border world of medieval *machismo* are found other jewels of balladry; songs of love and fidelity, and of the harsh sadness of marital jealousy; songs of what folk feel, not of what they do; of their states of mind when the big moments strike, offering them love or death, poverty, abandonment, despair.

In battle or brawl, it is the men who die, the women who clear up afterwards. The ballad of *The Hunting of the Cheviot* (Child, 162), for example, concludes with a roll call of the slain, and the sad procession on the following day when, as Earl Percy is led captive into Scotland, the women come to identify and fetch away their dead:

> Then on the morne they mayde them berrys
> Of byrch and haysell gray;
> Many a wydowe, wyth wepyng teyres,
> Ther makes they fette awaye.

How do simple people, living to a considerable extent without the comfort or support of religious faith, respond to the sudden infliction of violent bereavement; how do they endure the long loneliness that follows? The ballads seem to suggest that they do so with a stoical resignation rather than with resentment, and their stoicism is sustained by a deep but unsentimental sense of fidelity.

In *The Lament of the Border Widow* (a version of *The Famous Flower of Serving Men*, Child, 106) the account of the treachery and murder which have robbed the lady of her knight is conveyed with a skilled economy of language, a tone of mournful elegance and some delicacy of apprehension, though perhaps it owes much to Scott.

> My love he built me a bonny bower,
> And clad it a' wi' lilye flour,
> A brawer bour ye ne'er did see,
> Than my true love he built for me.
>
> There came a man, by middle day,
> He spied his sport, and went away;
> And brought the King that very night,
> Who brake by bower, and slew my knight.
>
> He slew my knight, to me sae dear;
> He slew my knight, and poin'd his gear;
> My servants all for life did flee,
> And left me in extremitie.
>
> I sew'd his sheet making my mane;
> I watch'd the corpse, myself alane;
> I watch'd his body, night and day;
> No living creature came that way.
>
> I took his body on my back,
> And whiles I gaed, and whiles I sat;
> I digg'd a grave, and laid him in,
> And happ'd him with the sod sae green.
>
> But think na ye my heart was sair,
> When I laid the moul' on his yellow hair;
> O think na ye my heart was wae,
> When I turn'd about, away to gae?

> Nae living man I'll love again,
> Since that my lovely knight is slain;
> Wi' ae lock of his yellow hair
> I'll chain my heart for evermair.

Such a ballad reflects on appropriate grief in a society where excessive lamentation was regarded with disfavour, and where action and mourning are consciously displayed without mawkishness or self-indulgence .

In *Clerk Saunders* (Child, 69) and the linked *Sweet William's Ghost* (Child, 77), we move from the vigorous sexual invitation of the opening:

> 'A bed, a bed,' Clerk Saunders said,
> 'A bed for you and me!'
> 'Fye na, fye na,' said May Margaret,
> 'Till anes we married me.'

Her refusal, however, is the result not of virtue, but simply of her fear that they will be caught by her 'seven bauld brothers', which in the event they are, and Saunders is killed by them as the two lovers sleep.

Later, he returns and begs her to declare her love once more. She invites him to kiss her, and he replies in words very like those of *The Unquiet Grave* (Child, 78), which is not a border song:

> My mouth it is full cold, Margaret,
> It has the smell now, of the ground;
> And if I kiss thy comely mouth,
> Thy days of life will not be lang.'

And eventually we reach the moving irony of her request for a place in his last bed:

> Is there ony room at your head, Saunders?
> Is there ony room at your feet?
> Or ony room at your side, Saunders,
> Where fain, fain, I wad sleep?'

but she is denied, and the ballad ends on this note of the bleak mutual

27

B

longing of the living and the dead. Throughout, the pair are envisaged as lovers; Saunders is described as dead, but never as a ghost. Nothing could be more realistic.

Parcy Reed betrayed and dying; the solemn rituals of the law made an occasion for a social outing; the re-enactment of ancient rites of blood; the grief of women, and the life of (but not beyond) the grave; in their preservation of such moments as these, the Border Ballads, however distorted by time, changing manners and editorial refinements, give us a brief but moving glimpse into the lives of an obscure, unlettered people. They remain precious, even in their corruption, because they are unique, and because their people are our image.

FOR FURTHER READING
1. *Border Ballads*
The classic collection, though it contains much of dubious provenance, with a valuable introduction on the Borders and its people, is Sir Walter Scott's *Minstrelsy of the Scottish Border*, Kelso/Edinburgh, 1802-3.

Commentaries devoted specifically to Border Ballads are few:
J. Veitch, *The History and Poetry of the Scottish Border*, Edinburgh, 1893.
James Reed, *The Border Ballads*, London, 1973.

2. *General Collections*
B. H. Bronson, *The Traditional Tunes of the Child Ballads*, Princeton, 1959.
F. J. Child, *The English and Scottish Popular Ballads*, 5 vols., Dover, 1965.
A. B. Friedman, *The Penguin Book of Folk Ballads*, London, 1977.
G. Grigson, *The Penguin Book of Ballads*, London, 1975.
M. J. C. Hodgart, *The Faber Book of Ballads*, London, 1965.
J. H. Kinsley, *The Oxford Book of Ballads*, Oxford, 1971.

3. *General Commentaries*
David Buchan, *The Ballad and the Folk*, London, 1972.
M. J. C. Hodgart, *The Ballads*, London, 1950.
A. L. Lloyd, *Folk Song in England*, London, 1967.

4. *History*
G. M. Fraser, *The Steel Bonnets*, London, 1971.
R. Hugill, *Castles and Peles of the English Border*, Newcastle, 1970.

T. I. Rae, *The Administration of the Scottish Frontier, 1513-1603*, Edinburgh, 1966.
D. L. W. Tough, *The Last Years of a Frontier*, Oxford, 1928.
H. G. Ramm et al, *Shielings and Bastles*, HMSO, 1970.

NOTES
1 G.M.Trevelyan's 'The Middle Marches' in *Clio A Muse* (rep. NewYork, 1968), pp. 33-4.
2 Ballad references follow the conventions established by F. J. Child, *The English and Scottish Popular Ballads* 1882-98, 5 vols. (reprinted New York, 1965).
3 *The Poems of Sir Richard Maitland of Lethington* (Bannatyne Club, 1830), pp. 52-55. Maitland's dates are 1496-1586.
4 See James Reed, 'The Long Memory', *Scotland's Magazine*, October 1975.
5 *Calendar of Border Papers*, (ed.) J. Bain, 2 vols. (Edinburgh, 1894-6), II, p. 163.
6 Walter Scott, *The Heart of Midlothian*, Everyman edition (London, 1901), p. 403.

Calvinism and the Survival of Folk
or 'Deil stick da minister'

EDWARD J. COWAN

There has been a strongly entrenched and widely held belief in Scotland, particularly among the *literati*, that the Reformation of 1560 engendered a cultural blight. As the late Fionn MacColla succinctly and characteristically put it, 'the essence of the matter is that, stripped of its theological trappings and all other accidentals, the Reformation represented the triumph of Mediocrity over Distinction'.[1] In another powerful articulation of the same idea Edwin Muir wrote,

> We were a tribe, a family, a people.
> Wallace and Bruce guard now a painted field,
> And all may read the folio of our fable,
> Peruse the sword, the sceptre and the shield.
> A simple sky roofed in that rustic day,
> The busy corn-fields and the haunted holms,
> The green road winding up the ferny brae.
> But Knox and Melville clapped their preaching palms
> And bundled all the harvesters away,
> Hoodicrow Peden in the blighted corn
> Hacked with his rusty beak the starving haulms.
> Out of that desolation we were born.
>
> *(Scotland 1941)*

If those gentlemen and the many others who joined their chorus are correct it is truly remarkable that Scottish folk song and music survived the traumas of the sixteenth and seventeenth centuries which happens to be the period in which so much of our extant song and

30

balladry were produced. This apparent paradox seems worthy of investigation. What was the relationship between the Kirk and folk culture during the first century and a half, or so, of Reformation? Definitions of folk already abound.[2] Suffice it to say that folk is defined by the milieu in which and for which it is produced and designed, while a ballad is simply a folk-song that tells a story.[3] Since the last century, Scottish historians, with a few honourable exceptions, have been strangely reluctant to investigate this great communal treasure-trove which stores the people's past and for their failure they are liable to be pilloried by posterity. Oral tradition has been largely ignored in favour of the supposedly more 'scientific' and less subjective historical evidence of record and charter, statute and account. Historians are inexplicably happier to quote the observations of foreign commentators, from Tacitus to Dr Johnson, than they are to utilise the native lore of the country. Consequently, Scottish historiography is, in certain respects, a chronicle of lost opportunities; volumes of carefully edited (and undeniably valuable) texts have accumulated as the irrecoverable oral history of the people has gradually disappeared. As Sir Walter Scott took Europe by storm the German poet, Heine, remarked on 'the strange whim of the people – they demand their history distilled back into the original poetry whence it came'. While such a demand undoubtedly still exists it is seldom satisfied. The problem was succinctly stated by the late Calum Maclean of the School of Scottish Studies. 'There are two histories of every land and people – the written history that tells what it is considered politic to tell and the unwritten history that tells everything.'[4] He thus beautifully encapsulated the endless appeal, as well as the importance, of the folk tradition.

It is not always realised that pre-Reformation Scotland was a most musical place. The earliest fragment of surviving Scottish vernacular poetry is a song lamenting the death of Alexander III at Kinghorn in 1286. John Barbour in his magnificent poem 'The Bruce', completed c. 1385, observed that it was unnecessary to describe a particular battle since

> wha sa liks thai may her
> young wemen quhen thai play
> sing it amang them ilk day.

Andrew Wyntoun, the fifteenth century's answer to William
McGonagall, obviously used ballads and songs in compiling his vast
metrical chronicle of Scotland, one of the first as well as one of the
lengthiest and most sustained experiments in the vernacular. He
was, for example, full of praise for MacBeth yet he felt bound to add,

> Bot as we fynd be sum storys,
> Gottyne he wes on ferly wys.

Having related that MacBeth was the product of a union between his
mother and the Devil, Wyntoun recounts a rival folk tradition that
Malcolm Canmore was the son of Duncan by his 'lemman lewyd', the
daughter of the miller of Forteviot. The tales of the three witches
which have their echoes in international folk motifs presumably
derived from similar sources.

Fifteenth-century poems such as 'Peblis to the Play' and 'Colkelbie
Sow' give the titles of songs and tunes, some of which could be
classed as folk.[5] Church and art-music flourished in the same period.
Sir Richard Holland's 'Buke of Howlat' (1451) contains an elaborate
catalogue of musical instruments. There were song schools
throughout the country. Poets like Robert Henryson and Gavin
Douglas were perfectly familiar with music theory.[6] William Dunbar
referred to the 'musicians, menstralis and mirrie singaris' at the court
of James IV where trumpeters, drummers, fiddlers, lutars, harpers
and pipers were also to be found.[7] The latter were, of course, professionals but there were others who could be described as folk
musicians .

'Wondor laith wer I to be ane baird,' wrote Dunbar, 'flyting to use
richt gritly I eschame.' The bard in the Highlands was a professional
who held an important and valued place in society but in the Lowlands the word was to become synonymous with vagabond. As early
as 1449 parliamentary legislation decreed that 'bards and other
runners' were to be nailed through the ear and their ears cut off
before their owners were banished. Eight years later the king ordered
an inquisition of 'sornars, bards and masterful beggars or fenyeit
fulys'.[8] It was the flyting tradition which earned bards such an
unenviable reputation. This element of argument or protest was to
remain an important characteristic of balladry until the end of the

seventeenth century, and it might be added, of all folk song right down to the present day. The word 'minstrel' was to undergo a familiar debasing metamorphosis to 'bard'. It was entirely respectable in the fifteenth century as for example in 1471 when knights, minstrels and heralds were excluded from a ban on the wearing of silks. But these *joculatores* were to become just as much of a menace, in the eyes of the authorities, the Latin being corrupted to Jockie. The last of the wandering Jockies were still to be found in Scotland in the eighteenth century.[9]

The Complaint of Scotland (1549) lists thirty-eight songs, some of which were undoubtedly ballads. Among 'the sweet melodious songs of natural music of antiquity' it mentions 'The Hunting of the Cheviot', 'The Battle of Otterburn' and 'The Battle of Harlaw'.[10] A number of popular songs, based upon existing folk songs and utilising folk tunes were put into circulation through performances of Sir David Lindsay's 'Satire of the Three Estates'. The Reforming Council at Linlithgow in 1549 responded by ordering enquiries in each diocese as to 'what persons have in their keeping any books of rhymes or popular songs containing calumnies or slanders defamatory of churchmen and church institutions, or infamous libels, or any kind of heresy: and when such have been discovered they shall be prohibited under the penalties inflicted by Act of Parliament and confiscated and burned'. Parliament in 1551 legislated against 'divers prentaris in this realme that daylie and continuallie prentis bukis concerning the faith, ballatis, sangis, blasphematiounis (and) rymes alsweill of kirkmen as temporall and uthers'.[11] The pre-Reformation church was thus considerably troubled about the circulation of such material.

One of the most persistent myths of Scottish history is that the Reformed church abolished ecclesiastical music and was positively hostile to music in general. Professor John MacQueen cites Sir Richard Maitland of Lethington in the 1560s as lamenting the demise of 'daunsing, singing, game and play ... all mirrines is worne away'. Maitland was the compiler of a well-known manuscript anthology. 'His motives as a compiler were probably mixed. He was certainly proud of the accomplishment of Scottish letters, but almost equally certainly he shared the additional impulse with his younger contemporaries and fellow collectors, George Bannatyne and the musician Thomas Wode, Vicar of St Andrews – the impulse to preserve something of an already suppressed culture which they felt to be in danger of complete disappearance. ' Wode in particular was possessed of the belief that 'musik will pereishe'.[12] Fears of the moment, however, are not the same as the longer term reality. As a matter of historical fact the reformed church did not outlaw music.

John Calvin himself adopted a pragmatic attitude to music as to so many other subjects. 'The natural qualities of things themselves demonstrate to what end, and how far, they may be lawfully engaged. Has the Lord adorned flowers with all the beauty which spontaneously presents itself to the eye, and the sweet odour which delights the sense of smell, and shall it be unlawful for us to enjoy that beauty and this odour? ... In short, has he not given many things a value without having any necessary use?'[13] The same point is made in another part of the *Institutes*. 'Although the invention of instruments has ministered rather to man's pleasure than to his actual needs, it is not on that account to be looked on as a superfluity, still less does it deserve to be condemned – so long as it is used in the fear of God and in the service of the company of mankind.'[14] It is also worth quoting Calvin's preface to the French Genevan psalter. 'Among other things which are suitable for the recreation of men and for giving them pleasure, music is the first, or one of the chief, and we should esteem it as a gift of God bestowed for that end. In truth we know by experience that song has great force and power in moving and inflaming the heart of man to invoke and praise God with more vehement and ardent zeal. It should always be seen to, that the song be not light and frivolous, but that it should have weight and majesty and also that there is a great difference between the music that is employed for the enjoyment of men at table and in their houses, and the psalms which they sing in church, in the presence of God.'[15] Calvin, to be sure, objected to the use of organs in churches though not, apparently, in private homes. The Council of Trent at the same period decreed, 'let them keep away from the churches those forms of music with which, either by the organ or by singing, anything impure is mixed, in order that the house of God may be seen to be truly a house of prayer'.[16] It is often forgotten that there was 'a general trend towards puritanism at this time' which embraced the church of Rome as well as the Protestants.[17]

When Mary Queen of Scots arrived at Holyrood in 1561, one of her courtiers, Brantôme, complained that as the queen was about to go to bed 'five or six hundred knaves of the town came under her window, with wretched fiddles and small rebecs, and sung psalms so badly and out of tune that nothing could be worse'. John Knox was more sympathetic, ' a cumpany of the most honest, with instrumentis of musick, and with musitians, geve thair salutationis at hyr chalmer wyndo. The melody (as sche alledged) lyked her weill, and sche willed the same to be contineued some nightis after'.[18] Knox was far from being the killjoy so often depicted. Edinburgh pubs were allowed Sunday opening in the 1560s. Knox had no objection to entertaining on the Sabbath and he is on record as having attended plays. His fiery and more extreme younger contemporary, John Davidson of Prestonpans, actually wrote one.

The reformers were as worried about the bards as their predecessors had been. Among those to be punished as vagabonds in legislation of 1574, which was doubtless ineffective since it was repeated five years later, were 'all menstrallis, sangstaris and taill tellaris not avowit in speciall service be sum of the lords of parliament or greit barronis or be the heid burrowis and cities for their commoun menstrallis'. Also in 1574 'na Irishe and hieland bairdis and beggaris' were to be brought into, or received in, the Lowlands, 'be boittis or utherwayis under the pane of £20 of the bringaris'.[19] Throughout the post-Reformation era many cities and towns continued to employ official minstrels, often gorgeously apparelled. Peebles hired a piper in 1554 and a minstrel in 1568. Glasgow employed two minstrels from 1574 to 1599 and in 1675 John M'Claine was engaged as the city's minstrel or piper who played through the town morning and evening. Stirling paid a piper and a drummer from 1681 to 1731.[20]

Professional musicians, church music and song schools, as well as folk, undoubtedly survived the Reformation. As Helena Shire has demonstrated, James VI's court was a centre of musical patronage and, as might be expected, there was some intercourse between folk and art music in the period.[21] Folk, in particular, so flourished that almost one hundred years after the Reformation, the Cromwellians felt compelled to legislate against 'profanation of the Lord's Day through persons dancing, or profanely singing or playing upon

35

musical instruments or tippling'. Furthermore, 'if any person or persons, commonly called Fidlers or Minstrels, shall be taken playing, fidling and making musick in any Inn, Alehouse or Tavern, or shall be taken proferring themselves, or desiring or entreating any person or persons to hear them to play, or make musick in any of the places aforesaid, that every such person and persons so taken shall be adjudged ... rogues, vagabonds and sturdy beggars and proceeded against as such'.[22] It would therefore seem that when Calvin came knocking at the door the ceilidh continued unabated. Indeed it could be argued that the Kirk inadvertently, and despite its own instincts actually managed to foster folk music.

When Robert Burns turned the 'Merry Muses of Caledonia' into some of the most beautiful and most moving of Scottish songs he was working within a long-established Scottish convention. The reformers early adopted the expedient which was quite widespread in Europe, of adapting profane songs and tunes for religious use. Around 1542 Mr John Wedderburn of Dundee 'translated manie of Luther's dytements into Scottish meeter. He turned many bawdie songs and rymes in godlie rymes'.[23] Those translations were to become popularly known as 'The Gude and Godlie Ballads', or to give the full title of the 1621 edition, 'Ane compendious Buik of godlie psalms and spiritual sangs, collectit furth of sundrie parts of Scripture, with divers uther Ballates changeit out of prophane sanges in godlie sangis for avoyding of sin and harlatry, with augmentation of sindrie gude and godlie Ballates not contained in the first edition'. Many of the pieces contained in this remarkable volume were Scots translations of German psalms and paraphrases. A number, however, were based upon native ballads or songs and some of these, given the originals, require an inspired leap of the imagination.

A few examples will illustrate the point. There was an old song of which the first stanza:

> John, come kiss me now, now, now
> O John come kiss me now!
> John come kiss me by and bye
> And make nae mair ado.

The singer is fairly explicit, somewhat impatient and quite emphatic.

The godly version starts with the same stanza but it continues:

> The Lord thy God, I am,
> That John dois thee call,
> Johne representit man
> Be grace celestiall.

Or consider another explicit theme about a couple spending the night together. The song is mentioned by both Dunbar and Douglas, the version here quoted being a revamping of Alexander Montgomerie in the reign of James VI.

> Hay! now the day dawis,
> The jolie Cok crawis,
> Now shroudis the shawis,
> Throu Natur anone.
> The thissel-cok cryis
> On lovers wha lyis,
> Nou skaillis the skyis:
> The nicht is neir gone.

The sacred version is very different.

> Hay now the day dallis
> Now Christ on us callis
> Now welth on our wallis
> Apperis anone:
> Now the Word of God Regnes
> Quhilk is King of all Kingis,
> Now Christis flock singis.
> The nycht is neir gone.

One last example is an adaptation of a song of which only a fragment survives:

> Till our gudman, till our gudman,
> Keip faith and love, till our gudman.

Whatever the original was about it could not have been like the later paraphrase.

> For our gude man in hevin dois regne
> In gloir and blis without ending,
> Quhar Angellis singis ever 'Osan'!
> In laude and pryse of our gude man.[24]

God the gudeman is a fine couthy image, reminiscent of the Deity in 'Kynd Kittock's Land' who when he saw Kittock slipping out of Heaven, past Peter, to visit the nearby tavern, 'Leuched his hairt sair'. God seldom laughs in any literature, stepping off his cottonwool cloud only to present a stern countenance to wretched mankind.

In 1568 the General Assembly objected that Thomas Bassandine, printer in Edinburgh, had appended to the 'Gude and Godlie Ballads' 'ane baudie song callit "Welcum Fortoun"', which he was ordered to delete from subsequent printings. The song is innocuous enough –

> Welcum, Fortoun, welcum againe,
> The day and hour I may weill blis,
> Thow hes exilit all my paine,
> Quhilk to my hart greit plesour is.
>
> For I may say, that few men may,
> Seeing of paine I am drest,
> I haif obteneit all my pay,
> The lufe of hir that I lufe best.
>
> I know nane sic as scho is one,
> Saw treis, sa kynde, sa luiffandlie,
> Quahat suld I do, an scho war gone?
> Allace! zit had I lever die.
>
> To me scho is baith trew and kynde,
> Worthie it war scho had the praise,
> For na disdaine in hir I find,
> I pray to God I may hir pleis.
>
> Quhen that I heir hir name exprest,
> My hart for Ioy dois loup thairfor,
> Abufe all uther I lufe hir best,
> Unto I die, quhat wald scho moir?'[25]

Bassandine was allowed to retain the cheerfully ribald 'The Paip that Pagan full of Pride', so coarse that its Victorian editor omitted several lines. Salacious humour directed against anti-Christ was permissible but Fortune was anathema to Calvinists. 'Fortune and adventure are the words of Paynims, the signification whereof ought in no wise to enter into the heart of the faithful,' wrote Knox echoing Calvin's *Institutes* – 'if all success is blessing from God, and calamity and adversity are his curse, there is no place left in human affairs for Fortune and chance'.[26] The interest of the good and godly ballads is that they explicitly appealed to, and attempted to exploit, the Scottish folk tradition. In so doing they very probably reinforced, rather than threatened, that tradition. The psychological effects of cloaking bawdy folk songs with a veneer of religiosity must be judged by those more qualified than the present commentator. Certain it is that the strange vein of eroticism which is common to most religions but which is so pronounced in Calvinism was present from the beginning. Tragically the innocent coquettishness of love imagery in these early ballads was to become a pathological obsession with sex itself, a subject fitter for private shame than public rejoicing.

Any doubts about the propriety of spiritualising profane songs were valiantly quashed by William Geddes, sometime minister of Wick who published his exquisitely wrong-headed anthology of execrable religious verse in 1683 under the title *The Saint's Recreation upon the Estate of Grace and Spiritual Songs*. William confessed to his readers that he had been 'much longing ... for reclaiming (if possible) our profane vulgar from obscene bawdy songs (which are most scandalous to our profession) to more Christian-like divertisements. I have not sought for a sublime lofty style, nor hunted after pedantick expressions, or Romantick phrases; partly that the treatise might be usefull and intelligible to the vulgar as well as to the learned; And partly because I supposed, that neither the whorish dress of human eloquence, or high flowing notions, nor yet the sluttish garb of rustick expressions, were suteable for the chast Lady of Divinity.' Geddes anticipated criticism from certain 'inconsiderate persons' who would say, 'we remember some of these ayres and tunes were sung heretofore with amorous sonnets, wherein were (may be) some bawdy-like or obscene-like expressions'. He answered that he followed the precedent of some of the most pious, grave and zealous divines in the kingdom who have composed godly songs to the tunes of such old songs as 'The Bonny Broom', 'I'll never leave thee' and 'We'll all go pull the heather'. 'It is alleged by some, and that not without some colour of reason, that many of our Ayres and Tunes are made by good Angels, but the letter or lines of our songs by devils. We choose the part Angelical and leaves the Diabolical.' In any case he thought it possible that those who 'composed amorous naughty sonnets had surreptitiously borrowed those grave sweet tunes from former spiritual hymns and songs so he was simply claiming his own.'[27] So there it is – the good and godly ballad tradition persisted until 1683 at least in Wick!

Not even Andrew Melville and his followers who were certainly less tolerant than Knox, were totally opposed to music. Andrew's nephew, James, had enjoyed a musical education and of Wedderburn's songs he 'lerned diverse *per ceur* with graitt diversitie of toones'.[28] There was a proclamation in 1583 against the unlicensed printing of books, ballads, songs, rhymes or tragedies[29] but music continued to flourish. Archibald Stewart, 'recusant' once interrupted a church service at Neilston when he 'brocht with him into the kirkyaird twa or thre pyperis and thairby drew ane gret nowmer of the people to danse befoir the kirk dur in tyme of prayaris'.[30] James Graham, future Marquis of Montrose, was generous with his tips to violers, drummers, trumpeters and pipers. When the invading covenanting army based itself at Newcastle in 1641 the Earl of Lothian, unable to find a sober fiddler in the entire force, diverted himself with pipers. 'I have one for every company in my regiment and I think they are as good as drums.'[31] Habbie Simson's pipes accompanied most social activity in the early seventeenth century.[32] Thomas Kirke who visited Scotland in 1679 testified that newly-weds were escorted home 'with loud ravishing bagpipes ... which enchant you with a loath to depart'.[33]

One practice to which the reformers did have a number of objections was dancing. John Knox informed Mary Queen of Scots that princes were more interested in "fiddling and flinging' than they were in reading or hearing God's blessed word. 'Of dancing Madam, albeit in Scriptures I find no praise of it, and in profane writers that it is termed the gesture rather of those that are mad and in frenzy than in sober men, yet I do not utterly damn it providing that two vices can be avoided.' Firstly dancing must not become an obsession overriding all other activities. 'Secondly that they dance not, as the Philistines their fathers, for the pleasure that they take in the displeasure of God's people. For if any of both do, so they shall receive the reward of dancers, and that will be drink in Hell, unless they speedily repent, so shall God turn their mirth in sudden sorrow.' What Knox had in mind was the 'immoderate dancing' of the courtiers though the reference to 'drink in Hell' may well allude to the potent refreshments which traditionally accompanied the dance.[34] In 1596 the General Assembly criticised Queen Anne's 'nightwaking and balling'.[35] In the minds of Calvinists the threat embedded in the dance was the abandonment of self-control. John MacInnes has tentatively revived the connection between 'erotic, lyrical songs and the dance'[36] and some identification seems to have motivated the ecclesiastical opposition to the folk dance which is well attested in the notorious witch hunts of the sixteenth and seventeenth centuries. In the records of the witch craze there are obvious elements of the fertility cult, of eroticism and of pornography, all of which had been associated with the dance since an early date. At Easter, 1282, John, the priest of Inverkeithing, collected young girls from his parish and made them dance in circles in honour of Liber, sometimes identified with Bacchus. John led the dance bearing a pole on which was mounted a phallic symbol and he urged the girls to lust and filthy language.[37] William Dunbar witnessed the 'Dance of the Sevin Deidly Synnis'.

> Me thocht, amangis the feyndis fell,
> Mahoun (Satan) gart cry ane dance
> Off schrewis that wer nevir schrevin.

The Devil's dance continued long after the Reformation.

A minister told George Sinclair, author of *Satan's Invisible World Discovered* (1685), that the Devil was the composer of several bawdy songs. A wizard claiming to be the Deil's piper had confessed to the anxious minister that 'at a ball of dancing the Foul Spirit taught him a bawdy song to sing and play and within two days all the lads and lassies of the town were lilting it through the street. It were abomination to rehearse it.' A husband and wife, both consequently executed for witchcraft, had been led to a dancing in the Pentland Hills by the Devil disguised as a 'rough tanny-dog ... playing on a pair of pipes'. The tune he played was 'The silly bit chiken, gar cast it a pickle and it will grow meikle'. 'And coming down the hill,' said the woman, 'when we had done, which was the best sport, the Devil carried the candle in his bottom under his tail, which played ey wig wag, wig wag.'[35] At the trial of Gellie Duncan for her part in the infamous sabbat at North Berwick in 1589, the accused related that she had played the tune 'Gyllatrypes' upon her Jew's harp. King James was so fascinated that he had Gellie play the tune for him 'in a wonderfull admiration ... in respect of the strangeness of these matters'.[39] The tune apparently caught on, for four years later three women at Elgin 'confessit thame to be in ane dance callit gillatrype singing a foull hieland sang'.[40] Music, usually provided by the pipes was an important feature in several alleged sabbats. Before his execution in 1659 John Douglas, also of Tranent and Auld Clootie's piper, informed his torturers that Auld Nick's favourite tunes were 'Kilt thy coat Maggie and come thy way wi me' and 'Hulie the bed will fa'.[41] Those who share King James's curiosity as to the type of tunes which excited the Devil will find 'Kilt thy coat Maggie' fortuitously preserved in the Skene manuscript.[42]

Alexander Keith who partially edited the papers of Scotland's greatest ballad collector, Gavin Greig, observed that the 'majority of ballads are so decidedly partisan in their attitude, and so frequently perverted in their statements, that we cannot but conclude that they were composed and circulated with a definite objective in view'.[43] In this respect the ballad would seem to parallel the poetical traditions of the *Gaidhealtachd* in the sense that it represents public poetry which is partly polemic. It was a well-established practice in Lowland Scotland in the sixteenth century to produce ballads, squibs, placards and posters designed to both reflect and mould public opinion. Thus, for example, in 1592 'contumelious verses were made in contempt of KingJames calling him Davie 's (i.e. Riccio's) son, a bougerer, one that left his wife all night *intactam*' and so on. In the aftermath of the Spanish Armada the Kirk objected to all Scottish trade with Spain but the merchants boasted that they would not desist from carrying victual to Spain under the threat of censure by the church and 'spread some infamous rymes and libells against the ministers'.[44]

Rhymes and songs circulated widely as a consequence of the well-known episode when, on 7 February 1592, the Earl of Huntly killed James Stewart, Earl of Moray, at Donibristle in Fife. Moray was widely regarded as the champion of the kirk as were all who had borne his title. What is less familiar is that three days before Moray's death, Sir John Campbell of Cawdor was assassinated in Argyll. It later transpired that Cawdor's slaying was part of a widespread conspiracy, in which Huntly was involved, to assassinate the young Earl of Argyll. The murders of Moray and Cawdor were thus connected in a conspiracy which aimed to destroy the two great champions of Scottish Protestantism. In the aftermath of the murders the whole of Scotland was seething. The affair has been largely ignored by historians although the plot was one of the most disruptive developments of the 1590s. It is most significant that the ballad commemorating the slaying of the 'Bonnie Earl o Moray' should open with an appeal to the widespread disgust which the affair generated throughout the Highlands and the Lowlands.

The ballad was almost certainly Kirk-inspired and it is to be noted that it attacks King James at several vulnerable points. The king alleged that his part was like that of King David when Abner was slain by Joab – he was 'guiltless before the Lord forever from the blood' of Moray. Huntly was the king's representative and so acted faithlessly in the king's name. It is suggested that Moray was a rival for the kingship and that he was the queen's true love, so reviving allegations of James's sexual inadequacy. It need hardly be stated that Moray was neither a claimant to the kingship nor the queen's lover but it was believed he had incurred James's jealousy because Anne 'more rashlie then wyslie' had commended Moray in the king's hearing 'with too maney epithetts of a proper and gallant man'.[45] James's popularity had never been lower. A contemporary English agent informed his superiors in London that there were 'open exclamations of the king general amongst all sortis of his subjects and daily such murder and havoc amonst his subjects who should be preserved under his protection, and a muttering amongst them for that the king doth nothing to it; in times past both in England and Scotland, kings have been deposed for less occasions than now are given them. They dislike the queen because she is not with child. People are saying that so long as this king reigns over them never any luck or grace will be in Scotland. ' The widows of slain fugitives had prayed God, he that made him king again to unmake him claiming he was more 'fit to be a king of tikes, dogges for hunteing, then of his people, being so careless of them'.[46] In the last comment is yet a further implication of James's unnaturalness, for the king of tykes was the Devil himself.

> Ye Highlands, and ye Lawlands,
> Oh where have you been?
> They have slain the Earl of Murray,
> And they layd him on the green
>
> Now wae be to thee, Huntly!
> And wherefore did you sae?
> I bade you bring him wi you,
> But forbade you him to slay.
>
> He was a braw gallant,
> And he rid at the ring:
> And the bonny Earl of Murray,
> Oh he might have been a king.
>
> He was a braw gallant,
> And he playd at the ba;
> And the bonny Earl of Murray
> Was the flower amang them a.
>
> He was a braw gallant,
> And he playd at the glove;
> And the bonny Earl of Murray
> Oh he was the Queen's love!
>
> Oh lang will his lady
> Look o'er the Castle Doune
> Eer she see the Earl of Murray
> Come sounding thro the town.   (*Child*, 181A)

So successful was this propaganda that James was forced to concede to the establishment of Presbyterianism in the so-called 'Golden Acts' of May 1592.

In their excellent anthology Pinto and Rodway have suggested that 'in Scotland rigorous repression tended to diminish printed and increase oral transmission, so that the distinction between folk song or folk ballad on the one hand and street song or street ballad on the other became blurred'.[47] If the 'rigorous repression' is less easy to detect than they pretend, the rest of the statement is perfectly tenable. The ballad 'Gilderoy', commemorating the Earl of Argyll's capture of the notorious MacGregor outlaw in 1636, contains a number of ornate features which might suggest that it originated as a broadsheet or street ballad. The song is interesting in that Gilderoy's sweetheart neither attempts to excuse her lover nor does she so much as mention Argyll but she does condemn a society which could hang a man for theft.

> Wae worth the louns that made the laws
> To hang a man for gear;
> To reave of life for sic a cause
> As stealing horse or mare!
> Had not their laws been made sae strick
> I neer had lost my joy;
> Wi sorrow neer had wat my cheek
> For my dear Gilderoy.[48]

A ballad which aimed at discrediting the Campbells and so the covenanting cause of which Argyll was the leader, was 'The Burning of the Bonnie Hoose o Airlie'. The song is usually thought to refer to Argyll's sacking of Airlie in 1640 but it may have originated in an earlier Campbell invasion of the Braes of Angus in 1591.[49] A study of 'Airlie' sheds some light on the thorny problem of ballad evolution. As Keith graphically stated the problem – 'The probability is that each ballad, in its initial form, was the conception of a single mind, simply because no crowd ever created anything but a noise or a disturbance, and not even that without individual prompting or guidance (pace Ken Logue elsewhere in this volume!). Whatever the capacity of the first author, the ballad, once taken to the people's bosom, was not long left unchanged. So many contingencies, mental, physical, moral, historical and topographical, arose to alter the character of the ballads, that they gradually acquired the stamp of

communal or collective authorship by their passage through generations of singers and by intricate processes of synthesis.'[50] By the
eighteenth century Charles I of the Airlie ballad had become identified with Bonnie Prince Charlie and Argyll had become a duke. The
ballad thus remained productive in the sense that it had something to
say about the contemporary situation from 1591 to 1746. The raid
took place on a beautiful summer day; the Campbells attacked in
August 1591 and in July 1640.

> It fell on a day, and a bonny simmer day,
> When green grew aits and barley,
> That there fell out a great dispute
> Between Argyll and Airlie.

In the version of the ballad cited here (Child, 199A) Lady Ogilvie not
only has to contend with an attack on the castle but also with an
assault upon her own person. The plundering of the castle is accompanied by the symbolic rape of the lady. That the strait-laced,
presbyterian Argyll should have asked for a kiss, let alone anything
more ambitious, seems utterly fantastic from all that is known of him,
but the sexual innuendo greatly blackens Argyll's crime. Historically
he also ravished the countryside, destroying the crops of the Ogilvie
tenants, burning their standing timber, carrying off livestock and
altogether causing an estimated £7,000 worth of damage so that the
Earl of Airlie received no rents for fourteen months.

> Come down, come down, my Lady Ogilvie,
> Come down and kiss me fairly:
> O I winna kiss the fause Argyll,
> If he should na leave a standing stane in Airlie.

> He hath taken her by the left shoulder,
> Says, Dame where lies thy dowry?
> O it's east and west yon wan water side,
> And it's down by the banks of the Airlie.

> They hae sought it up, they hae sought it down,
> They hae sought it maist severely,
> Till they fand it in the fair plumb-tree
> That shines on the bowling-green of Airlie.

He hath taken her by the middle saw small,
And O but she grat sairly!
And laid her down by the bonny burn-side,
Till they plundered the castle of Airlie.

Gif my gude lord war here this night,
As he is with King Charlie,
Neither you, nor ony ither Scottish lord,
Durst avow to the plundering of Airlie.

A. L. Lloyd is rather dismissive of 'the sport of tracing ballad stories to some literal historical source ... The fact is, well substantiated or ill, this kind of historical attribution tells us nothing essential about the ballads'.[51] This 'sport', like many others, is irresistible and one might counter Lloyd by suggesting that the real interest lies in *which* historical events captured the popular imagination, and the reason why they did so. It must be significant that such well-remembered figures as Earl Bothwell, Edom o' Gordon, James MacPherson of 'MacPherson's Rant', the Bonnie Earl o Moray, Dick o the Cow, Kinmont Willie and Archie o Cawfield were all contemporaries. These big ballads represent the epic of the Scottish people. Lloyd further asserts that the historical ballads 'seem to have remained more interesting to the scholars than to the folk ... the high affairs of state rarely caught the imagination of lower-class singers and their listeners because such affairs were seldom in their interest'.[52] His statement may hold true for England but it is the very antithesis of what happened in Scotland. Here the strength of the kin-ties, the appeal to the blood and the name, the bonds of vassalage and tenancy, all combined in Highlands and Lowlands alike to ensure that the interests of a Gordon or a Moray or a Campbell were identified with the interests of those who depended upon them. Society in pre-covenanting Scotland was largely classless because in a sense it was totally aristocratic.[53] King James failed because he did not comport himself as a 'kyndly king' where the adjective is related to the word 'kin'.

The ballad literature of the late sixteenth and early seventeenth centuries was produced by a society which believed itself to be under siege. Such awareness of change is arguably one of the great themes of human history experienced from generation to generation; it is the means used by men to protect themselves against the unknowable that differs from period to period. At the time under discussion the folk became aware that the traditional way of life was disappearing as the crown steadily made inroads into the old society, notably on the kingdom's southern frontier and on the borders of the Highlands, and they took refuge in a literature which enshrined the values of the past. Since such ballads are born in difficult, not to say painful, circumstances, the child is depicted as more perfect than reality. When men gaze into the mirror of Time they are seldom seeking a reflection of their own mundane world but rather a roseate representation of what, in happier circumstances, might have been for them possible. The common observation that many of the ballads are deplorably unhistorical does not necessarily detract from their historical value. Like all great literature they are concerned with universals which now and again afford some comfort to bewildered humanity in its endless endeavour to come to terms with its own predicament. It must be recognised that the historian's notion of linear time is alien to non-literate agricultural communities, wherein history consists of the relentless cycle of birth, copulation and death, seed-time and harvest, winter and summer. Ancestral characteristics are reborn from generation to generation. Knowledge of a man's father tells much about his son. History, for good or ill, *does* repeat itself. Yet this is a dimension of which conventional historians seem barely aware. Who can say whether the phantom of reality is more readily recoverable in the folio or the folk tradition?

Just as the reformed Kirk may be said to have fostered the folk tradition through the good and godly ballads convention so it was not above encouraging the circulation of ballads to achieve political ends although it must be admitted that its greatest encouragement was given to psalms. A rendering of the twentieth psalm welcomed King James to Edinburgh in 1579. At a banquet, following the baptism of Prince Henry in 1594, 'there was sung the 128th psalm, with diverse voices and toones and musical instruments playing'. Psalms greeted the banished followers of Andrew Melville on their return to Edinburgh. The reception given to John Durie was as unprecedented as it was memorable for the numbers who greeted him. 'As he is coming to Edinburgh there met him at the Gallows Green 200, but ere he came to the Netherbow this number increased to 400, but they were no sooner entered but they increased to 600 or 700, and within short space the whole street was replenished even to Sanct Geiles Kirk: the number was estimated to 2,000. At the Netherbow they took up the 124th psalm and sung in such a pleasant tune in four parts, known to the most part of the people that coming up the street all bareheaded till they enter in the kirk with such a great sound and majestie that it moved both themselves and all the huge multitude of the beholders, looking out at the shots and overstairs with admiration and astonishment.'[54] Between 1564 and 1644 sixty editions of the psalm book were published. That period produced such glories as William Kethe's version of Psalm 100, 'All People that on Earth do Dwell'. In the third line of the second verse Kethe originally wrote 'we are his folk, he doth us feed', which early metathesis rendered 'flock'. The psalm book of 1650 was printed without tunes so initiating what one authority calls 'the dark age of Scottish psalmody''.[55] The relationship between Scottish psalmody and Scottish folk would be a worthwhile subject for investigation. Such covenanting ballads, still identifiably entrenched in the flyting or polemical tradition, as 'Philiphaugh' (Child, 202), 'Loudon Hill' (Child, 205), or 'Bothwell Brigge' (Child, 206) may well have originally been composed to psalm tunes.

But it was not only the ballad tradition which survived. A manuscript of 1670 or 1680 preserves the titles of a number of folk songs, some of which were undoubtedly bawdy. There is no suggestion that only the folk were capable of producing bawdy songs – Shakespeare's groundlings doubtless relished the philosophical reflections of Lear while the courtiers screamed at the clowns – but such songs are simply easier to recognise. The titles include, 'The nock is out of Johne's bow', 'Thy love leggs sore bunden-a', 'Whaten a yeapin carle thou arte', 'In the cool of the night came my lemman/ And yellow haire above her brow', and 'I and my cummer, my cummer and I shall never part with our mouth so dry'.[56]

This paper cannot claim to have even scratched the surface of a large, complex and under-investigated topic. Perhaps celebration is a one-word definition of what all music is about. The problem of whether a tune is best fitted for the praise of God or for the edification of the Devil is probably best answered in the deepest recesses of the

Scottish psyche. The church at least did not succeed in suppressing the folk music of Scotland in the period under review, nor is there much evidence that it attempted to do so. All too often Knox, Melville and their successors are viewed through the smokescreen of the evangelical revival of the early nineteenth century by which time it was possible for Thomas Carlyle to distinguish 'bare old Calvinism under sentence of death'.[57] After four hundred years the impact of Calvinism on Scottish history still awaits serious investigation.

The great bulk of our surviving folk tradition is concerned with the celebration of the people's past. The fascination of such a vast and little-tapped reservoir is perhaps epitomised by the astonishing works of the Reverend Zachary Boyd, sometime minister of Glasgow who died in 1653 and who has some claim to the distinction of having been one of Scotland's most prolific folk poets. His translation of the psalms was rejected by the General Assembly but, nothing daunted, he produced some 26,000 lines of verse under the title 'Zion's Flowers', an encyclopaedic collection of biblical lore in metrical translation and known as Zachary Boyd's Bible. His doggerel gained for him a reputation, not altogether undeserved, of being a kind of seventeenth-century ecclesiastical Billy Connolly. He was spuriously attributed with such stanzas as,

> And Jacob made for his wee Josie,
> A tartan coat to keep him cosie,
> And what for no? there was nae harm
> To keep the lad baith saft and warm.

In one passage he has the daughter of Herodias dance a Strathspey. Yet Zachary Boyd like Andrew Wyntoun or the much misunderstood MacGonagall and anyone else who has ever tried to put pen to parchment or paper, was simply trying to comprehend the meaning of man's experience on this planet and in particular that lovely little patch named Scotland. In a profound passage he discusses the fascinating business of how words come into fashion and are, as quickly, forgotten or, alternatively, how words survive when their original meaning is forgotten. Similarly songs, orally transmitted throughout the generations can enshrine fragments of history long after the singers have forgotten the original circumstances in which the songs were conceived.

> The wordes which whilom all men did admire
> Loath'd in a trice may hence foorth not appear,
> No more than changing French with gallant shewes
> Could be content to weave the Irish trewes.
> Our wordes like clothes, such is vain man's condition,
> In length of time doe all weare out of fashion.
> We are like echo which by voices begot
> From hollow vales speakes words it knoweth not. [58]

As with words, then so with folk, which enables us to catch the echo of the people's past across the wide valleys of Time.

NOTES
I am grateful to David Stuart for providing the musical illustrations to this paper, when first delivered, for suggesting the Shetland fiddle tune as an appropriate subtitle and for helpful comments on the content.

1 David Morrison (ed.), *Essays on Fionn MacColla* (Thurso, 1973). Mac Colla's views are much elaborated in his *At the Sign of the Clenched Fist* (Edinburgh, 1967).

2 The most useful are to be found in the introductory chapters of Francis Collinson's, *The Traditional and National Music of Scotland* (London, 1966), A. L. Lloyd, *Folk Song in England* (rep. St Albans, 1975), David Johnson, *Music and Society in Lowland Scotland in the Eighteenth Century* (London, 1972).

3 David Buchan, *The Ballad and the Folk* (London, 1972) I.

4 Calum MacLean, *The Highlands* (London, 1959), p. 117.

5 William Dauney, *Ancient Scottish Melodies from a Manuscript of the Reign of King James VI with an Introductory Enquiry Illustrative of the History of the Music of Scotland* (Edinburgh, 1838), pp. 44-7.

6 John MacQueen, *Ballattis of Luve* (Edinburgh, 1970), xiii.

7 R. L. Mackie, *King James IV of Scotland. A Brief Survey of His Life and Times* (Edinburgh, 1958), pp. 121, 124.

8 *Acts of the Parliaments of Scotland* (A.P.S.), (eds.) T. Thomson and C. Innes, 12 vols. (London, 1814-75) II, pp. 36, 51.

9 Dauney, *Melodies*, p. 85.

10 *The Complaynte of Scotlande*, (ed.) J. A. H. Murray (Early English Text Society, 1872), pp. 64-5.

11 David Patrick (ed.), *Statutes of the Scottish Church* (Edinburgh, 1907), p. 127.
12 MacQueen, *Ballattis, xi-xii.*
13 John Calvin, *Institutes of the Christian Religion*, trans. H. Beveridge, 2 vols. (London, 1962), II, p. 32.
14 Quoted Percy A. Scholes, *The Puritans and Music in England and New England* (London, 1934), p. 344 in a useful section on 'Calvin and Music'.
15 Quoted William Cowan, 'The Scottish Reformation Psalmody', *Records of the Scottish Church History Society*, I (1926), pp. 38-9.
16 Scholes, *Puritans*, pp. 336-9.
17 Gordon Donaldson, 'John Knox: the first puritan or the victim of puritan mythology?', *New Edinburgh Review*, No. 3 (August 1969), p. 21.
18 D. Hay Fleming, *Mary Queen of Scots* (London, 1898), p. 44.
19 A.P.S. III, pp. 87, 89, 140.
20 *Scottish Burgh Records Society, Charters and Documents relating to ... Peebles* (1872), pp. 306-7, 411; *Extractsfrom the records ... of Glasgow* (1876), pp. 454, 469; *Extracts from ... Stirling* (1889), pp. 12, 52, 200, 339.
21 Helena M. Shire, *Song, Dance and Poetry of the Court of Scotland under King James VI* (Cambridge, 1969), p. 231.
22 A.P.S. VI (2), pp. 865, 909.
23 David Calderwood, *The History of the Kirk of Scotland*, (ed.) T. Thomson, 9 vols. (Edinburgh, 1842-9), I, pp. 141-3.
24 *The Gude and Godlie Ballatis*, (ed.) A. F. Mitchell (Scottish Text Society, 1897), pp. 158, 192, 198.
25 *Gude and Godlie Ballatis*, p. 222.
26 Quoted Edward J. Cowan, *Montrose for Covenant and King* (London, 1977), p. 227.
27 William Geddes, *The Saints' Recreation upon the Estate of Grace in Spiritual Songs* (Edinburgh, 1683), preface.
28 *The Diary of Mr James Melville* (Bannatyne Club, 1829), p. 18.
29 *Register of the Privy Council of Scotland* (R.P.C.), 14 vols. (Edinburgh, 1877-98), III, p. 587.
30 R.P.C., III, p. 273.
31 *Correspondence of Sir R. Kerr, Earl of Ancram and William Earl of Lothian*, 2 vols. (Bannatyne Club, 1875), I, p. 108.
32 For an interesting short discussion of this poem see Kenneth Buthlay, 'Habbie Simson' in *Bards and Makars*, (ed.) A. J. Aitken, M. P. McDiarmid and D. S. Thomson (Glasgow, 1977), pp. 214-220.
33 P. Hume Brown, *Early Travellers in Scotland* (Edinburgh, 1891), p. 258.
34 John Knox, *History of the Reformation in Scotland*, (ed.) W. C. Dickinson, 2 vols. (London, 1949), II, pp. 44-5, 64. On the significance of drink see

Dauney, *Melodies*, p. 260.
35 Calderwood, *History*, V, p. 409.
36 John MacInnes, 'The Oral Tradition in Scottish Gaelic Poetry', *Scottish Studies*, 12, 1968, p. 38.
37 *Chronicle of Lanercost* (Bannatyne Club, 1839), p. 109.
38 George Sinclair, *Satan's Invisible World Discovered* 1685 (Edinburgh, 1871), pp. 163, 219.
39 R. Pitcairn (ed.), *Ancient Criminal Trials in Scotland*, 3 vols. (Bannatyne Club, 1833-), I, pp. 230-41.
40 Quoted MacInnes, 'Oral Tradition', p. 40.
41 George F. Black, *A Calendar of Cases of Witchcraft in Scotland 1510-1727* (New York, 1938), p. 65.
42 Dauney, *Melodies*, p. 220.
43 Alexander Keith, *Last Leaves of Traditional Ballads and Ballad Airs* (Aberdeen, 1925), xxxix.
44 Calderwood, *History*, V, pp. 171, 177.
45 James Balfour, *Historical Works*, 4 vols. (Edinburgh, 1824), I, p. 390. For a discussion of the conspiracy against Cawdor and Moray see Edward J. Cowan, 'Clanship, Kinship and the Campbell Acquisition of Islay'.
46 *Calendar of State Papers Relating to Scotland 1547-1603*, 13 vols. (London, 1901-1969), X, pp. 573-5.
47 V. de Sola Pinto and A. E. Rodway (eds.), *The Common Muse. Popular British Ballad Poetry from the 15th to the 20th Century* (Harmondsworth, 1965), p. 21.
48 John Spalding, *Memorialls of the Trubles in Scotland and in England*, 2 vols. (Aberdeen, 1850), I, p. 446. The ballad is discussed pp. 437-46.
49 Edward J. Cowan, 'The Angus Campbells and the Origins of the Campbell-Ogilvie Feud'.
50 Keith, *Last Leaves*, xxv-vi.
51 Lloyd, *Folk Song*, p. 129.
52 Lloyd, *Folk Song*, p. 137.
53 For an excellent discussion of this theme see Buchan, *Ballad and Folk*, chapter 5.
54 Calderwood, *History*, III, pp. 458-9, 646-7; V, p. 345.
55 Cowan, 'Reformation Psalmody', pp. 46-7.
56 Dauney, *Melodies*, pp. 56-8.
57 William Ferguson (ed.), *An Anthology of Carrick* (Glasgow, 1925), p. 46.

Traditional Music: The Material Background

GAVIN SPROTT

There is no song, no pipe or fiddle tune, which does not have a material base. The relationship may not be immediately obvious or direct, but it is always there. The reason is self-evident. If there is no land or work there are no people, no livelihood, no stories and no music.

Here it is not proposed to demonstrate a series of mechanical linkages between certain bits of music and the precise circumstances of their composition. Rather, the object is to illuminate the material base in a general way, and provide something of a context into which people can put the heritage of folk music with which most people are familiar.

As L. P. Hartley[1] remarked, the past is like a foreign country. If you regard the particulars of people's daily lives, at every turn into the past, you tumble back into different words and different experiences. Sometimes this feeling of differentness is so strong, such a sensation of moving in a half-light, that it is difficult to know whether the perception is of reality or imagination.

How then can you enter into the experience of past generations and get the feel of their expectations and mental horizons? This is a thing on which the study of material culture can shed some light, in an attempt to reconstruct the physical world in which people lived.

Here the world encountered is the world of work. To begin with, work dominated family relationships. It governed the choice of mate and when people married, which in turn affected the size of the family, and consequently that of the population.[2] Childhood is almost a modern invention. The young worked as soon as they could herd a beast or gather bait for a line.

Behind all this was the rhythm of the seasons – seed-time and harvest, the hay, the peats, the lambing, the summer grazing, the long winter nights, Beltane and Halloween, Lammas and Martinmas the old holy days which marked the ritual starts and ends of season and the holding of markets. Even with the genius of a von Ranke, it is doubtful that it will ever be seen as it really was, but by reconstructing the physical world, it is the nearest you will get to it. There you begin to form some conception of the cradle in which people's experience was contained and the framework in which it was matured.

There is good reason for doing it this way round. Folk culture does not resurrect the experience of the past, but recycles it into the present. It is a bit more living and less traditional than is commonly supposed, and often what we hear reflected in music and language is not the past's imagination but the present's. For example, in a recent – and indeed interesting – anthology of Co. Antrim and Co. Down weavers' poetry, the editor, John Hewitt, discusses the Lowland Scots tongue. Take the lines of Thomas Given of Cullybackey:

> The blackbird keeks out frae the fog at the broo
> Gees his neb a bit dicht on a stane.

'To *keek* means something more precise than simply to look! There is always a furtiveness about it ... *Dicht* ... means something more exact than 'to wipe'; it means rather a flock-of-a-wipe.'[3] Now to a native speaker of *Scotch* (as native speakers call it) this is pure imagination. *Dicht* is wipe, and if it is to mean a special kind of wipe then it depends on the way you say it. Folk culture and folk music, like a folk language (for want of a better description) is implicit. It rests in the eye and ear of the performer or beholder, and paradoxically, in that way it lives entirely in the present. If you are to seek historical significance and insight in folk music, you must also ferret out the experience of the past quite independently.

Now, many people are rather silly, even paranoid, about change. It is certainly not in the monopoly of our own experience. It does come and go, and the particular interest of modern times is not that society is in the middle of change, but rather nearer the end of a

55

distinct period of change. Industrialisation of this part of the world is only becoming substantially complete today. It is out of two or more centuries of this specific change that much folk music has come.

The initial step towards industrialisation in the countryside was farming improvement. At the root of this was not new technology, but a change in the way land was used and people's work disposed. Instead of separate ground for arable and grazing, these two functions were integrated on the same ground through new rotations and from this flowed two remarkable results – vast social upheaval, and in the areas concerned, the end of famine.

Famine has a very crushing effect. It knocks the stuffing out of everything. The last full-scale famine in Lowland Scotland was in the last decade of the seventeenth century, and although it often barely rates a mention in the history books, it must have been one of the main elements that led to the Union of 1707. The last major famine in the Western Highlands and Islands coincided with the Great Famine in Ireland, between 1845-50. Again, you wonder if this has not had a lot to do with the decline of popular Gaelic culture. Although that is a difficult one to pin down in detail, the experience of starving monoglot Gaelic speakers seeking work in the Lowlands is not one they would have let their children forget. By contrast, the much despised Lowland Scots tongue, with a less well-defined literature and no agreed orthography has yet somehow survived the assault of lunatic teachers and social fashion, although maybe not for much longer. Underlying this is the corollary to the experience of famine. Prosperity takes the lid off and encourages cultural development.

That was certainly so in Lowland Scotland in the eighteenth century. This change was so startling with regard to the internal fitting out of the house that it is worthwhile going into more detail. The key to change was the ready availability of timber. In 1795 Sir John Sinclair remarked on the improvement in houses over the previous thirty years 'because timber is more easily got'.[4] The last of the great native forests in Rannoch, Speyside, Deeside and Affric were being commercially exploited and the product floated down the rivers, much of it already reduced to rough deals by water-driven sawmills. The East Coast burghs were in a position to import Scandinavian and Baltic timber on what would previously have been a prodigal scale, as the booming Lowland economy could now easily afford it. Houses could now be lined, ceiled, and provided with basic items of furniture such as tables and chairs which are now taken for granted. Perhaps most important of all, the timber enabled people to construct box beds. Like a tent within the house, they must have seemed a marvellous innovation at the time, and perhaps the immediate additional comfort they afforded stalled pressure to improve the main fabric of the house. It stood people away from damp floors and walls, provided a refuge from leaking roofs, provided warmth, and not least, a novel experience of privacy.

An improvement which often preceded the introduction of the box bed was the construction of a *hallan*, which partitioned the byre end from the living end of the house.[5] But the box bed was the main cause of the subdivision of the house, and descriptions of this trend occur over the whole country. This was following precedents set by the more well-to-do.[6]

The box beds could themselves be used to form the *hallan*[7]. More common, the box beds divided the living area itself in half, thus creating the *but* or outer room, and the *ben* or inner room which could only be reached through the *but* room. There is a whole range of alternative terminology to describe this simple division – for instance the *Kitchen and Spence* in Stirlingshire,[8] the *Kitchen and Farm Room* in Lanarkshire,[9] the *Trance* (for *hallan*), *Inseat and Spence* in Ayrshire, *But-hoose and Ben End* in Orkney [10] and so on.

The possession of a but and a ben became a mark of dignity[11]. The ben room was the place where the heads of the family slept and visitors of consequence were received.[12] Later, in the last century, the ben room was succeeded by the *best room,* which in slightly bigger houses often became a curious mausoleum of family photographs and fancy furniture.

By way of contrast, what was the alternative to these improvements? Some idea is gained by looking at descriptions of eighteenth and early nineteenth-century Western Highlands and Islands houses, where timber for domestic use was hard to come by. Bed spaces were often built into the thickness of the wall round the fire[13] and the remains of stone outshot beds are to be found as far apart as Shetland and Bute.[14] In early nineteenth-century Skye, a distinction in wealth lay in whether your fireside bench was of wood or a row of turf covered with stones.[15] In fact, the benches served as seats or beds.

57

Many small vestiges of stone furniture still survive – binks and recesses for storage, salt holes by the hearth, and so on.

But in general, the lack of timber for internal fitments drew everything to the fireside, including the sleeping arrangements. In the mid-eighteenth century in Wester Ross it was noted that they put brushwood around the central fire 'behind which they lay long heath for beds, where the family sleep promiscuously, few of them having any other covering than their body clothes'.[16] Perhaps the most spectacular evidence of the old stone and turf house-cum-furniture are the ruined old shieling huts still to be seen in the hill grazings in the Western Islands, and there are people scarcely of middle age who have used them. Something of a stone tent, these huts contained a heather bed, held in by a low turf wall, which capped with a plank, also served as a fireside bench.[17]

Although it would be rash to assert that these later style arrangements were uniformly uncomfortable, nevertheless, a lack of plenishings could spell out misery. For instance, earlier last century in Barra, according to the minister, 'the natives have little or no idea of cleanliness or comfort. They have seldom much furniture to boast of: sometimes not a chair to sit upon, or bed clothes to cover them from the severity of the night air.'[18]

All this serves to underline a simple point. Pictures such as Wilkie's *Penny Wedding* (with Neil Gow playing the fiddle and his brother Donald playing the cello) show an apparently traditional and homely interior of a prosperous old-style farmer's house. The homeliness, however, was entirely due to its modernity. Furthermore, the musical culture of Scotland in the eighteenth century was in dramatic contrast to that of the previous century.[19] The weakening of traditional strictures against dancing and public entertainment had something to do with it,[20] but also the great increase in prosperity and a flowering of musical activity is more than coincidental.

One interesting thing about the new prosperity is the degree of diversity that eventually came out of it. To illustrate what happened in the countryside in the course of farming improvement, one must at least touch on what went before. In the early eighteenth century, both Lowland and Highland farming were basically the same, although there was greater emphasis on arable in the former, and on pastoral in the latter. The common features were the ways in which the ground was used. For the most part it was either continuously cropped (the infield) or in permanent pasture (the common grazing) with some periodically used for arable and grazing (the outfield). For the most part it was a country of joint farming communities, which in turn formed the units of which estates were made up. It was a society of small farmers. The bigger farmers had lesser farmers as sub-tenants. In this set-up a man seeking a livelihood sought ground from which to produce a subsistence. Whatever tradesmen there were also had their ground, and people providing a common service were rewarded either wholly or in part with ground. Occasional place names are reminders of this – for instance, *Mammiesroun*, the midwife's holding, in Errol parish. By pre-improvement standards, many ministers with their glebes were substantial farmers. Local and estate administration and officialdom (which were much the same thing) were almost all drawn from among the farmers who were estate tenants. It is not that there were no servants, but their relation-ships to their masters were different. This all made for numerous communal arrangements – composite plough teams, common graz-ing, shared fuel resources and so on. At the same time it was the great age of do-it-yourself. Every man was a Johnny A'thing. He had to be able to make and mend his own implements, his plough graith, build and thatch his own house, provide his own fuel, and so on. Life, far from being the simple one, must have been full of endless compli-cations, for at every turn people had to fall back on local resources and their own ingenuity.

Ramshackle though the old-style farming was by the eighteenth century, it embodied a highly distinctive social structure, and one that was not without its merits. An appreciation of the old-style farming communities gives a far sharper sense of the actual change which took place when they went.[21]

With the new rotations that integrated arable and grazing into the same ground in improved farming went reorganised farms, greatly increased in size and blocked into single units. Tenant farmers be-came a small and comparatively privileged class, and to seek a livelihood most men now looked not for land, but for employment and a wage.

Out of this came the various groups of farm servants, *fee'd or* contracted for a year or half-year, living in purpose-built accom-

C

modation provided by the farmer or the laird, moving from one place to another as fancy or the labour market dictated.

The improved farming generated new skills of husbandry, and ploughing became a skill in its own right, encouraged by ploughing matches and identified with the horse, which now replaced the ox in the Lowlands. The *horsemen* or *hinds* offered their services at feeing markets or hiring fairs. In the South-East they were mainly married men, and a man was often fee'd on the strength of his wife and daughters being able to work as *bondagers* or women outworkers. In the late eighteenth century the fashion developed in parts of Central Scotland, Fife, Angus and the North-East of feeing single men, and out of this grew the traditions of the chalmer and the bothy. Besides the horsemen there were also the cattlemen, shepherds and the whole range of milkmaids, kitchie deems, farm lasses and domestic servants. The cattleman's wife usually had milking duties, sometimes had to attend to the bothy, and in the dairying counties of the South-West, women formed a major element in this new class of farm servants.

So great were the returns from farming improvement that the estate took on a new complexion. Besides the tenant farms which generated the basic income, widespread plantation developed new woodlands to manage. The big house itself had an economy of its own with the butler, footman, housekeeper, maids, and so on, and round the house were gardeners, coachmen, gamekeepers, estate tradesmen and, of course, the factor himself.

This new differentiation brought new prospectives. The lairds no longer raised a countryside in revolt in support of their religious and political views, for like Cincinnatus of old, they had beaten their swords into ploughshares. But by the same token, their servants no longer ate at their tables. As Burns wryly commented: 'Surely did those in exalted stations know how happy they would make some classes of their inferiors by condescension and affability they would never stand so high ...',[22] and on the strength of the opposite experience he asserted *A man's a man for a' that.* The old feudal familiarty, so well portrayed by the Baron of Bradwardine in *Waverley* and old Lady Bellenden in *Old Mortality,* had gone. Paradoxically, now that the apparatus of servitude is now vastly diminished in the countryside, the old feudal familiarity is returning.

But farming improvement created another distinctive group in the countryside which has largely passed away in our own day, but whose memory lingers with a distinct flavour – the tradesmen. The change in land use brought a technological revolution in its train. Sown grass could never thrive on the sour, weed-ridden, stony soil of the old-style farming. As it was drained, cleared of stones, cleaned and reduced to a fine tilth, it became feasible to work with much lighter ploughs, requiring a fraction of the old forms of draught. The consequences in terms of manpower can be seen in the case of a farm in Monikie parish in Angus. About the 1750s the ground was worked by five ploughs, each employing five pair of oxen, requiring an absolute minimum of fifteen people in all to work them. By the 1790s the same ground was being worked by lighter, improved ploughs, each with a yoke of two, and increasingly one pair of horses. In the latter case, the plough was guided and the horses driven by the same man, resulting in a fivefold reduction in manpower.[23] But as the numbers required to work the soil dropped considerably, other employment developed to service the new farming. Iron-framed ploughs on James Small's model were turned out in local smiddies, solid carts built by joiners replaced pack horses and slypes, the new trashing mills and improved corn mills required skilled hands to set them up and maintain them. Harness was no longer home-made but turned out by the saddler. Building the new farm houses, steadings and cottar houses employed numerous masons and wrights. Other trades such as weaving, tailoring and shoemaking prospered in their train. By early last century, the numbers directly tilling the ground in the lowland countryside were often less than half the total population, and equalled in numbers by the tradesmen. Another sizeable component now comprised people engaged in numerous casual labouring jobs, working for small tradesmen, building and maintaining roads and other public works which were now commonly available for the first time.[24]

In many ways these tradesmen inherited the character of the old-style farmers. Many feud small plots in the new villages that the lairds encouraged, or often they had crofts or pendicles scattered between bigger farms. Where the farm servants and their families often moved from one fee to another, the tradesmen remained settled, leaving them in possession of a certain position in local society.

They were a strong element in the kirk sessions and masonic lodges, often on an equal footing with the smaller tenant farmers. Thus they could afford to cultivate a certain independence, enjoying the benefits of a modest prosperity and a strong family life. Because they were not so mobile, their children could reap the advantages of education often denied to the farm servants' children. Their situation and housing enabled them to maintain an extended family and all the cultural continuity that goes with it.

Yet in the Lowlands, there is in large degree a break between the culture of the old townships, even among the tradesfolk, and the more differentiated society bred of improved farming. By the end of the eighteenth century, what had happened to the bellows pipes and the stockenhorn? Even though there are some remarkable survivals in the Lowland oral tradition, they are subterranean phenomena – they were discovered. Fancy discovering a tradition! Burns, himself acutely aware of this break in continuity, talked of 'old pieces (of balladry which) are still to be found among the peasantry of the West . . . the shattered wrecks of these venerable compositions'. He collected and preserved some of them in the Scots Musical Museum. He also unwittingly assisted in their decline. George Younger recalled an old man saying that 'Burns had come on the carpet and spoilt the market for common Scotch poetry'.[25] What has survived has a more abstract appeal. How many pre-eighteenth-century Lowland songs to do with work survive as more than the name of a fiddle tune? An isolated example is a *pleugh sang* – and it survived only because it was noted as a curiosity after it had been reared into a late fifteenth-century part-song.[26]

My grandfather, who must have been among the last to serve on square-rigged sailing ships, was a singer of chanties, even though, as he modestly asserted, he hadn't a note of music in his head. Even when he sang them or wrote them down, he noted that there was a taboo that existed that kept the songs for working occasions alone.

So, when the work changed and the social set-up changed, the songs changed, and sometimes there were no songs. This essay only touches on a small part of that complex situation bred of farming improvement, but what I suggest is that it was in certain ways an aggregate of subcultures with overlapping areas of experience. They are the songs of fisherfolk, bothymen, weavers, sailormen, tradesfolk and so on, the products of two unique centuries of change. The Highlands and Islands are different. Left to the old-style farming much longer, they were then subject to drastic and often barbarous change in the form of the Clearances. Yet the population that remained, crowded into the new crofts, to carry on the old farming, often on marginal land in a changed and stunted form, retained much of the old homogenous character. The do-it-yourself habits and neighbouring customs have today been eroded by the influx of cheap industrial goods and partial mechanisation. Nor should it be regretted, for in material things, as an octogenarian Highlander remarked, there are no good old days. Yet an older social ethos is passing away that began disappearing in the Lowlands two centuries earlier, although even there it lingers in neighbourhoods of moorland crofts not an hour's drive from Edinburgh. In the Highlands and Islands there will not be that uniquely rich interval between the start and full consequences of industrialisation being felt. As new work patterns mature into a different age, both Highland and Lowland, who knows what may come of it?

NOTES

1 L. P. Hartley, *The Go-Between.*
2 The relationship between the economic base, marriage patterns and population is ably demonstrated in *The Northern Isles,* Alexander Fenton, 1978, and *The Making of the Crofting Community,* James Hunter, 1974.
3 John Hewitt, ed. and intro., *Rhyming Weavers and other Country Poets of Antrim and Down,* 1974, pp. 15 and 16.
4 J. Sinclair, *Agric. N. Counties,* 1795, p. 50.
5 J. Headrick, *Agric. Angus,* 1813, p. 128.
6 R. Dinnie, *An Account of the Parish of Birse,* 1865, p. 14.
7 Rev. C. Findlater, *Gen. View Agric. Peebles,* 1802, pp. 45-6.
8 P. Graham, *Agric. Stirling,* 1812, pp. 77-78.
9 N.S.A. 1845 VI, pp. 831-2, Wandell and Lambington.
10 A. Fenton, *Northern Isles,* 1978, p. 148.
11 R. Dinnie, *An Account of the Parish of Birse,* 1865, p. 14.
12 J. Headrick, *Agric. Angus,* 1813, p. 128.
   P. Graham, *Agric. Stirling,* 1812, pp. 77-78.
13 Martin [1695], 1884, p. 281.
14 A. Fenton, *Northern Isles,* 1978, sections 15-16.

15 N.S.A. 1845 XIV, p. 292, Snizort.
16 A J. Warden, 'The Linen Trade', 1864, quoting 1754 report to Board of Manufacturers.
17 C.L.A. and Information, *Peigi MacLeod*, Shawbost, 1874, *Donald Macdonald*, N. Tolsta, 1976.
18 N.S.A. 1845 XIV, p. 212, Barra.
19 G. Emmerson, *Rantin Pipe and Tremblin String*, 1971, p. 49.
20 D. Johnson, *Music and Society in Lowland Scotland in the Eighteenth Century*, 1972, pp. 11, 111 and 121.
21 This neglected subject has been tackled in Ian Whyte's excellent *Agriculture and Society in Seventeenth Century Scotland, 1979*.
22 J. De Lancy Ferguson, *The Letters of Robert Burns*, 1931, Vol. I, p. 43.
23 O.S.A. 1792, Vol. IV, p. 348, Monikie.
24 N.S.A., Vol. X, p. 411, Longforgan.
25 G. Younger, *Autobiography*, 1881, p. 178.
26 See *Tools and Tillage*, A. Fenton, Vol. 1/3, 1970, 'The Plough Song'.

The Ballad, The Folk and The Oral Tradition

HAMISH HENDERSON

1

'Eighteenth-century Scotland, there is no doubt at all, was a nation of ballad singers and ballad lovers. How much earlier it had been so, no one knows; but it is a fact that what we today know as British balladry at its best is a mass of texts taken down by interested persons from living Scottish tradition in the latter half of the eighteenth century, or learned then and transmitted to print or manuscript early in the following century.'

Thus Bertrand H. Bronson, polymath editor of the music of the classic or Child ballads, writing in the *California Folklore Quarterly*, Vol. IV, No. 2, in 1945. One reaction to this sort of praise may well be, of course, to ask: are the Scots ballads, the muckle sangs, really as good as all that? Are they better, for example, than the English versions of what in many cases are virtually the same songs? How do they relate to the oral literature of other countries? What is their connection with the ballads of the Scandinavian countries, which seem to resemble many of them quite closely? In fact, the question narrows down to: What are they? What makes them tick?

For about half a century the sound of their ticking was almost swamped, so to speak, by the furious din of a controversy about their nature and origins – about what one might call ballad identity; one lot of scholars supporting the idea of 'communal' composition (the ballads the result of a sort of team effort of some ill-defined semi-mystical kind, sometimes visualised as a dancing throng), and others, regarding themselves as very hard-headed and down-to-earth, supporting the idea of some degree or other of individual authorship. An appalling racket went on for years, and on some remote campus – maybe the University of the Grand Canyon – it is no doubt going on still.

The book that at long last began to get the main problems into focus was *The Ballad of Tradition* by Professor Gordon H. Gerould; this was published in 1932, and it led to a breakthrough on several fronts.

At about the same time it appeared, Bronson began to get interested in these same 'big ballads' whose texts Professor Child had edited in five massive volumes in the latter half of the nineteenth century; and a growing realisation of the interdependence of ballad tunes and texts led him to devote himself to his life work – the completion of the 'other half' of Child's thesaurus.

'Nothing but the apparent unreason of history could justify the absurdity of recommending at this date that for their proper comprehension it is necessary to study texts and tunes together. For that is so logically and so obviously the initial point of departure!'

In his ballad researches, Bronson looked back curiously, like so many others, at that extraordinary late eighteenth-century Scotland which had given so much folksong – and so much else – to the world and, disregarding the 'dancing throng' and other strictly non-terrestrial ballad-ferlies, his gaze came to rest on a sober manse in Fife, where the minister's wife continued, off and on, to sing the ballads she had learned as a child in the highlands of Aberdeenshire. This lady, Anna Gordon (better known, from her husband's charge, as Mrs Brown of Falkland), was the daughter of the Professor of Humanity at King's College, Aberdeen, and she appears from her letters and the accounts of others to have been a well-educated, indeed a very literate person, who read Ossian and wrote verses; not, therefore, at first sight the sort of person likely to emerge as source-singer of priceless orally transmitted (and orally recreated) folksong. However, as Bronson noted, her importance can be readily suggested by means of a few figures: of the nearly three dozen ballad texts which she preserved, Child allowed every one a place in his canon. Four of these are the only extant versions. Twenty others are Child's A, or primary texts; and four more his B texts. 'Her records,' adds Bronson, 'offer besides a rare opportunity for the study of variation in classical balladry'.

It is this last sentence which served as a springboard for the researches of Dr David Buchan, formerly of Stirling University and now of Memorial University, St John's, Newfoundland, who in 1972 published what is probably the most important single book on the textual side of the Child ballads since Gerould. His *The Ballad and the Folk* is itself an expression of that reawakening of interest in the oral tradition which has been one of the major cultural phenomena of the mid-century. Apart from Bronson, two books clearly influenced him: Albert Lord's *The Singer of Tales,* an analysis of the techniques of oral composition in the light of research among the singers of Yugoslavia, and Marshall McLuhan's complementary study, *The Gutenberg Galaxy.*

It is the first of these which undoubtedly had the most palpable effect on Dr Buchan's thought. *The Singer of Tales* is the fruit of intensive fieldwork, by Milman Parry and Lord himself, among the Yugoslav epic singers, the Homerids of modern Europe. These virtuosi are able to 'compose' orally (i.e. recreate, using traditional techniques) songs which can be thousands of lines long. The Serb epic singer does not start out with an immutable text, but with a story and a highly flexible system of techniques for telling it. Thus every new rendering is in a sense a new composition. 'Oral poems frequently possess quite complex architectonic patterns. These latter patterns manifest themselves, structurally and conceptually, in all kinds of balances and parallelisms, contrasts and antitheses, chiastic and framing devices, and in various kinds of triadic groupings. A conceptual pattern called by Lord the 'tension of essences', whereby certain narrative elements automatically cohere, would suggest that there are other hidden patterning forces, as yet undissected, working within oral tradition. Just as the aural patterns reflect the non-literate person's highly developed sense of sound, so these architectonic patterns reflect how this mode of apprehension is spatial as well as simply linear and sequential'(*The Ballad and the Folk,* p. 53).

The central part of Dr Buchan's own work, therefore, is a revaluation of the great Scots ballad texts – and specifically the variants provided by Mrs Brown of Falkland – in the light of the findings contained in a *Singer of Tales.* And he has also taken a cue from the structuralist studies which followed in the wake of the translation into English of Vladimir Propp's *Morphology of the Folktale.*

Does it come off? One major snag is that Mrs Brown has been dead these many years, and it is now, alas, impossible to hear her re-creating her ballads at every singing. On the other hand, we have the sometimes strikingly different texts of the same ballad which she sang or dictated at different periods. Bronson was moving towards the position Dr Buchan adopted when he wrote (referring to the versions of the 'Lass of Roch Royal' – Child 76 – recorded at an interval of 17 years): 'Is it not clear that what Mrs Brown was trying for in the version of 1800 was not to recover her own text of 1783 but to recover, or recreate, the ballad itself, the essential, ideal *Lass of Roch Royal*, as it exists in the sum of all its traditional variations? ... What was it she had carried in her memory? Not a *text* but a ballad: a fluid entity soluble in the mind, to be concretely realised at will in words and music.'

Child, on the other hand, was more prosaic (or just unenlightened, in those pre-Lord days?) when, commenting on these discrepancies, he contended that the version of 1800 was to be regarded 'as a blending of two independent versions known to Mrs Brown, which no doubt had much in common.'

Then again, the Yugoslav singers recorded by Lord were unlettered, and Mrs Brown (as we know) wrote verses. Dr Buchan gets over this one by pointing out that 'it is possible, at a certain point in the tradition, for a person to be both literate and an oral composer ... born one generation earlier, she would probably have remained unrecorded: born one generation later, she would not have been able to compose her ballads by the old oral method.'

Throughout his book Dr Buchan is very much alive to the long march of North-East Everyman, from the arrival of the 'beaker folk' to the fading out of the bothy system. He provides a lot of valuable information on the old homogeneous 'clannit society' which lasted in certain areas into the eighteenth century, and then charts in considerable detail the social transformation which came in the wake of the agrarian and industrial revolutions, describing the changes wrought in the life and mentality of 'the folk' by education and increasing literacy. One of the strengths of the book is that it is so firmly established in its Buchan base. One detects, however – off and on – a tendency to think of the North-East in a kind of artificial isolation, overlooking the ease with which many ballads must have moved from one part of Scotland to another.

When Dr Buchan's book was published (1972), a singer widely

regarded (by scholars, as well as by the 'folk' public) as one of the finest modern exponents of traditional ballad-singing was still living in her native city of Aberdeen – the great Jeannie Robertson. This was the singer of whom Alan Lomax wrote that she was 'a monumental figure of world folksong', and of whom A. L. Lloyd remarked that she was 'a singer sweet and heroic'. Although Jeannie is now dead, her vast repertoire of traditional balladry is fully documented in the sound archive of the School of Scottish Studies, many of the songs recorded over and over again. Several of the foremost ballad scholars of the mid-century met her, and marvelled at her. Her performances of songs like 'Lord Donald' (Child, 12) and 'The Battle of Harlaw' (Child, 163) are a living memory for thousands of people. Can such performances – in the intimacy of her own home or in the dramatically different situation of public 'folk' events – be of any assistance in elucidating the problems raised by Dr Buchan's chapters on oral composition?

It can be said at once that Jeannie was an exceedingly 'fluid' ballad singer, in the sense that she would readily incorporate fresh verses or phrases in her songs if she heard a previously unknown version that pleased her; would adopt a new tune or set new words to an old one; make songs of her own; and learn completely new items with comparative speed if they took her fancy. But she did not recreate her ballads afresh every time she sang them, as was the case with Mrs Brown (if Dr Buchan's contention is right). However, Jeannie was a singer who did sing her favourites over and over again, either with or without an audience – and I personally would submit that it is inherently *unlikely* that a singer relating the stories of what Dr Buchan rightly calls these 'tight-knit ballad-dramas' would, in fact, vary them to any great extent if the performances actually were frequent. Take 'Son David' (Jeannie's version of 'Edward'); it begins with three questions and three answers ('O what's the blood that's on your sword' etc.), and after the revelation that David has killed his brother John, the denouement follows swiftly. If the ballad is sung with any frequency, is it not more likely that the singer will sooner or later make his or her own version, and that this will eventually 'gel'?

Jeannie, then, displayed what Bronson calls 'active participation' in her ballads, but was not a ballad-composer (or recreator) in the style Dr Buchan adumbrates for Mrs Brown.

But *was* Mrs Brown a ballad-composer in this style? Her versions certainly bear the hallmark of orally recreated folk song, as Dr Buchan shows very convincingly in his three chapters on the structure of the ballads. But not everything we hear about her, from her father, her friends, and indeed (via her letters) from herself would encourage us in the belief that a casual visitor to the manse in Falkland would ever have been likely to hear a ballad, whether orally recreated or just remembered.

We know who her sources were, all right – the principal one, apparently, was an aunt (Mrs Anne Farquharson, née Forbes) who had married into that redoubtable, staunchly Jacobite, Deeside clan which still spoke Gaelic, told stories about the 'Black Colonel' who had fought for King James VII at Killiecrankie, and had many memories of blood feud with the Gordons. Anne learned her songs from the nurses and old women who lived 'among flocks and herds at Allan-a-quoich, her husband's seat', so here we have a tradition of Lowland balladry which had found its way into the haunts of the Gaelic-speaking Aberdeenshire highlanders. (If anyone finds this curious, or prima facie unlikely, it is only necessary to point to the regions of the Irish Gaeltacht such as the Aran Islands and the Dingle Peninsula, which in the last two decades have yielded beautiful versions of Anglo-Irish folk song to collectors like Seamus Ennis; the songs are a *lingua franca* which actually precedes the incoming language.)

Mrs Farquharson, it seems, was Anna's main source, but she also heard songs from her own mother, and from an old servant-maid of the Forbes family. This is, therefore, a 'woman's tradition', and we probably should not expect too much of it to have reached the males of the family. Her father certainly knew she could sing her aunt's songs because it was he who told William Tytler, the Scottish historian and antiquarian, about the ballads she retained in her memory. But what are we to make of a remark the professor made in a letter to Tytler's son which he wrote in 1793: 'Both the words and the strains [tunes] were perfectly new to me, as they were to your father'?

Mrs Brown herself wrote several letters to the same man (Alexander Fraser Tytler) in 1800, the year when – at the request of Sir Walter Scott – he approached Mrs Brown in order to obtain more ballads. Here are quotations from these letters, which Dr Buchan prints in Chapter 7 of *The Ballad and the Folk*:

> You judge rightly in supposing that I should take pleasure in recalling those scenes of infancy and childhood which the recollection of these old songs brings back to my mind, it is indeed what Ossian call(s) the joy of grief the memory of joys past pleasant, but mournful to the soul – but enough of this prattle ... I dare say I may have fragments of others, but I could not so easily recollect them, except the ballads they belonged to were mentioned.
>
> I have lately by rummaging in a by-corner of my memory found some Aberdeenshire ballads which totally escaped me before they are of a different class from those I sent you not near so ancient but may be about a century ago.

The following year, in a letter to Robert Jamieson, she wrote: 'I doubt not that in the course of conversation I might recollect something that might be new to you, tho' I do not recollect anything at present.'

Does this really sound like a ballad singer who frequently performs a song? Dr Buchan states categorically (p. 87): 'These stories we have been discussing were recreated by Mrs Brown at each singing'. But what if these separate singings were few and far between? One finds oneself toying with the idea that maybe – *pace* Bronson – Child was right after all, and Mrs Brown, in 1783 and 1800, was actually remembering two different versions – one her mother's, possibly, or one from that old maidservant, as well as Anne Farquharson's (if one was indeed hers). There would no doubt be interaction between them in her memory, in any case.

It is, of course, true that Child (who never wrote an introduction for his great collection) left, among his notes for it, the following directive: 'Remark on the differences between Mrs Brown's earlier and later versions.' Dr Buchan acclaims this as an example of his 'unerring instinct'. It may well be so. But Child's observation, as well as his instinct, might surely have led him to think, and think again, about certain characteristics of Mrs Brown's versions which Bronson himself mulled over and summarised as follows: 'There are almost no real obscurities of phrase or idea, such as often appear in pure oral transmission. There are occasional moral observations and pious reflections, especially at the ends of her ballads, which are little above the broadside level and which jar our sense of fitness. It can hardly be an accident that where the erotic note is bluntly struck in other versions, in Mrs Brown's it is side-stepped or soft-pedalled.' He also draws attention to 'false notes, artifical touches, pretty sentimentalities, and a specious neatness that puts one on guard'.

* * * * *

From Mrs Brown, still able – according to Dr Buchan – to compose ballads using techniques available first and foremost to nonliterate ballad singers, we pass to the much maligned Peter Buchan, 'vain and volatile' Peterhead printer and ballad editor who was very much Professor Child's whipping-boy when difficult questions of admission to the canon arose. For years almost anyone who wanted an Aunt Sally to shy things at had Peter Buchan at his disposal, because he had actually paid a blind ballad singer to collect songs and stories for him – thus opening the door wide, obviously, to all sorts of imposture, as well as setting an unwelcome precedent for other researchers in the public domain – and had printed as genuine a fake ballad two hoaxers had foisted on him. Also, the ballad versions he printed were mostly longer than anyone else's, and you know what *that* must mean. Will Walker, skeely antiquarian, and Alexander Keith, editor of *Last Leaves*, began the necessary job of rehabilitating Peter Buchan many years ago, but Dr Buchan's chapter on the controversy presents the case for the defence with a fine Philpot Curran-like flourish. Peter leaves the dock without a stain on his name, but unfortunately in the end of the day he is left carrying a different sort of can.

It is Dr Buchan's contention that it was the growth of literacy which spelt the doom of ballad making and remaking, in the old high style. Why, he asks, do Peter's versions seem so slack, so diffuse, so inchoate, so *vulgar*, compared to those recorded from a lady who had learnt her songs in the mid-eighteenth century? Not because Peter's ballads are not genuine – their 'vulgarity', as Grundtvig pointed out, is the best proof of their material authenticity – but because they are the first fruits of a fumbling and imperfect literacy among the 'folk' themselves. With the break-up of the homogeneous society, with improvements changing the face of the old lawless North-East, where 'life was short and death was violent', and with literacy everywhere rearing its bespectacled head, it was only to be expected that singers would gradually lose the knack of oral composition, and that ballad texts collected by Peter in the 1820s would seem tawdry, insipid and unattractive compared to the productions of non-literate eighteenth-century singers. So runs the argument, and it has a familiar ring. Dr Buchan's thesis from this point on – one might dub it 'The Disuse of Illiteracy' – is, in fact, just another version of the old familiar 'descending graph' of ballad scholarship – it was good once, now it is thinning out, we'll have to remember to send a wreath – which produced titles like *Last Leaves* and elegiac prefaces quoting 'les lauriers sont coupés'. Let us take a close-up view of a piece of thin-ice skating in Dr Buchan's chapter about his volatile namesake.

On page 216 he quotes the introductory note to a collection of chapbooks and broadsheets in the British Museum: 'This Collection was made by me, James Mitchell, at Aberdeen in 1828. It may be considered as the Library of the Scottish Peasantry, the works being sold by itinerant Chapmen about the country, especially at fairs. No such collection could now be made, and *Chambers Edinburgh Journal* and similar publications have superseded the writings of our forefathers.'

Included in this budget of 'curious tracts' is a version of 'Bessy Bell and Mary Gray', which starts off with four lines of the old ballad but is shortly purveying a completely different idiom:

> And Mary's locks are like a craw,
>   Her een like diamonds glances;
> She's aye sae clean, redd up and braw,
>   She kills whene'er she dances;
> Blyth as a kid, with wit at will,
>   She blooming, tight and tall is;
> And guides her airs sae gracefu' still.
>   O Jove, she's like thy Pallas.

Dr Buchan leads into this quotation by remarking that 'the language of the songs now sung by the folk was in a very unsettled state', and he then goes on to say: 'In this song, which is actually reprinted from the works of Allan Ramsay, there are three linguistic varieties; there is poetical English, ordinary vernacular Scots, and in the first quatrain the formulaic language of the old tradition. The language of the songs the folk were singing was in a state of flux. It is in the light of this fact that linguistic vulgarities and incongruities of Peter Buchan's ballads must be considered.'

Sung by the folk ... the fact that a song is printed in a chapbook is in itself no evidence that it was actually sung by the 'folk'. Furthermore, this version of the song was in print a quarter of a century before Mrs Brown of Falkland was born, and was almost certainly better known to that lady (who herself wrote verses) than to the informants who gave blind Jamie Rankin their ballads. There is no evidence whatever, in fact, that this ludicrous, wishy-washy, pedantic ditty (reprinted almost word for word from *Ramsay's Poems*, 1721) was ever sung by the 'folk' in Aberdeenshire, although it was no doubt hawked around at feeing markets and elsewhere by enterprising colporteurs.

* * * * *

One curious feature of *The Ballad and the Folk* is its almost total omission of any consideration of that large and entertaining part of our Scottish ballad heritage, the bawdry – although this omission may perhaps reflect Professor Child's own prejudices on that score. All the same it is strange, because Peter Buchan himself (whose reputation Dr Buchan is concerned to vindicate) put together a fascinating collection of songs of the *Merry Muses* persuasion, most of them couched in the most delectable Scots ballad idiom, called *The Secret Songs of Silence*; the MS is now in the library of Harvard. Several of Peter's texts illustrate techniques of oral composition at least as well as any of Mrs Brown's texts – with the added advantage that the occasional moral observations and pious reflections alluded to by Bronson, are totally absent. Here is 'The Wanton Trooper':

There came a trooper to this town
I thank you for your gentleness,
He would hae maidens nine, or ten,
To cure him o' his wantonness.

Then out it speaks the millar's lass,
I thank you for your gentleness,
I think, says she, I well may pass
To cure you o' your wantonness.

The firstan night he wi' her lay,
I thank you for your gentleness,
He gain'd her love nine times a day
Now gane was some of's wantonness.

The second night he wi' her lay,
I thank you for your gentleness,
He gain'd her love six times a day
And gane was mair of's wantonness.

The thirden night he wi' her lay
I thank you for your gentleness,
He gain'd her love three times a day
And gane was a' his wantonness.

As he gaed through her father's ha',
I thank you for your gentleness,
The peats and clods they gart him fa'
And gane was a' his wantonness.

O peats and clods lat me alane
I thank you for your gentleness,
Gin ye had been where I hae been
Ye'd gotten fley the wantonness.

As he came through her father's close,
I thank you for your gentleness,
The peacock pinch'd him by the nose,
And gane was a' his wantonness.

O peacock, peacock, lat me alane,
I thank you for your gentleness,
Gin ye had been where I hae been
Ye'd gotten fley the wantonness.

As he came through her father's fields,
I thank you for your gentleness,
The windlestraes turn'd up his heels,
and gane was a' his wantonness.

O windlestraes lat me alane,
I thank you for your gentleness,
Gin ye had been where I hae been
Ye'd gotten fley the wantonness.

The millar's lassie lay and leuch,
I thank you for your gentleness,
I think mysell now fit eneuch
To cure you o' your wantonness.[1]

This strapping hizzie belongs to a very old Scottish (and indeed
Celtic) tradition. The girl in the next song is well and truly of high
degree, as befits a ballad heroine, but she is well equipped to deal
with even the most taxing ballad situation; one feels that if she
happened to encounter the treacherous Elf-Knight, or indeed any
other predator, human or supernatural, she would have no trouble in
blowing him where he belonged in double-quick time.

There was a duke's daughter,
She was a gallant farter,
Steer well the wind, steer well the wind;
There was a duke's daughter,
She was a gallant farter,
Steer well the wind and blow.

She farted till her sisters three,
A bonny ship to sail the sea,
Steer well the wind, steer well the wind;
She farted till her sisters three
A bonny ship to sail the sea
Steer well the wind and blow. .

Most of the pieces are the most disarmingly anonymous of folk
song, but here and there one detects a work of individual authorship,
in a different idiom. One such is *The Farto-Turdoniad; A Ballad addressed to Alexander Tumbleturd Esq.* The author of this scatological
squib was none other than the celebrated James ('Balloon') Tytler,
radical publicist and aeronaut, whose life has been written by Sir
James Fergusson of Kilkerran, and whose portrait will be found on

the cover of Michael Donnelly's *United Scotsman* (Vol. 1, no. 3, Dec. 1972).

As D. K. Wilgus has pointed out, the bawdy ballad is important for study, because 'it tends to remain the oral possession of even the collector'. Peter shared some of his finds with other interested parties, and no doubt enjoyed the favour of reciprocal benefaction. He wrote in the dedicatory epistle to William Gordon of Fyvie and Maryculter: 'My worthy and valued friend Sir Walter Scott has some of them, which are stored up with pious care – he values them perhaps more than he ought – but he is the better judge.'

The bawdy anonyms have a further advantage in that they reveal, almost better than the tragic or romantic ballads, the nature of the ballad-Scots – the flexible formulaic language of the older Scottish folk song – which grazes ballad-English along the whole of its length, and yet is clearly identifiable as a distinct folk-literary lingo. David Buchan, referring to Mrs Brown's language, says that it is a '*Kunstsprache* (art language) for it is no one dialect but composite', and points out that it subsumes words from mid-Scots and English, as well as northern Scots. This is true, as far as it goes, but it does not really illuminate the nature of the simple, dignified and muscular folk-literary language which carries the best of our ballads. Ballad Scots merges into ballad-English, for the simple reason that England and Scots-speaking Scotland – and indeed English-speaking Ireland – really form one single great ballad-zone. Here an over-emphasis on the isolation of the North-East can be seriously misleading. The ballads moved around with astonishing ease, and breached dialect and language boundaries like an underground army. What makes much of the Scottish balladry so very different in feel from the English is that our ballad composers really do seem to have had what has been called a 'fierier imagination' than their English counterparts, and also that so many of the tunes they used were ultimately of Celtic origin.

And another vital point: one should not underestimate the influence of the King James's Bible in stabilising ballad-Scots. Dr Buchan, in his chapter on the ballads of James Nicol, one of Peter's informants, notes that in some cases the English of the Bible as well as the English of chap literature infiltrated ballad language . This is true, in the sense that individual words and turns of phrase seem biblical, but it overlooks the far deeper and all-pervading influence that the arrival of the 'New Testament in Inglis tung' exerted from the sixteenth century onwards. The language of Luther's Bible exerted a similar influence, on the language of much German folk song, as scores of texts in *Des Knaben Wunderhorn* testify.

The items of patently English origin which turn up in this hyperbolean *galère* are very revealing. Here is another Secret Song:

> There were three lads in our town,
> Slow men of London!
> They courted a widow was bonny and broun,
> And yet they left her undone.
>
> They went to work without their tools,
> Slow men of London!
> The widow she sent them away like fools,
> Because they left her undone.
>
> They often tasted the widow's cheer,
> Slow men of London!
> But yet the widow was never the near,
> For still they left her undone.
>
> Blow ye winds, and come down rain;
> Slow men of London!
> They never shall woo this widow again,
> Because they left her undone.

In the North-East this would be sung *more Boreali,* and the occasional Scots turn of phrase might well find its way into the text. Indeed, in spite of the place names, the singer would probably think of it as a Scots song. And yet it is plainly in a rather square-arsed ballad English.

Bawdy ballads, such as 'The Minister's Wether' and 'The High Notes of Bangor' (both in Peter's *Secret Songs* collection) were, together with oatmeal brose, the staple diet of the Aberdeenshire bothies. The couthie farmyard ditties slanging tight-fisted farmers and poking good-humoured fun at the local 'crew' which found their way into Gavin Greig's column in the 'Buchanie' and were later sung in church halls and the WRI by popular entertainers like Willie Kemp and George Morris of Old Meldrum, are mildly amusing in their way, but they are not a patch on the gorgeous gargantuan-pantagruelian bawdry which was the Buchan farm servant's answer to the uncouth life-denying puritanism of the Kirk and the harsh reality of existence as an underpaid hired hand. The bothies and chaulmers where the farm labourers were housed acted as a sort of folk-song incubator in Victorian and Edwardian Scotland, and the lads naturally sang everything, from classic ballads to rhymes thought up while hoeing neeps or whistling at the plough. Among the popular bothy favourites were 'Let Me In This Ae Night', 'The Muckin' o' Geordie's Byre', and 'Roy's Wife of Aldivalloch', racy versions of which were on the go long before Mrs Anna Brown was a glint in her father's eye.

The bawdry was ritualised in the secret society of the ploughmen which was called The Horsemen's Word; this was a kind of cross between a farm-servant freemasonry, a working-class Hellfire Club, and a 'primitive rebel ' trade union. The sessions of The Horseman 's Word – particularly the initiation ceremonies, when youthful recruits to the industry were given the works – could boast their own orally transmitted freemason-type ritual, scarifying oaths and all, but they rapidly turned into uproarious drinking bouts in which the bluest of bawdy toasts were exchanged, and 'The Ball of Kirriemuir' was the order of the day. Nothing could be more curious and ironic than the contrast between the world of Bell Robertson, Gavin Greig's princi-pal ballad informant, with her pietistic poems and hymns, and the orgiastic underground of the Horseman's Word, with its enormous rumbustious folk-song repertoire, sub-literate and super-oral. One moves in thought from a douce parlour, with 'Crimond' being played on the harmonium, to a riotous bottle-strewn cauf hoose where the 'Rantin' Roarin' Willies' of half a dozen fairm toons are giving a lusty rendering of 'The Duke's Daughter', or barracking while one of their number proposes a toast like this:

> Here's to the swan that sweems in the dam
> And dips her neb in adultery.
> Here's to the bonny lass that lies on her back
> And fucks for the good of her country.

And maybe down the road, in a quarry or on a patch of waste ground, singing would be going on too – inside the hump-backed tent of a tinker encampment, with ragged children happed in plaids stretched out on the ground, and tousle-headed, hawk-faced men sitting on kists and listening intently, while a weather-beaten old matriarch raised 'The Baron of Brackley' or 'The Dowie Dens of Yarrow'. These were the members of another fraternity, also with its unwritten rules, shibboleths and rituals, who loved the old ballads, and sang them often. The Scots travelling folk had preserved their own 'clannit society' into Gavin Greig's day – indeed, they have to quite a big degree preserved it into ours – but collectors seldom went among them seeking ballads. Even Greig himself, one of the most energetic and successful collectors of all time, appears practically to have ignored them. And yet their vast ballad repertoire, distinctive singing styles, and aptitude for making up their own songs offer much of interest to the folklorist, not least because many of the older generation of tinker singers are completely or almost completely illiterate.

In his chapter 'The Oral Ballad: A Summing Up', Dr Buchan writes: 'Ideally, of course, one would like to have available the tape-recorded texts of a non-literate ballad composer, but rather than 'rax for the meen' (reach for the moon) we should perhaps rest thankful for what we have.' Here Dr Buchan is being far too modest in his ambitions, for this particular moon landing was made quite a number of years ago – in 1952 and 1953 to be precise, when concentrated fieldwork started among the travelling people, and hundreds of songs and stories from non-literate informants were recorded. At camp fires in the berryfields of Blairgowrie, in council houses at Perth, and in the heart of secret-looking woodlands in the Mearns (an ancestral hideout) members of the travelling fraternity, young and old, sang rare Child ballads, lyric love-songs, execution broadside ballads, kids' rhymes, contemporary pop songs, you name it, they sang it. The only trouble (if you can call it trouble) was that everyone sang, or wanted to sing, right down to the smallest children: at an encampment near Laurencekirk, in 1953, a teenage girl who was tone deaf sang a long version of a classic ballad into the microphone for the Kentucky singer Jean Ritchie; the other travellers were far too well-mannered to pass any comment while the song was being recorded – or indeed afterwards – although I intercepted some embarrassed glances.

What one encountered, in that drystick wood, in Jeannie Robertson's house in Causewayend, and at the Standing Stones berry field on the road to Essendy, was this wonderful fluid thing representing the actual world of the ballad singers, a shared sensibility still artistically vital and fertile. Singers who *are* singers remake their own versions, which may gel for themselves and others, or may dissipate again ... The greatest thrill is to hear one's own songs sung in new variants by singers who feel themselves totally free to remake them in any old way – or in any new way – that seems good to them.

'Ineluctably,' writes Dr Buchan in his concluding chapter, 'the ballad is descending in the social scale, passing from the tenant-farmers to the ploughmen to, nowadays, the 'travelling folk' and the keeping of such a superb singer as Jeannie Robertson.' Although it is quite true that one must, moving along these linear and sequential lines, take reluctant cognisance of a dwindling heritage, it is also possible to have recourse to still-operative spatial awareness in order to redress the balance. From Jeannie, and from people like her, the ballads have now moved – thanks to the present folk revival – to Allan Glen's schoolboys, Dick Vet students, Lochee housewives, Clydebank shop stewards, and indeed probably to a wider section of the Scottish people than ever before. (When I say they have moved from the traditional singers, I do not mean of course that these singers have in any sense lost them, or relinquished their hold on them, for folksong is one of those agreeable zones of human experience in which it is possible to give all, and retain more – hence the folly of attaching to it any form of copyright symbol.)

And, most significantly, the ballads have moved to wide new sections of society as *songs*, and therefore packing the whole and not just the half of their formidable punch. There will be scope in the future for ethnomusicological studies of ballad variation, not only among traditional singers of Jeannie's type, but also in the fluid and still evolving world of the folk revival.

2

After the Revolution of 1688, when King Billy (known in Scotland as 'Willie Wanbeard') arrived to succour the Protestant religion, and King James VII and II beat it in haste to the Continent, there was a strenuous attempt in Scotland to restore the house of Stuart. Graham of Claverhouse ('Bonnie Dundee') raised the Jacobite clans, and died while leading them to victory at Killiecrankie. The following year his successors (Cannon and Buchan) were routed on the Haughs of Cromdale and two months later the Battle of the Boyne settled James's hash for good and all. These stirring events were watched with the keenest of interest by the partisans of the two opposing Protestant systems of church government – the Episcopalians and the Presbyterians – because their own power, influence and privilege depended on the outcome of the conflict. In the event the Presbyterian system was restored, and this meant that over half the ministers in Scotland lost their charges. Among these was the ingenious Robert Kirk, Episcopalian minister of Aberfoyle (earlier of Balquhidder), who made the first complete translation of the Psalms of David into Scots Gaelic, and was the author of a fascinating work on Highland folklore, *The Secret Commonwealth of Elves and Fairies*.

It can well be imagined with what frustration, gall and fury the dispossessed Piskies reached for their pens and discharged molten satire and polemical slingstones on the heads of their victorious opponents. Among the numerous tracts published at that time there is one – *The Scotch Presbyterian Eloquence* (of 1692) – which is of major interest for folklorists as well as for historians. The identity of the author of this curious pasquinade is not known – he called himself 'Jacob Curate' – but it is clear he was a minister of strongly Episcopalian persuasion who had spent a considerable time 'collecting' the sayings and doings of the Covenanting zealots, in order to hold them up to ridicule. In doing so he performed a real service to connoisseurs of the vernacular, for the anecdotes and aphorisms he put on record are a gold-mine of old, exuberant, freespoken Doric. Here are one or two examples:

> Mr William Guthry, preaching on Peter's confidence, said, 'Peter, Sirs, was as stalliard a fellow as ever had cold iron at his arse, and yet a hussie with a rock feared him.'

Mr Robert Blair, that famous presbyterian preacher at St Andrews, was very much thought of for his familiar way of preaching. He preached often against the observation of Christmass, and once in this Scotch jingle, 'You will say, Sirs, 'Good old Youleday'; I'll tell you, 'good old Fool-day'. You will say, it is a brave Haly-day; I tell you, it is a brave Belly-day. You will say, these are bonny formalities; but I tell you, they are bonny fartalities.'

Mr John Levingstone in Ancrum, once giving the sacrament of the Lord's Supper, said to his hearers, 'Now, Sirs, you may take Christ piping hot,' and finding a woman longsome in taking the bread out of his hand, he says, 'Woman, if you take not Christ, take the meikle devil then'.

(The reference to St Peter recalls a story told about a Methodist lay preacher in nineteenth-century Cornwall who is reputed to have addressed the apostle as follows: 'Ah, Peter, no wunder ye danied the Lawrd. He went down to the ketchen, my friends, after the sarvent maids, a-coortin of 'em – *and him a married man!*')

The following is 'Jacob Curate's' version of an incident which became famous throughout Scotland, and which spawned one of the most delicious songs in the *Merry Muses:*

A party of King Charles II, his guards being sent to apprehend Mr David Williamson (one of the most eminent of their ministers now in Edenburgh) for the frequent rebellion and treason he preached then at field meetings; and the party having surrounded the house where he was, a zealous lady, mistress of the house, being very solicitous to conceal him, rose in all haste from her bed, where she left her daughter of about eighteen years of age; and having dressed up the holy man's head with some of her own night cloaths, she wittily advis'd him to take her place in the warm bed with her girl; to which he modestly and readily consented; and knowing well how to employ his time, especially upon such an extraordinary call, to propagate the image of the party, while the mother, to divert the troopers' enquiry, was treating them with strong drink in the parlour, he, to express his gratitude, applies himself with extraordinary kindness to the daughter; who finding him like to prove a very useful man in his generation, told her mother she would have him for her husband; to which the mother, though otherwise unwilling, yet, for concealing the scandal, out of love to the cause consented, when the mystery of the iniquity was wholly disclosed to her.

The version of the song-offspring of this encounter which appears in the first known edition of the *Merry Muses* (circa 1800) goes as follows:

> Being pursu'd by the dragoons,
> Within my bed he was laid down
> And weel I wat he was worth his room,
> My ain dear dainty Davie.

> O leeze me on his curly pow,
> Bonie Davie, dainty Davie;
> Leeze me on his curly pow,
> He was my dainty Davie.

> My minnie laid him at my back,
> I trow he lay na lang at that,
> But turn'd, and in a verra crack
> Produc'd a dainty Davie.

> Then in the field amang the pease,
> Behin' the house o' Cherrytrees,
> Again he wan atweesh my thies,
> And, splash! gaed out his gravy.

> But had I goud, or had I land,
> It should be a' at his command;
> I'll ne'er forget what he pat i' my hand,
> It was a dainty Davie.

Another version had been printed earlier by David Herd in his *Ancient and Modern Scots Songs, Heroic Ballads &c.* (1776) with a note which reads: 'The following song was made upon Mess David Williamson on his getting with child the Lady Cherrytree's daughter, while the soldiers were searching the house to apprehend him for a rebel.' The story goes that when Charles II heard of this exploit of Dainty Davie's, he exclaimed: 'Odd's fish! that beats me and the oak!

Find me that man and I'll make him a bishop!'

In his MS collection *The Secret Songs of Silence* (mentioned above),
Peter Buchan supplies a version – characteristically the longest – of
the same song. As it will be new to most readers, I subjoin it here:

> Amang the Presbyterian race,
> Some gweedly men's come to this place,
> But nane o' them that kent my case,
>   Not guess'd my doubts like Davie.

>> Well's me on his curly pow,
>> Davie laddie, Davie laddie,
>> Well's me on his curly pow,
>> My bonny, Dainty Davie.

> When first my Davie I did see,
> The very smile blink'd in his e'e,
> He was a blythsome sight to me,
>   I thought I lov'd my Davie.

> O little did my minnie dread,
> Of what I stood in greatest need,
> It was my fancy for to feed,
>   Upo' my Dainty Davie.

> Some says he has some muckle pelf,
> Horse and cattle, lands and wealth,
> But I wou'd rather hae himself,
>   My bonny Dainty Davie.

> The last time he and I did meet,
> It was upo' the open street,
> Where kindly he did me saleet,
>   My bonny Dainty Davie.

> As we came thro' my father's glen,
> He gae me kisses nine or ten,
> And something else, ye sanno ken,
>   Because he was my Davie.

> As we came by yon water side,

He stopt the stream, and then did ride,
But yet for a' I did him bide,
    Because he was my Davie.

As we were walking up the hill,
And there o' me he gat his will,
But yet for a' I lay me still,
    Because he was my Davie.

When twenty weeks were come and gane,
Now my stays wou'd no less on,
It's now my time to sigh an' moan,
    All for my Dainty Davie.

Next time we met upo' the lee,
The very saut tear blint my e'e,
And mony heavy sigh did gie,
    Unto my Dainty Davie.

O Davie lad, well may ye mind,
Sin' I reliev'd you out o' pine,
And now to me ye will prove kin,
    My bonny Dainty Davie.

Then Davie pledged his faith and vow,
To me he ever wou'd prove true,
And I shou'd ne'er hae cause to rue,
    He was my Dainty Davie.

Then to the kirk we quickly went,
And married were wi' sweet content,
And aye sinsyne I'll ne'er repent,
    I lov'd my Dainty Davie.

There are several anecdotes in *The Scotch Presbyterian Eloquence*
which suggest comic ballad-situations; here is one, which follows
close upon the story about Dainty Davie Williamson:

> A gentleman of good reputation and credit ... confessed to me,
> with regret, that in the heat of his youth he had been guilty of the
> sin of fornication with a gentlewoman of that holy sect. He says,

that being with her in a garret, and she hearing some body coming up stairs, she said to him, 'Ah, here's my aunt. I must devise a trick to divert her.' Upon which, she fell a whining and howling aloud, as these people used to do at their most private devotions. 'Oh, to believe, to believe! Oh, to have experience!' said she. And by that means she diverted her aunt's further approaching, who instantly retired, commending her niece's zeal and devotion.

Anyone who has heard a version of the classic ballad 'The Keach in the Creel ' (Child, 281) will feel a tug of recollection at this point, for part of it is strikingly similar. Here are four verses from the version recorded from Willie Mathieson, Ellon, Aberdeenshire, in 1952:

> The auld wife couldna sleep that nicht
> Tho late late was the 'oor.
> I'll lay my life, says the silly auld wife,
> there's a man in my dochter's boo'er.

> The auld man he jumped oot-ower the bed
> To see if the thing was true,
> But she's tae'n the wee clerk in her arms
> And covered him owre wi' blue.

> 'Ts oh father, dear father,
> Oh faur are ye gaun sae late,
> Disturbing me frae my evening prayers
> And oh but they were sweet.

> Oh ill betide ye, ye silly auld wife,
> And an ill death may ye dee,
> For my dochter is lying wi' the Bible in her airms
> And she's prayin' for you and me.

In that extraordinary sinister masterpiece, James Hogg's *Private Memoirs and Confessions of a Justified Sinner,* which is set in the period immediately prior to the Act of Union (1707), there is a scene which may well owe something to Jacob Curate's anecdote, or stories resembling it. The wife of the Laird of Dalcastle has a 'favourite pastor', a 'flaming predestinarian divine', who encourages her in her severe and gloomy bigotry. 'Hers were not the tenets of the great reformers, but theirs mightily overstrained and deformed.' The pastor makes free with the upper quarters of the house, much like Tartuffe (although against the laird's wishes), and he and the wife sit up all night 'for the sake of sweet spiritual converse'.

> In the course of the night, they differed so materially on a small point somewhere between justification and final election that the minister, in the heat of his zeal, sprung from his seat, paced the floor, and maintained his point with such ardour that Martha [the maid] was alarmed, and, thinking they were going to fight, and that the minister would be hard match for her mistress, she put on some clothes, and twice left her bed and stood listening at the back of the door, ready to burst in should need require it ... If the listener's words were to be relied on, there was no love, no accommodating principle manifested between the two, but a fiery burning zeal, relating to points of such minor importance that a true Christian would blush to hear them mentioned, and the infidel and profane make a handle of them to turn our religion to scorn.

Eventually the lady presents her husband with a second son, but the laird refuses to acknowledge him as his own progeny, and after a year and a day he is baptised Robert Wringhim, after his 'adoptive' father. This Robert grows up to become the antinomian 'justified sinner', who – under the influence of an uncanny doppelgaenger called Gil-Martin – commits many crimes (including murder) 'in the cause of Christ and his church'. Gil-Martin, a great potentate among the Elect, who proclaims his orthodoxy by totally rejecting the notion of salvation by good works, turns out to belong to the other camp.

It is the charge of duplicity which is levelled most constantly against the Presbyterians by their opponents, and nowhere with more flamboyant fury than in *The Grameid*, an 'Heroic Poem' in Latin composed by James Philip of Almerieclose, Dundee's standard-bearer in the campaign of 1689. Philip provides us with a wonderful description of the mustering of the clans at Dalcomera, but he never gets as far as Killiecrankie in the poem, partly because he devotes an enormous stretch of his fifth book to a denunciation of the Presbyterians and all their works. This he puts into the mouth of his hero, the handsome charismatic general:

The miserable presbyterian, the fatal fury of his country, hated by the gods, the disturber of peace, prone to wrath, the student of avarice, earnest master of lust, wanton as a goat, infamous in guilt, a very Greek in deceit, and well known on Scottish shore for Grecian fraud, distinguished in artifice and in the arts of hypocrisy, like the crab of the sea or the tortoise, he directs his steps hither while he looks the other way ... While the deceiver seeks to impose upon the foolish common people, he assumes an expression of hope, and with palms spread open to the heavens he seems by mouth, eyes, and gestures to be uttering divine things, yet amid tears and sobbing words he skilfully lays his plots, and by his arts kindles strife. Presently you may see his face distorted, and his vast gaping mouth howling after the manner of hoarse wolves, and while he pours out long prayers, he raises up horrible wars upon his country and against his country's father. Thus in the feigned name of religion he plays upon the stupid people.

And the Scotch presbyter, the most notorious in the world, presents the fatal specimen of the incorrigible tyrant whose sad name never comes with any note of joy – envious, cunning, lazy, faithless in friendship, unfilial, subtle, anointed Pharisee, a true disciple of Machiavellian guile, loving lies as a lawyer loves a lawsuit.[2]

While Philip was composing this singular invective, the anonymous author of *The Scotch Presbyterian Eloquence* was putting the finishing touches to his collection of Presbyterian sayings and sermons ostensibly 'taken in Writing from their Mouths'. One of these actually lists a number of the songs which were circulating at the time, and puts them into some rather unexpected categories:

Mr Kirkton ... told the people; 'There be four kinds of songs, Profane Songs, *My Mother sent me to the Well, She had better gone her self, for what I got I dare not tell, but kind Robin loves me.* Malignant Songs, such as *He, ho, Gillichrankie,* and *The King Enjoys his own again;* against which I have not much to say. 31y. Allowable songs, like *Once I lay with another man's wife* ... Lastly Spiritual songs, which are the Psalms of David; but the godless prelates add to these, *Glory to the Father,* the worst of all I have yet spoken of.

Much of this hilarious material is clearly art and part of that same old compulsive grotesquerie which one finds blooming luxuriantly in odd corners of an off-beat Scoto-Irish literary tradition. Its atmosphere is very different from that of the harsh self-confident prepotent Calvinism which Burns was later to recognise as a deadly enemy of his art (and of art in general):

> Ye are sae grave, nae doot ye're wise;
> Nae ferly tho' ye do despise
> The hairum-scairum ram-stam boys,
> The rattlin' squad:
> I see you upward cast your eyes –
> Ye ken the road.

The point is that the religion pilloried, parodied and satirised by 'Jacob Curate' was a religion not persecuting but persecuted; like many sects in similar cases, it was a fertile breeding-ground for eccentricities and oddities of every description. It was not until the opening of the eighteenth century that dominant Calvinism was really in the saddle, and probably not until the nineteenth that its numbing effect on the Scottish psyche became most marked, and an *idea* of Scotland began to circulate outwith our borders that no nation on earth could possibly covet. (In June 1893 *The Studio* published a rhyme which characterised Scotland and Scotsmen as follows:

> Land o' careful cunning bodies
> Foes of a' ungodly fun
> Land that sums up man's whole duties:
> Heaven, the Deil and NUMBER ONE.

Of course, Burns had expressed the same general idea much more trenchantly and in much better verse, a hundred years previously, but it would be idle to deny that this sort of taunt still rankles.)

Several scholars – among them the late Dr Mary Ramsay – have attempted to show that Calvinism was not in fact antagonistic to the arts. It would be misleading to suggest that we are faced here with a 'black and white' situation, and Ted Cowan presents forceful arguments in support of the Ramsay thesis in his contribution to the present volume. However, some of the attempts to defend the cultural record of Scots Calvinism seem to me reminiscent of the not dissimilar attempts to whitewash 'bawdy Burns', and deny against all the evidence that he had any hand in *The Merry Muses*. There is in the archive of the School of Scottish Studies a notebook containing the notes made by an Aberdeen antiquary called Alexander Mutch for a lantern lecture on Robert Burns. These include a passage on Burns's sentimental rewrite of the old bawdy song 'John Anderson My Jo' which goes as follows:

> It is indeed an exceptional production when we consider the dross out of which it was rescued. A very old song with this name had existed in Scotland since *before the Reformation* (my italics), but the words, in addition to being mere doggerel, were rude, licentious and offensive. Burns could not tolerate an indecent song ...

The reason why people like Mutch could write such arrant nonsense was that Burns just could not be allowed to be one of the Damned – he just *had* to be one of the Elect. The theology of the Calvinist zealots divided mankind into two irreconcilable camps, the Elect and the Damned, and made it plain that the second of these was by far the more numerous. The Damned were known by their irreverent laughter, and by a frank delight in the ordinary pleasures of living. What was worse, the self-elected Elect seemed by an aggravation of predestinate unfairness to be exactly those who, in this world, were in more comfortable circumstances than their neighbours. Who can wonder, in the face of all this, that those who were made to believe that they were the 'Damned' felt the need to organise?

It was in the North-East – Aberdeenshire, Banffshire and the Mearns – that one could still find in the 1950s the remnants of the clandestine organisation of the Damned – and in quite a good state of preservation, at that. Aberdeenshire has always been a noted place for balladry, and it was no surprise for researchers from the School of Scottish Studies to find that the county still contained many fine ballad singers, some of them quite young. What did come as a definite surprise was that the organisation of the non- (or anti-) Elect – which looked as if it had some sort of link with the witch cult of the

D

seventeenth century – was a going concern all over the Scottish North-East until roughly the period of World War I, and that its fantastic ritual was still fresh in the minds of a good number of the older people.

The name of the cult – as stated earlier – was the Horseman's Word, and it embraced virtually the entire farm-labourer population of the North-East. Its principal ceremony, which was most often celebrated around Martinmas, was an elaborate initiation rite in the course of which the young lads of the neighbourhood were made 'Horsemen'.

> Between the manger and the greep
> 'Tis there that I do hang my whip.
> Between the stable and the cartshed
> 'Twas there a Horseman I was made.

The number of initiates taking part in the capers had to be an odd number, preferably 13; the place chosen was always a barn a good bit off the beaten track. To avoid detection, the locale of meeting was changed frequently. When the seniors of the cult had collected the names of sufficient novices, they passed round the word to attend; this was sometimes done by sending a single horse-hair in an envelope to the brother invited.

Each novice was told of the summons to attend by a 'made Horseman'. He was also told that he had to bring with him a bottle of whisky, a jar of berries (or jam), and a loaf of bread. There is a verse of *Nicky Tams*, often sung and seldom understood, which puts the matter succinctly:

> It's first I gaed on for baillie loon,
> An' syne I gaed on for third:
> An' syne of course I had to get
> The Horseman's grip an' Word...

On the appointed night, when the rest of the farm-world were safely bedded, the novices were roused and convoyed across country to the barn selected for the ceremony. On the way they were blind-folded. When the horsemen got to the door of the barn, they gave the

'Horseman's knock' (three measured raps), pawed three times on the door with hands or feet, and whinnied like horses. Inside the door stood the 'minister', and the following interrogation took place:

> 'Who cometh? In the name of the Word speak your name.'
> 'A brother.'
> 'A Brother of what?'
> 'Of horsemanry.'
> 'Who bade ye come here?'
> 'The Devil.'
> 'What way did ye come? The crooked way, or the straight way of the path?'
> 'By the hooks and crooks of the road.'
> 'In what light did ye come?'
> 'The stars and the light of the moon.'
> 'What's the tender of the oath?'
> 'Hele, conceal, never reveal: neither write, nor dite, nor recite: nor cut, nor carve, nor write in sand.'

Towards midnight the ceremony began. The novices, still blindfolded, knelt in a circle around the 'minister', each with his left foot bare and his left hand raised. The 'minister' rehearsed the mysteries of the Word: he told the lads the name of the first Horseman, which was Cain (Tubal Cain?), and gave them the Word itself, which was another word written backwards. He also revealed the two verses of the Bible which were to be read backwards when a Horseman wished to invoke the aid of the Devil.

As the novices received the Word they swore 'neither to write, nor dite, nor recite' it. Immediately afterwards the 'minister' tried to trick them into breaking their oath. The blindfold would be raised slightly to allow each boy to see paper in front of him, and the command would be given – 'Now you have the Word: write it'.

Occasionally a sharp lad would be fly enough to refuse, but the average greenhorn fell for the trick. He would take the proffered pen or pencil to write the Word, but before he could write the first letter, he would be given a 'lick' over the fingers with the backchain of a cart or the stock of a horsewhip. Several old men to whom I have talked in Buchan and Stra'bogie still bear the marks of this 'lick' on their fingers.

After this – the ritual infliction of pain – the novices were pushed one by one into the cauf-hoose of the barn for 'a shak o' Auld Hornie'. No horseman was a right 'made Horseman' if he had not shaken hands with the Devil, so everyone had to go through it. Sometimes the 'Deil' was a man dressed in a calf-skin rubbed with phosphorus; sometimes he was a live calf or goat. In either case, the novice felt a hoof pressed into his hand, and he was ordered to shake it.

This completed the initiation. After it the bottles of whisky were uncorked, and the meeting became less formal. The newly initiated Horsemen were given 'information' by their seniors, in which practical hints on the managing of horses were mixed up with the wildest of supernatural folklore. Stories were related of the prowess of some famous Horseman, who with the Devil's assistance could make stallions dance around the corn-yard, and follow at his heels wherever he went.

If a Horseman who had signed himself over to the Deil had trouble with some coarse, ill-natured mare, all he had to do was this: take her collar and bridle to the crossroads, 'say over his lessons' (i.e. recite two verses of the Bible backwards), and a horse would appear. He would have good cause for fear, because the horse would be the Devil – but if he took courage, slipped the collar over the uncanny cratur's head and mounted it, he would never afterwards have trouble from his pair of horse.

('The Deil is a gey handy man' – as one old chap put it to me – 'a gey handy man.')

As the drinking got going, the Horsemen would challenge each other on points of horsemanry and rehearse a number of esoteric shibboleths. One question often put was – 'Where were ye made a Horseman?'. To this the correct answer went as follows:

> In a Horseman's hall
> where the sun never shone
> where the wind never blew
> where a cock never crew
> and the feet of a maiden never trod.

(In this, as in some other rhymes associated with the Horseman's Word, there are reminiscences of the classical balladry. The first verse

94

of *Leesome Brand* (Child, 15) in Peter Buchan's collection goes:

> My boy was scarcely ten years old
> When he went to an unco land
> Where wind never blew, nor cocks ever crew –
> Ohone! for my son Leesome Brand.

A question put to the greenhorns, and which they were now supposed to be able to tackle, was 'Fat d'ye need maist?' (What do you need most?). The correct statutory answer here was 'More light' but other, more ribald answers were suggested by senior Horsemen.

The whisky was now circulating freely, and the time had arrived for the drinking of toasts. The puritanism of the Kirk was 'sent up' in verse toasts every bit as outspoken as *The Merry Muses*.

One of these neatly brings together all the basic necessities of rural life:

> Here's to horn,
> Corn, lint an' yarn,
> The pintle and the ploo –
> Corn mills
> And whisky stills
> An' cunts wi' curly 'oo.   ('oo=wool)

Sooner or later during the proceedings the ceremonial Horseman's toast was given:

> Here's to the horse wi' the four white feet,
> The chestnut tail and mane –
> A star on his face and a spot on his breast,
> And his master's name was Cain.

Drinking and revelry went on until dawn, when the Horsemen staggered off to their own farms – to Auchnamoon, say, or Satyrhills or Cairnadellie – to cope with horses in the cold light of day.

Although, as I said, it seems to have links with the witch cult of the seventeenth century, the Horseman's Word did not admit the woman witch. Indeed, its members swore never to reveal the mysteries to 'anyone who wears an apron, except a blacksmith or a farrier'.

Great interest attaches to another phrase, 'hele and conceal', which occurs in the oath. In the old Scottish kingdom this was part of the oath of homage ('I sall ... your counsell conceil and heill, that ye schaw me '), but it is also part of the ritual of Freemasonry, and Joyce uses it at a dramatic moment in *Ulysses*, towards the end of the Walpurgisnacht section, when Bloom addresses Stephen Dedalus (his 'pre-ordained and self-appointed son') for the first time by his Christian name.

That the Horseman's Word was a kind of Freemasonry, at any rate in the obligations of help and counsel which it imposed, cannot be doubted. In the nineteenth century many of the horses used for farm work in the North-East were crossbreeds between Galloways and Highland shelts, and these were inclined to be restive, recalcitrant brutes. At a time when a farm servant's fee for a six-month term might be as little as ten shillings and when farmers had small mercy for the labour they employed, it was more than a man's job was worth to seem incompetent in dealing with his pair of horse. So the experienced 'Horseman' helped his younger mate break horses that were giving him trouble.

The organisation of the cult was so widespread that virtually every farm-hand was in fact a brother. The seniors had no difficulty in finding recruits, because the young lads knew that until they were made Horsemen they were not regarded as men.

Although the Horseman's Word corresponds to a definite period in the social history of the North-East countryside – the so-called 'bothy' period, when farm workers were lodged and fed in communal living quarters called bothies – it seems to have developed out of two earlier cults called the Ploughman's Word and the Miller's Word, which were also custodians of diabolism. Since it was consciously anti-farmer, the cult suggests in certain of its manifestations a kind of 'primitive rebel' trade unionism which is employing the organisational forms, the centuries-old cadres of the witch cult.

One thing is certain. In the shape in which it persisted until the 1914 war, it cannot be older than about 1820, because until then oxen and not horses were used for farm work in Buchan. (In a village near Banff, for example, the only horse in the parish around 1830 was a Highland garron belonging to the minister, and ploughing was done with the 'twal ousen plough'.) What seems to have happened is that the Horseman's Word developed out of the earlier cults during the first half of the nineteenth century.

That the cult was exported to Ireland by Scots planters and later settlers seems likely in view of the statements in a letter I received after I had sent a short letter about folklore survivals to the *Manchester Guardian* (August 1954). My correspondent, a London businessman, wrote:

> Your letter in today's *Manchester Guardian* made my hair stand on end. It sent my mind flashing back to a strange bewitching evening on the sands at Portobello when – over 40 years ago – I heard my grandfather talking to my father about the 'Brotherhood of the Horseman's Word'. My parental grandfather had served for 32 years in the 6th Inniskilling Dragoon Guards (Heavy Brigade); he and apparently many other troopers were 'Brothers' of this association. Years later, when he was dead, I discovered quite accidentally that my maternal grandfather (who came from Fife) was also a 'Brother'!
>
> In asking my own father about all this I (and my nine brothers) were told such terrifying and fascinating things about the 'Brothers' that we came to believe – in the end – that the whole thing was sheer fiction. But when my father was an old man, I heard him talking to a horse-dealer (from Enniskillen) about this same thing. I didn't realise until days later that this very serious conversation was about the Brothers and that it was not at all concerned with Trade Union (or similar) activities; it was purely connected with black magic, the occult, the language of horses, horse-worship, &c., &c.
>
> My father, in this conversation, was talking of the days he had spent in Tain and the Glenlivet countryside where, I gathered, this business was very much alive (circa 1895-1900). I think ... that certain horse-copers had some solid active connection with this cult ... I am quite sure that the Brotherhood of the Horseman's Word was in essence and practice an occult organisation; I feel that this would repay serious research and scholarly examination.

Initiations into the brotherhood of the Horseman's Word were still being carried out after the end of World War II in Angus, and there are still a fair number of 'Made Horsemen' in Perthshire, Stirlingshire and Lanarkshire. The most northerly outpost of the brotherhood seems to have been Orkney.

After the turn of the century the cult began to wither, and with the coming of the tractor it became – on the mainland at any rate – a museum-piece. What the Kirk had for generations failed to do, the tractor accomplished in little more than a decade.

Nevertheless, the fact that it survived so long and so lustily raises a number of interesting questions. It used to be thought that the seventeenth-century warlock, Major Weir, who by day prayed 'with a fervent groan' among the Covenanting saints and after dark presided at the revels of the witch cult, was an isolated example of depraved monstrosity. The facts that we have been examining suggest that in the douce and decorous kirkyards of Angus, the Mearns, Kincardine, and Aberdeenshire, there lie many thousands of Scots countrymen who went to the Kirk, and were buried according to its rites, after having had a 'shak o' Auld Hornie'.

The Horseman's Word may also offer a clue to the reason why the great classic ballads, many of which are full of supernatural folklore, have lived on longer in the North-East than anywhere else.

3

Turning once more to these same Scots classic ballads – the 'Muckle Sangs' – it is maybe worthwhile pointing out yet again (at the risk of seeming to labour unnecessarily an often stated truism) that they are folksongs, linked by countless ties to others of the species – and linked also (as we have seen) to the esoteric rhymes of the Horseman's Word, and the bawdy ballads of the *Secret Songs of Silence*. Many of them are also living and evolving folksongs. David C. Fowler puts it well when he writes (at the conclusion of his *A Literary History of the Popular Ballads):*

> An earlier generation looked upon modern times as an era of decline and fall for the ballad tradition. But those of us who have been privileged to live through the singing sixties know better. Thanks to the artistry and dedication of modern minstrels like Peter Seeger, a new vitality has been restored to ballad and

folksong. Even the element of radical social protest, largely dormant since the rhymes of Robin Hood in the fifteenth century, has made a strong comeback. The current revival, aided enormously by the electronic revolution, has sketched by Josh Dunson in *Freedom in the Air* (New York, 1965). I continue to hope, however, that a scholar of sufficiently catholic taste will be found who can chronicle the evolution of balladry from Sir Walter Scott to Bob Dylan.

The mention of Sir Walter Scott brings us to the nub of the whole question, for Scott was the canny heritor of a rich but highly idiosyncratic national-cultural patrimony. There has for centuries been a constant, fruitful cross-fertilisation in the fields of literary and 'folk' poetry in Scottish cultural tradition; one has the impression that many ballads which now exist in numerous variants must have stemmed from original versions composed by craftsmen-balladeers who took the inherited skills of their art very seriously indeed. By the same token, art-poets have often operated like folk-poets, appropriating opening lines or even whole stanzas from earlier or contemporary authors – or from popular tradition – and using them as a basis for their own productions. The best known example is, of course, Robert Burns, who on one occasion borrowed two lines which he thought were old, but which were actually the work of a poet (John Mayne) who survived him by close on forty years.

These interactions can be observed at their most revealing when one examines the narrative songs which are 'true ballads' for the historian as well as for the folksinger – i.e. those which, like The Laird o' Drum, The Fire o' Frendraught and Mill o' Tifty's Annie (Andrew Lammie), can be tethered fairly confidently to an actual historical incident: something which can be documented from contemporary records as well as from oral tradition. Here it is maybe not too sanguine to postulate an original song-poem composed by an unknown folksinger who was a virtuoso in the techniques of his craft – and also, in some cases at least, a literate man, with a certain amount of knowledge of his country's written poetry. In the ballads connected with actual events, particularly those of the seventeenth and eighteenth centuries, we find consequently a *mélange* of various kinds of poetic and musical experience: on the one hand we encounter unmistakably ancient folk motifs and images which are the common patrimony of orally created and transmitted poetry everywhere, and on the other, not seldom, a sensibility more usually associated with art-poetry. Clear evidence that techniques of composition more proper to non-literate composers survived among the literate or semi-literate has to be balanced against just as definite manifestations of organisation and management which bespeak a tutored and lettered intelligence – often a quite sophisticated one, at that. Viewed in this light, the phenomenon of Mrs Brown of Falkland – the professor's daughter who read Ossian, wrote verses and was also source-singer of ballad versions which have been described as priceless examples of orally transmitted (and orally recreated) folksong – becomes much more comprehensible. Far from being unique, Mrs Brown seems to me to have been merely an outstanding exemplar of a *type* of creative literate folksinger which is one of the most characteristic types of folksinger on the Scottish scene, and one which certainly did not die out during the course of the nineteenth century. Few will be surprised to learn that in the thirty years that the School of Scottish Studies has been prospecting for songs in Lowland (or Scots-speaking) Scotland, we have been encountering this type of folksinger all the time.

The first traditional singer to record his entire repertoire for the School was Willie Mathieson, a septuagenarian retired farm-servant who had devoted much spare time throughout his life to collecting songs. In his kist, which he transported from farm to farm when he got a new fee, were three large ledger books full to overflowing with songs of all kinds, from classic ballads through lyric-love-songs to place-name rhymes and bairn songs. Willie had either collected songs on the spot from his fellow ploughmen, or had diligently followed up his informants by correspondence. He had also tried his hand at versifying, and one of the poems which he wrote down alongside ballads and bothy songs was a moving elegy for his dead wife. Willie Mathieson was quite capable of discoursing knowledgeably about different 'weys' of a ballad, and he would often quote 'what Gavin thocht aboot it' – giving the great collector his first name, in familiar Scots style – but the ballads, especially the tragic love ballads, were closer to him (and 'truer') than they could possibly be to the mere scholar; when he referred to Barbara Allan's callous cruelty to her luckless lover on his death-bed, he would shed tears. If the arguments in an earlier part of this article may have seemed critical of David Buchan's *The Ballad and the Folk*, this in no way diminishes my general appreciation of Dr Buchan's fine scholarly book – which is not only splendidly documented, but is also a real pleasure to read, being exceedingly well-written (a bonus one does not always receive from works on the folk arts). The big ballads have aye been damnt slippery eels to catch, and it is not surprising that even in a book as perceptive as David Buchan's there are reaches where one can catch a glimpse of more than one escaping tail. Nevertheless his book has already taken its place as a major contribution to ballad scholarship. I emphatically recommend it as a 'must' to everyone over whom the great songs have cast what Davie felicitously calls their 'enigmatic glamourie'.

NOTES

1 Sheila Douglas of Scone, one of the best modern composers of songs in the Scots folk tradition, has made an excellent song on the same theme. It is called 'On Monday nicht he cam tae ma door' and can be heard (sung by Alison McMorland) on Tangent TGS 125.

2 The translation is by Canon Alexander D. Murdoch, who edited *The Grameid* for the Scottish History Society in 1884. In his book, *Glencoe*, John Prebble makes liberal use of Canon Murdoch's translation, though nowhere mentioning him by name.

Eighteenth-Century Popular Protest: Aspects of the People's Past

KENNETH LOGUE

An appreciation of folk culture must be, as Gavin Sprott has shown, firmly founded on an understanding of the material culture and conditions of the people. The folk tradition is, however, not only illuminated by that understanding but, because the material and folk culture are so closely bound up, the material culture is itself illuminated by the folk tradition. In a period of great and fundamental change – such as the eighteenth and early nineteenth centuries, similar perhaps to that which we are now experiencing in the last decade of the twentieth century – there is a tendency for popular song to look backwards, to hark back to the days when everything was supposedly peaceful, everyone allegedly contented and prosperous. Popular songs of the eighteenth century reflect that tendency: popular politics for some did so also – and these two come together most notably in Jacobitism. We are all familiar with the stirring songs about the regal charms, martial ardour and aristocratic beauty of Bonnie Prince Charlie. Not surprisingly we need to have that pictured 'balanced' by less enthusiastic Hanoverian opinions which remind us that Charles Edward Stuart had many of the Stuart family failings and few of its talents.

Jacobitism, however, was a rather vague form of popular protest. This was true particularly of the romantic version of Jacobitism which did not require any action –

> Ye Jacobites by name
> Your fautes I will proclaim
> Your doctrines I maun blame –
> You shall hear![1]

More definite forms of popular protest did, however, take place throughout the eighteenth century and beyond. It was a period of great change, a period when agricultural life was disrupted, when industrial and commercial activity began to increase rapidly and to affect the lives of hundreds of thousands. It was a period in which the pressure for political change began to build up – slowly at first but as the eighteenth century wore on, and into the nineteenth, more and more rapidly. Not only that, but there was a time, during the first half of the eighteenth century at least, when the fact, in many cases the unpleasant fact, of the Parliamentary Union hung in the background of every Scot's life. We should not, perhaps, exaggerate the apparent pace of social, economic and political change since events generally seem less significant to those experiencing them than to those commenting on them several centuries later.

Elsewhere in this volume the early traditions and history of folk music and culture as well as more recent developments in the field are discussed. In a period of such change as described, the people not only sang songs about their life, their plight or their work, but they began to try to do things about those conditions. The eighteenth century was a period of popular direct action, of popular protest. That protest was sporadic, largely spontaneous and short-lived and in many senses just a trial run for working-class struggles in the nineteenth century; but it was real enough at the time.

Although popular protest is a significant part of popular folk culture there is a notable dearth of folk songs referring to the many instances of popular direct action. A possible explanation is that popular protest was relatively short-lived, often quite spontaneous and, with the exception of food riots, often quite localised in its immediate causes. Folk songs which have survived for that period tend to have had universal themes which collectors or the keepers of the oral tradition felt worth preserving. Like other areas of the folk tradition which have not survived from this period – the bawdy songs for instance – it is difficult to believe that no such songs ever existed. Like the bawdy songs, the songs about the people's struggle for fair prices, against local tyrants or in support of political reform were sung.

In a period of great change, one of the most significant political developments was quite clearly the Parliamentary Union between

Scotland and England in 1707. This has been a very fruitful source of folk songs ever since, perhaps most evocatively and notably in Burns' *A Parcel of Rogues in a Nation:*

> Fareweel to a' our Scottish fame
> Fareweel our ancient glory!
> Fareweel ev'n to the Scottish name,
> Sae famed in martial story!

> 'We're bought and sold for English gold' –
> Such a parcel of rogues in a nation![2]

The event did not pass at the time, however, without popular outcry on the streets of Edinburgh, Glasgow and elsewhere. Throughout much of the period from October to December 1706, when the Scots Parliament was debating the Articles of Union, the Edinburgh crowd demonstrated vociferously against the Union, fêting those they believed opposed to the Act and attempting to rabble those who were not. The crowd indicated quite clearly that it did not want Union. Daniel Defoe, a government agent in Edinburgh at the time, reported that the crowd marched through the streets

> with a drum at the head of them, shouting and swearing and crying out all Scotland would stand together. 'No Union, No Union', 'English dogs' and the like.[3]

This resentment was not restricted to the capital. On the contrary, the government was more worried about the outlying areas especially the West and South-West, where there was a fear – amazing as it may seem – that the presbyterian Cameronians would ally themselves with the episcopalian Highland Jacobites against Union. Whether this was ever a real possibility or not, there were scenes of violent popular action against the Union in Glasgow, Hamilton, Stirling and the Galloway area. In Glasgow the crowd were led by two men, Finly ('a mean, scandalous, scoundrel fellow ... and a professed Jacobite' according to Defoe), and Montgomery. The crowd seized the Bishop's House in the city as a strong-point and it required the intervention of dragoons from Edinburgh to dislodge them. In Edinburgh itself, the Town Guard had to clear a protesting crowd out of the Provost's house but it required the assistance of the Lord Commissioner's Guard to clear the High Street, even temporarily, of popular opponents of the Union. Clearly there was a real and deep hostility among ordinary people to the Union which they saw as being imposed upon them.

Anti-English feelings were not new in 1706. A year or so earlier, popular disturbances inflamed by such prejudices had resulted in the execution for piracy of three innocent English seamen. The men were the captain and two crew members of an English merchant ship, the *Worcester*. They were charged with a piratical attack on the *Speedy Return*, a Darien Company ship which had been missing for some time. At a crucial point the English government stepped into the matter, in a way particularly unhelpful to their countrymen, by passing the Alien Act which threatened to cut off trade between Scotland and England unless negotiations for Union were begun. By the time that Captain Green and his crew were charged with piracy the Edinburgh crowd were in no mood for justice far less mercy. On the day the Privy Council met in the Parliament House to consider a reprieve, the crowds were thick on the High Street. In spite of evidence that the *Speedy Return* had not been attacked at all, the crowd succeeded in panicking the Privy Council into refusing to save the seamen's lives. 'It was good it went so,' commented one Privy Councillor, 'for otherwise, I believe, the people had torn us to pieces.'[5] Thomas Green, John Madder, and James Simpson were taken from the Tolbooth and led through a throng of people lining the streets all the way to Leith sands. There the discreditable episode came to an end amid a jeering crowd when three innocent men died on the gallows.

Opposition to the Union was a factor in eighteenth-century Jacobitism and as late as 1797 crowds opposed to the Militia Act said that the Act was 'contrary to the Union'. As an issue, however, it was most closely connected with two essentially urban riots – the Shawfield riots in Glasgow in 1725 and the Porteous Riot in Edinburgh in 1736. Despite the significance, not to say the notoriety, of these events, there seems to be no evidence of popular songs inspired by them – at least none which have survived.

The background to the Shawfield or Malt Tax riots in June 1725 was a still general discontent at the Union, which had failed to produce the great economic advances promised by its supporters. The specific cause was the imposition of threepence a bushel on malt, which was half the English rate, a concession which failed to prevent a hostile reception being given to the tax. Disturbances were reported at Glasgow, Hamilton, Stirling, Ayr, Paisley and Dundee, while at Edinburgh the brewers refused to brew. It was in Glasgow that the most serious and best-known outbreak occurred. When the revenue officers went to assess the maltsters, 'a parcell of loose disorderly people'[6] barred their way. On 24 June the Glasgow crowd attacked the house of Duncan Campbell of Shawfield who, it was thought, had supported the Malt Tax in Parliament. Troops sent by the Lord Advocate, Duncan Forbes, were not at all welcomed by the Provost, who refused to employ them in quelling the disturbances. Eventually the military were attacked by the rioters and the soldiers opened fire. As many as eight civilians were killed and the Provost ordered the troops to withdraw, which they did with difficulty. The magistrates then spent much more time investigating the tragic deaths of the civilians than in trying to catch those responsible for the riotous attack on Shawfield House. Duncan Forbes, alarmed at this turn of events, went to Glasgow, arrested the magistrates and took them back to Edinburgh. After an unsuccessful prosecution by the Lord Advocate, the magistrates were released and returned to Glasgow, where they were enthusiastically welcomed by the crowd.

Perhaps the most famous Scottish example of crowd action in the eighteenth century, or any other century, was the Porteous Riot, immortalised by Walter Scott in his novel *Heart of Midlothian*. Following the execution in Edinburgh's Grassmarket of Andrew Wilson, a convicted smuggler, stones were thrown by some of the crowd and the Town Guard, under the command of Captain John Porteous, fired on the crowd killing several innocent bystanders. Porteous was quickly arrested, tried for murder and, despite a lack of definite proof, found guilty at the High Court of Justiciary. He was sentenced to be hanged on 8 September. After petitions from both Porteous himself and from some of Edinburgh 'society', he was granted a six-week reprieve. On the evening of 7 September, however, a large crowd gathered in the Portsburgh, entered the city through the West Port which they secured by nailing it up, and marched east through the Grassmarket and along the Cowgate, preceded by a drummer. As they went, they secured the minor gates to the city. The Netherbow Port was then safely locked, isolating the city from the troops in the Canongate. The crowd could then turn its attention to the Tolbooth prison. In the absence of opposition from the Town Guard, the magistrates or the military, the Tolbooth doors were burned down and John Porteous was dragged out. He was taken down the West Bow to the Grassmarket where, after several attempts, he was lynched from a dyer's pole near the official place of execution. Having achieved their macabre purpose, the crowd slowly dispersed. Despite efforts by the government to track down those responsible, only one man, a footman of the Countess of Wemyss, was tried for taking part in the disturbance, and he was acquitted. The Porteous Riot, as well as being the most famous of Scottish riots, was also the most successful. John Porteous was an unsavoury and unpopular Captain of the Town Guard and this, added to his guilt in the popular mind of the slaughter of several innocent civilians, resulted in a collective but single-minded act of revenge, a daring but successful coup which sent ripples through the whole fabric of British politics.[7]

Towards the end of the eighteenth century, political change of a fundamental kind became an issue in Scotland. By its nature – pressure for a democratic political system to replace the old, corrupt, oligarchic one – this was an issue in which a large proportion of the population of Scotland had an interest, in both senses of the word. The first signs of a political awakening in Scotland can be traced to the era of the American War of Independence. The failure of the British government to crush a small colonial uprising was seen as evidence of mismanagement by an unresponsive and unrepresentative administration. At the same time attention was drawn to the democratic ideals for which the American colonists were fighting. It was not, however, until revolution broke out in France that the broad mass of Scottish people began to show an active and widespread interest in political reform. The events in France were followed assiduously in the newspapers. In 1789 most sections of the community welcomed the French Revolution which many believed was similar in nature to Britain's so-called Glorious Revolution and few saw it as a threat to the status quo. It was only slowly that the propertied classes in Britain began to realise the potential threat posed by the new political order which had emerged in France. The bulk of the poorer sections of society – for whom the French Revolution was something like a revelation – were assailed by no such doubts. There existed in Scotland a deep-rooted egalitarianism and, with the example of France before them, many Scots saw that this could be translated into political democracy.

Tom Paine in his *Rights of Man,* which by 1793 had sold over 200,000 copies, showed that a democratic society was possible. In Scotland the main 'official' vehicle for parliamentary reform was the Society of Friends of the People. The first branch of the Friends of the People was established in Edinburgh in July 1792. Popular and democratic, with low subscriptions and no social barriers to membership, other branches followed throughout central Scotland. The strength of the Friends of the People was its broad base and wide membership but it was, of course, this, which alarmed the government. Commenting on the establishment of the Glasgow Society, a government spy put his finger on the fear which would lead to the downfall of the Friends of the People when he reported that

> the success of the French Democrats has had a most mischievous Effect here ... it has led them to think of founding societies into which the lower Class of People are invited to enter – and however insignificant these leaders may be in themselves, when backed with the Mob they become formidable.[8]

The government did not fear a few political renegades like Thomas Muir, a young, radical lawyer,[9] but it was almost panic-stricken by the thought that, with such leadership, the ordinary people might emulate their French counterparts. Events in France showed that, no matter how innocuous initial moves towards reform might be, the people soon demanded more radical changes. Early in 1793, the government moved against the reformers and arrested Thomas Muir. Eventually, following a visit to France to try to save the doomed Louis XVI, Muir was tried and sentenced to fourteen years transportation to Botany Bay. Other 'Political Martyrs' were also tried and similarly sentenced, joining Muir on the prison ship to Australia. The reform movement, almost crippled by the loss of much of its leadership and further harassed by the government, went underground.

As well as the 'official', there was also the 'unofficial' voice of reforming zeal. In 1792 the Tree of Liberty, the French symbol of liberty, equality and fraternity, was planted in towns and villages all over Scotland. Burns celebrated in song the planting of the Tree and caught the atmosphere surrounding the many popular disturbances accompanying these events:

> Heard ye o' the Tree o' France,
>   And wat ye what's the name o't?
> Around it a' the patriots dance –
>   Weel Europe kens the fame o't!
> It stands where ance the Bastile stood –
>   A prison built by kings, man,
> When Superstition's hellish brood
>   Kept France in leading strings, man.
>
> Wae worth the loon wha wadna eat
>   Sic halesome, dainty cheer, man!
> I'd gie the shoon frae aff my feet,
>   To taste the fruit o't here, man!
> Syne let us pray, Auld England may
>   Sure plant this far-famed tree, man;
> And bythe we'll sing, and herald the day
>   That gives us liberty, man.[10]

The planting of Trees of Liberty was often accompanied by the burning in effigy of Henry Dundas, the Home Secretary and political manager of Scotland. In June 1792 Aberdeen, Perth, Dundee 'and almost every village in the North of Scotland', according to one report, burned Dundas in effigy. At Peebles 'the Right Hon. Secretary has twice undergone fire ordeal, and passed through the flames unhurt'.[11] Earlier, in May, Lanark was 'in a very disagreeable State of Tumult and disorder' and 'one or two Guns or Pistols, loaded with Balls were discharged at the Windows of the Provost's house'. 'The real cause', the magistrates stated,

> is, an almost universal Spirit of Reform and opposition to the Established Government and Legal Administrators, which has

wonderfully diffused through the Manufacturing towns of this Country [12]

In November another wave of disturbances saw Trees of Liberty erected at Stonehaven, Aberdeen, Fochabers, Auchtermuchty and Strathmiglo. At Perth an unidentified effigy – probably Dundas himself but his correspondent was too polite to say so – was carried around the streets by a journeyman dyer dressed in woman's clothes. It was also not uncommon, apparently, to hear boys in the streets of Perth crying 'Liberty, Equality and No King'. An anonymous correspondent asserted that the people in Perth had gone 'quite mad about Liberty and Equality ...'

> The Lower Class of People talk of nothing but Liberty and Equality – 'No Dundas – No Bishops – and No King. Nothing but a Republic for us'. Such is the Spirit of the Times. [13]

Dundee was also the scene of extended popular action in November 1792. A fir tree was planted on the High Street but this Tree of Liberty was pulled down by some 'young gentlemen'. A few days later handbills circulated in the town urging all to meet to avenge this insult to the people. Several hundred gathered and became 'somewhat riotous': several effigies were burned, including one of the young men who had uprooted the Tree of Liberty, while a 'stout man' was made to carry a blazing tar-barrel at the head of the crowd through the streets. In an unsuccessful attempt to attract an even larger gathering, the town bell was loudly rung while the crowd which remained built a large bonfire in the High Street. The fire was kept alight all night and the Tree of Liberty was paraded around it before being fixed to the front of the Town House. It was removed the following day, but shortly afterwards another tree was put up in the market place where it remained until removed on the provost's orders two days later. [14]

Perhaps the most spectacular demonstration of popular democratic feelings occurred in Edinburgh in June 1792. [15] Traditionally, the King's official birthday was an occasion for boisterious and inebriated celebration by the people of Edinburgh. While the Edinburgh establishment was inside the Parliament House toasting the King, the crowd outside tore a sentry-box from its place in the High Street and carried it off to the Netherbow where it was burned. The High Street above the Netherbow was full of people, squibs and sky-rockets were set off and four Dragoon officers on foot were forced to mount and retreat before a threatening section of the crowd. When the Provost appeared on the scene the Dragoons tried to clear the street but the crowd simply ran down the narrow closes or up stairs until they had passed, then safely re-emerged. Only when the bonfire at the Netherbow had been extinguished and the military withdrew to the Cross near St Giles did the crowd disperse. About six in the evening of the following day, Tuesday, a small crowd escorted an effigy of Henry Dundas from the Newington area through Cross Causeway and into George Square. The effigy, suspended on two poles and held aloft by the masons who had constructed it, was set alight outside the house of Dundas's mother to the accompaniment of insulting epithets and gestures along with a few more substantial missiles. By the time the Sheriff arrived in the square to disperse the crowd it had swollen to a considerable number and his attempts were met with 'foul language and a volley of stones and a squib' which hit him on the chest. After the Riot Act had been 'read' – the Sheriff forgot to bring a copy and recited it from memory – he ordered the troops to prepare to fire. The crowd retreated a little at this, but edged forward again when no shots were fired. This lulled the crowd into a false sense of security, believing the troops had not been issued with shot. Meanwhile, a party of soldiers outflanked the crowd through the back alleys and, with bayonets fixed, came upon it from behind. The tactic was successful and the crowd dispersed for the moment. The troops were then sent off to St Andrew Square in the New Town where a further disturbance was reported. This did not materialise and the peace in George Square was short-lived. Having seen the troops march off towards the Castle and the New Town and having pursued them some of the way, part of the crowd returned to the Lord Advocate's house in the square. There they broke all the windows on the ground floor. When the remaining troops attempted to disperse this crowd two volleys were fired; the first produced no effect but the second killed one man and left at least six seriously wounded. Not surprisingly, the crowd ran off in all directions and the protest was over for the night. The fatality, however, did not prevent another large crowd assembling in and near George Square for a second night. The crowd of upward of two thousand, fearing the strong guard's fire-power, 'disappeared in a moment when the troops moved to disperse them'. Far from dispersing, they 'rolled like a torrent along both bridges' to the New Town where they attacked the Lord Provost's house in St Andrew Square. Within twenty minutes every single window in the house, front and gable-end, was shattered, while the Provost's terrified wife and two daughters remained trapped inside. By the time the troops arrived from the Castle the crowd had melted away and the King's Birthday Riot was over. It was, in terms of expressing popular anti-government sentiments and demonstrating at least the beginnings of democratic opinions, a dramatic success.

If anything the economic and social changes undergone in the eighteenth century were even greater than the political. It is usually remarked of this period of Scottish social history that there was a remarkable absence of 'Luddism' as a response to industrial change. While this is no doubt true it merely reflects the different nature of Scottish industry and the different developments which were taking place. There were, for instance, quite widespread examples of loom smashing during the 1787 and 1812 weavers' strikes – but these were aimed at blackleg weavers rather than against capitalist new technology. As a response to the development of the increasingly capitalist orientation of the Scottish economy the more common and widespread 'reactionary' response was the meal mob. Almost invariably when prices began to increase above a certain level in many places the population took matters into their own hands. It can be strongly argued that one of the most important parts of folk culture in the eighteenth century could have been what Edward Thompson has described as the 'Moral Economy' of the crowd.[16] This involved a popular determination that the people should not starve, that meal or grain which was known to be in storage should not be held by its owners at the people's expense, and that the people should not have to pay exorbitant prices at a time of scarcity but that 'a just price' should be paid.

This attitude is best illustrated by the conversation which took place between some of the crowd from Errol in the Carse of Gowrie and Robert Eason, a local farmer. John Bruce, a weaver from Errol, went to Eason's front door 'having a poke in his hand to carry meal', and asked the farmer to sell him meal, explaining he had a bag to carry it in and money to pay for it. Eason told him he had no meal to sell, at which Bruce complained that it was very hard that he and his children could get no meal after working hard and that his children were so badly off for food that 'they were seen picking the haws from the bushes'. Mrs Eason did not improve the situation by commenting that this was not so bad 'as eating grass like the brute beasts'. Undeterred, however, Bruce remonstrated that 'as God had blessed them with a good crop it was improper in him (Eason) to keep up his meal'. Equally adamant, Eason insisted that he had no meal and furthermore even if he had any he would not be forced to sell it by 'the menaces of a canaille'. It was only at this point that tempers were lost in the crowd and they then threatened they would burn his house unless he sent meal to Errol at an unspecified price fixed by them.[17] It is evident that here the people were concerned to convince the farmer that it was immoral on his part to withhold meal in this situation, especially when the harvest had been relatively good. While other examples of *taxation populaire* – the practice of forced sales and price-fixing or 'the imposition of price control by riot' – are less explicit in stating what the crowd felt, their actions revealed a similar attitude to the question of food supply.

Meal mobs took place intermittently throughout the eighteenth century. Such disturbances almost certainly occurred in 1709-10, 1727, 1740, 1756-7, 1767 and 1770-4, when prices rose above the average. There is certainly evidence of disturbances in 1739-40 and in the 1770s with much more definite information about food riots in 1780, 1783, 1784, 1792, 1793, 1795-6 and 1799-1801 when prices rose dramatically and progressively towards the end of the century. Three basic types of popular direct action recur throughout the food riots of the eighteenth century: the prevention of the export or movement of meal, grain or potatoes; the fixing of prices and the enforced sale of these commodities; and attacks on meal-sellers and grain dealers or their premises. Meal was sometimes simply seized from farms and granaries but these were a minority of incidents. In some cases in the 1790s the local Volunteers – supposed supporters of the established order – intervened on the popular side. One of the most common practices was to prevent the export of food by sea; by preventing loads of grain from reaching the harbour; unrigging and disabling the ships involved; attempting to intimidate or win over the crews of the ships; unloading ships in harbour; and even putting ships to sea before they could be loaded.

A traditional norm of behaviour in a situation of scarcity operated among the people and they sought to impose this norm on local farmers, meal-sellers and exporters. All the economists, all the substantial farmers, all the grain dealers and all the members of the government executive saw the manifest advantages to the country at large, and in some cases to themselves in particular, of the free internal movement of grain. What the theorists and entrepreneurs left out of the equation was the supply of those areas from which the grain came and through which it was exported. The townspeople of those areas – tailors, weavers, wrights, shoemakers, blacksmiths, labourers, fishermen – earned their keep by providing their skill or their services or their produce to the town and its hinterland and received in return money wages, from which they had to provide for themselves and their families. They depended for their supply of food on the local market. When meal and grain began to be shipped from the surrounding area through their town, and at the same time prices in the market rose and supplies dropped, the only resort was to direct action. Popular tradition told them what to do to protect, or to reassert, the 'moral economy'. Direct action here, as elsewhere, seemed to be the only effective response, not only, it was hoped, ensuring a better and possibly cheaper supply of food, but also releasing the tensions and frustrations created by lack of control over events that were of the greatest importance to people's lives.[18]

Turning to a completely different aspect of people's lives, one of the great traditions of Scottish folk and popular song has been the Scottish military tradition. A fair proportion of this tradition may be kailyard in origin and style but it certainly exists now and there is no reason to suppose that it did not exist in similar vein in the eighteenth century. It was not, however, necessarily the complete picture. John Prebble's book, *Mutiny*, has shown that the eighteenth-century tradition of Scottish, and particularly Highland, military service was not universally or gladly accepted at the time.[19] As early as 1743 the Black Watch mutinied near London while in 1778 Lord Seaforth's 78th Highlanders mutinied and occupied Arthur's Seat in Edinburgh for a while. In the latter year also, Lord MacDonald's 76th Highlanders mutinied at Burntisland rather than board transports for North America and sixty of Fraser's Highlanders shot it out with a Lowland regiment rather than be drafted into it. There were mutinies of the Gordon and Grant Fencibles at Edinburgh and Linlithgow in 1794. These were mutinies within established regiments of the army and should perhaps not be regarded as part of a more general popular culture. There are, however, examples of popular direct action which do seem to indicate a popular attitude contrary to the generally accepted one.

With the outbreak of the French Revolutionary Wars in 1793, MacKenzie of Seaforth was given approval to raise a Fencible regiment for the internal defence of North Britain. When he got to Lewis where he expected the bulk of his recruits to come from, Seaforth found 'evil-minded people' spreading 'pernicious doctrines' so that 'a few hundred turbulent people in the parish of Uig had assembled, and threatened to impede the recruiting service'. Three hundred or more Lewismen had armed themselves and had

> taken to a hill, where they had taken an oath to stand by each other, and vow death to any Serjeant, Drummer or other Recruitor, who dares enter the parish, and also threaten with death whoever dares Inlist.[20]

The men of Uig explained that they had no complaints against Seaforth as landlord but they would not disperse peacefully until all recruiting was over in Lewis since, 'as the Publick had Broken Faith with the late 78th Regiment, there was no saying but they might do the same by this regiment'.[21] When the 'old' 78th was raised in 1778, the men were told that they would be brought back to Rossshire for discharge. In the event they were discharged in the East Indies and attempts were then made to force them to enlist for a new term. Only those with more money than most soldiers or who managed to work their passages got home, while the rest were doomed to remain. It seems to have been a few old soldiers of the 78th who had struggled back home who were leading the refusal to be recruited. It is clear that enlistment into Seaforth's Fencible Regiment was not, in any real sense, voluntary. To resist recruitment meant to risk the eviction not only of the reluctant soldier but of his family as well. Highlanders and Islemen may have made good soldiers, but they did not necessarily make willing ones. In this case, after a few weeks of resistance it seems that solidarity began to crumble and eventually Seaforth was able to leave Lewis with at least some recruits: possibly enough to save his face but few enough to save the Lewismen's as well.

If popular culture is still felt to be in favour of military service, then this romantic notion must be shattered by another more fundamental popular belief. The people did not like to be forced to many things against their will but to be forced to serve in the army was intolerable, particularly when voluntary service was offered and refused, service was restricted to a certain age group, selection was by ballot and substitutes could be 'bought' by the rich. In the autumn of 1797 there was an eruption of popular protest against the imposition of the Scottish Militia Act.[22] After years of British government refusal to give the Scottish gentry the right to lead a local militia force in the Scottish counties because of the fear first of Jacobitism and then Jacobinism, the government was eventually forced to do so because other sources of military support were drying up. The Act provided for a militia force in each county drawn by ballot from among those eligible men between the ages of eighteen and twenty-three. From 17 August until 19 September 1797, local meetings to decide whose names were to go into the ballot were disrupted by angry and protesting crowds. Beginning in Eccles in Berwickshire, opposition spread into central and west Scotland, around Glasgow and Stirling, down into Galloway, across into Fife, north into Perthshire and then, finally, into Deeside. In almost all cases the lists of those young men eligible for the ballot were seized by the crowd and the local gentry who were responsible for executing the Act were forced to make declarations that they would play no further part in putting it into practice. At least forty-two separate incidents took place and the government felt itself in very real danger, moving troops northwards into Scotland but unable to take effective action because of the scattered nature of the resistance. There was, however, no revolution, no concerted attempt, even, to pursue the aim of getting the Militia Act repealed. In a sense this too was part of the tradition of popular protest. Action of this kind had little or no long-term political aims; it was short-term in its objectives and people felt, whatever experience should have told them, that the simple act of opposing the Militia Act would force the authorities to pay attention to their demands and act accordingly. Two incidents illustrate the difficulties of sustaining opposition even where attempts were made to do so and also the determination of the government to resist the popular will.

On 29 August 1797, the Deputy-Lieutenants for the parishes of Saltoun, Ormiston, Prestonpans and Tranent met in John Glen's public house in Tranent to draw up the ballot-list for the area. On their way through the large crowd which had gathered to object to particular names on the list and to oppose the Act generally, the Deputies were jostled and may have been threatened. Soon after they got inside the meeting-room the constables on guard outside reported that they needed military assistance because of the great press of people. A platoon of six men and a sergeant were sent in support. Shouts of 'No Militia' punctuated the general hubbub, a few stones were thrown and the soldiers were jostled and insulted. Others shouted that 'there must be no Militia, that none had ever been in Scotland' and 'a Militia was against the Union'.[23] Tempers on both sides began to fray as the narrow street of Tranent seethed with people hurling abuse at the soldiers, the Deputies and the Militia Act. When the cavalry tried to clear the street, the crowd simply retreated up the convenient alleys while at all times the troops were exposed to volleys of stones thrown from the street, from stairheads and from the rooftops. The Riot Act was read and shortly after that the soldiers opened fire on the crowd.

The first targets were the men on the rooftops. One man, William Hunter, was shot dead from the roof, George Elder and Joan Crookston were shot dead on the street, and Isabel Roger was killed 'within a door of a house ' where she had been pursued by a dragoon. These can be said to be the 'legitimate' casualties of the Tranent riot: while they are not necessarily excusable, they are understandable. Worse was to follow. Having been on the receiving end of a great deal of verbal and physical abuse for over an hour, some of the dragoons ran amok, venting their frustrations on the dispersing crowd which was now at their mercy. They turned this dispersal into a bloody rout and massacre. Peter Ness, a sawyer who probably played no part in the riot, was cut down and shot as he flew through the standing corn behind Tranent. Stephen Brotherstone, a farm labourer from Pencaitland who was on his way *to* Tranent to look for his son, was sabred to death behind a hedge. Peter Lawson, a wright on his way innocently into Tranent, was approached by a soldier, 'a stout lusty man pitted with smallpox and a remarkable Scar upon one of his cheeks' as he described him before he died, who shot him 'upon his right side, a very little above his Foot Rule'. Not close enough to save his life. William Laidlaw, a farm labourer, was found dead in a field near the Haddington road while James Moffat, a brewer's servant, was shot while retrieving a dragoon's helmet for him. D. Kemp, a thirteen or fourteen-year-old, was found dead, stabbed in the chest 'with the upper part of his head … nearly cut from temple to temple'. John Adam did not leave his work at St Germain's colliery until after the end of the riot in Tranent but he was still shot by one of the dragoons. Robert Dundas, the Lord Advocate, would admit later only that Lawson and Adam 'appear to have been entirely innocent and to have lost their lives most unjustifiably'. The others were, in his opinion, either 'actually engaged in the Mob, or on their way to join it'. No action was, however, taken or even contemplated against the soldiers involved.

At Weem, near Aberfeldy in Perthshire, on Sunday, 3 September, the parish list was torn down from the church door as soon as it was nailed up.[24] This was the beginning of over a week of popular action in the whole Strathtay and Strathtummel area which indicates the difficulties of sustaining such action. Once it had begun much of the activity was directed by Angus Cameron, a Lochaber man employed by a Glasgow company to build a factory and houses in Aberfeldy. Fluent in Gaelic and English, well informed, a reader of anti-government newspapers, he had the reputation of being a great orator 'who could beat the Gentlemen, ministers and Schoolmasters in Speaking'. On the morning of 4 September crowds visited most of the gentry in the area demanding their word not to execute the Act. Contingents of people arrived from all over Strathtay at the gates of Castle Menzies, the home of Sir James Menzies, the local Deputy Lieutenant. Early in the afternoon the crowd of between fifteen hundred and two thousand pushed the gates open and surrounded the main door of the house. They clamoured for the repeal of the Militia Act and eventually Menzies agreed to sign a bond to take no further part in the execution of the Act. The crowd then withdrew as far as the park gates where Angus Cameron asked them to raise their right hands and swear to be true to each other in their opposition to the Militia. Later that afternoon the crowd, with Cameron at its head on a white horse according to some reports, moved eastwards from Weem along the north bank of the Tay, forcing the gentry to sign the Castle Menzies bond. At Boat of Tummel that night the crowd from Weem were joined by a large contingent from Atholl and spent much of the night drinking and dancing. The next day the Atholl people marched north again to Blair Atholl but the Duke managed to muster enough of his tenants to deter the anti-Militia crowd which dispersed. The rest of the people visited the remaining large houses on the east bank of the Tay and Tummel before beginning to drift back to their own homes, having succeeded, as far as they could see, in stopping the Militia Act's execution.

During these few days there was much heady, democratic talk among the people as well as potentially revolutionary advice from Angus Cameron. He told the people that the government intended to turn the British Constitution into an arbitrary military government and pointed to the barracks in the towns and cities as evidence, crowned by the Militia Act. He is, moreover, said to have talked of arming the people from Lord Breadalbane's armoury, from Glenlyon House and from Castle Menzies, of seizing the great guns at Taymouth Castle and, if necessary, of taking to the hills to fight a guerilla campaign. The people themselves talked of liberty and equality. One man told Sir James Menzies' factor 'that the Lords and Factors were very fat and living very well and he thought they would bring them down and have time about with them'. Another reported hearing 'murmurs about reducing the Lairds' rent and the ministers' stipends and about making the King reside at Edinburgh'. At Glenlyon House, one of the crowd, when asked what they were doing, answered that 'they wanted to make this like France'.

The people of Strathtay would, however, have to wait a long time before it was 'like France'. On 10 September, Angus Cameron addressed a group in the churchyard at Kenmore. Speaking in Gaelic, he told them that there was to be a meeting at Glenlyon House near Fortingall the next day and that fifteen or sixteen thousand people from Grandtully, Strathtay, Atholl, Foss, Rannoch and Glenlyon were to attend to petition the King and Parliament for a repeal of the

Militia Act. He then left Kenmore and travelled north to Kinloch Rannoch where he repeated his attempts to ensure a large turn-out the following day at Fortingal. He told the innkeeper that

> there would not be a man betwixt the foot of Loch Tumble and the head of Loch Rannoch on both sides but would turn out before the Sun set tomorrow ...

The Fortingall meeting was a complete anti-climax and Cameron's high hopes for further popular action against the Militia Act were not realised. Very few turned up and, possibly disheartened by the small numbers, even they drifted away. With them went Angus Cameron's popular support. A party of Windsor Foresters had been waiting at Blair Atholl for some days, unable or unwilling to act because of the large numbers involved in the disturbances. Three days after the Fortingall meeting a platoon of the Foresters marched in bad weather twenty miles over the hills to Weem and seized Angus Cameron and his lieutenant, James Menzies, from their beds at five in the morning. They were bundled into a post-chaise and then whisked away to Perth, before being sent on to Edinburgh to await trial. The 'revolution' in Strathtay was over but the people had for a few days been in complete control of the area, paralysing the local gentry. Only when the people believed they had achieved their purpose was the government able to reassert its control and remove their leader.

1792 is, in Highland tradition, *Bliadhna Nan Caorach*, 'The Year of the Sheep'. On 31 July, following a few months of increasing opposition to the introduction of sheep farms, about two hundred men from Ross and Sutherland gathered in Strathoykel, a northern part of Ross and Cromarty. They then proceeded to drive all the sheep they could find southwards through the county. All that week an ever-increasing flock of sheep made its way southwards until on Saturday, 4 August, a huge flock of upwards of ten thousand sheep was gathered near Strathrusdale where the original opposition had begun. The plan was to drive the flock further south to the Inverness border where they hoped the Inverness people would take up the job of driving the hated sheep even further south and finally out of the Highlands. The plan was frustrated by the arrival at Dingwall on Saturday of three companies of the Black Watch. The gentry of Ross had written desperately to Edinburgh for assistance:

> We are at present so completely under the Heel of the Populace
> that should they come to Burn our houses, or destroy our prop-
> erty in any way their Caprice may lead them to feel we are
> incapable of Resistance.[25]

With the aid of the Black Watch they were capable of resistance and
a party led by the Sheriff-Deputy accompanied the soldiers to the
spot where the sheep were gathered. At one in the morning they
came upon six thousand sheep grazing unattended; the soldiers
rested and the gentlemen galloped off to capture the 'rebels'. By
midday twelve men had been arrested and *Bliadhna Nan Caorach* was
over. This was remembered not as a great success, but as an heroic
attempt to reverse the trends which were going to mean the destruction of a way of life in the Highlands.

Like the direct action in Ross, much of the popular action described above was an attempt to reverse trends, to assert the 'moral
economy' and its equivalents in other areas of life. Folk music and
folk song are of great importance in telling about aspects of the
people's past. They do not, however, tell the whole story. A lot of
popular history is not told in the ballads and songs of the eighteenth
century and in a time of great change there may be very good reasons
for songs not to have survived. The oral tradition was for a time at
least interrupted, especially in the lowlands. Collectors in that period
– and since – may have looked for the song with the universal theme
and it may be suspected that they also looked for the ones which
confirmed their views of society – i.e. not songs of protest. Although
Robert Burns ought to be excepted from the latter generalisation, it is
difficult to imagine someone like Walter Scott being very keen to
collect folk material about popular protest. Interestingly, however,
Scott was connected with two examples of such protest: he wrote
about the Porteous Riot in *Heart of Midlothian* and he defended one of
those accused of taking part in the Eccles militia riot.

Between 1805 and 1810 Malcolm of Poltalloch cleared eighteen
families from Arichanan in Argyll. An anonymous poet wrote (in
Gaelic) at the time:

121

A wicked man is Malcolm
And I will ever say it
When the French come
Across to rout him,
Who will stand up for Malcolm
In the rabble round about him?
Everyone will be wild
Desiring to strike him
And I myself will be there
Urging on the conflict.[26]

The poem illustrates the culture shock of life in a time of great change, indicating the extent of the disillusionment of the once loyal clansman. Another response was popular protest of the kind we have discussed. Popular protest was an important and integral part of popular culture in eighteenth-century Scotland. In many ways it is the people's past.

NOTES
1 Robert Burns, 'Ye Jacobites by Name', verse 1, lines 1-4.
2 Robert Burns, 'A Parcel of Rogues in a Nation', verse 1, lines 1-4 and verse 3, lines 7-8.
3 *H.M.C. Portland*, iv, 340.
4 *Ibid.*, 364.
5 *Jerviswood Correspondence*, Bannatyne club, lxii, 75.
6 *Culloden Papers*, p. 80.
7 See H. T. Dickinson and K. J. Logue, 'The Porteous Riot: A Study of the Breakdown of Law and Order in Edinburgh 1736-1737', *Journal of the Scottish Labour History Society* x 1976; 'The Porteous Riot', *History Today*, xxii, 1972.
8 (S.R.O., Home Office Correspondence) RH2/4/64, f. 369, 12 October, 1792.
9 See K. J. Logue, 'Thomas Muir' in Gordon Menzies, ed., *History is My Witness* (London, 1976), pp. 13-37.
10 Robert Burns, 'The Tree of Liberty', verses 1 and 11.
11 H. Meikle, *Scotland and the French Revolution* (Glasgow, 1912), p. 81. See also K. J. Logue, *Popular Disturbances in Scotland 1780-1813* (Edinburgh, 1979), pp. 148-153.
12 RH2/4/63, ff. 32-32v., 8 May, 1792.

13 RH2/4/67, f. 438, 15 December, 1792.
14 RH2/4/66, f. 259, 8 December, 1792.
15 Details from precognition into disturbances, RH2/4/63, *passim*. See also Logue, *Popular Disturbances* pp. 133-143.
16 E. P. Thompson, 'The Moral Economy of the English Crowd in the Eighteenth Century', *Past and Present*, 1, 1971.
17 S.R.O. Justiciary Papers, JC26/313, H.M. Advocate v. John Bruce *et al.*
18 Logue, *Popular Disturbances* pp . 18-53.
19 John Prebble, *Mutiny: Highland Regiments in Revolt 1743-1804* (London, 1975) on which this paragraph is largely based.
20 RH2/4/207, p. 465, 27 April, 1793.
21 RH2/4/71, f. 238v., 23 May, 1793.
22 37 Geo. III, cap. 103.
23 RH2/4/81, 'An Account of the Tranent Riot', and precognition into the riot, Sept./Oct./Nov. 1797. See also K. J. Logue, 'The Tranent Militia Riot of 1797', *Trans. of East Lothian Antiquarian and Field naturalists Society*, xiv 1974.
24 S.R.O., Lord Advocate's Papers, AD14/25/127, Strathtay Precognition, on which the following paragraphs are based.
25 RH2/4/64, f. 258-258v., 31 July, 1792.
26 *The Oban Times* 3 January, 1885. I am indebted to James Hunter for bringing the poem to my attention and to Donald Meek for this translation.

E

Old and Plain: Music and Song in Scottish Art

DUNCAN MacMILLAN

Mark it, Caesario; it is old and plain,
The spinsters and the knitters in the sun,
And the free maids that weave their thread
with bones,
Do use to chant it.

Shakespeare's *Twelfth Night*

Robert Fergusson's epigraph to
Elegy on the death of Scots Music, 1772.

The period of most striking originality in Scottish art coincides with that of the most widespread interest in Scottish traditions in music and poetry. This is not a coincidence for these two aspects of Scottish cultural history were closely connected, and their interaction is recorded in a striking way. For whatever reason, images of popular music-making seem largely to disappear from European art in the mid-eighteenth century. Such images as there are in the later part of the century refer clearly to formal, or classical, music, and the theme of informal music-making only returns to what is generally regarded as the mainstream with Courbet in the *Après dîner à Ornans,* the picture which could be said to have launched the new movement in French painting at the revolutionary Salon of 1849. During this period of a century when popular music was absent from the imagery of the rest of European art it was central to that of art in Scotland. David Allan, Alexander Carse, William Lizars, David Wilkie, Walter Geikie and several others all produced pictures of popular music and dance. Raeburn made his masterpiece the portrait of Neil Gow playing his fiddle.

At the simplest level the pictorial evidence indicates that music featured importantly in daily life at all levels in society, and this is certainly true; but it seems that the matter is more complex, for the choice of this kind of subject and the style in which it was treated reflected a deeper intention upon the part of the artists.

The first image to spring from this relationship is not one that has an obvious bearing upon the representation of music-making. It is a drawing by Alexander Runciman of an ancient Celtic bard sitting playing his harp beneath windblown trees.[1] It was done in Rome about 1770. It probably represents Ossian and was followed in 1772 by Runciman's Ossianic paintings in Penicuik House of which the centrepiece showed Ossian singing. Runciman, in painting these pictures, used a deliberately rapid and abbreviated style to emulate what was believed to be the primitive style of Ossian, invoking the Rousseauesque idea of the simplicity and directness of life in the original state of human society. Although Rousseau did not extend his ideal of simplicity to art, Runciman did, following the example of literary theorists like Hugh Blair. He was effectively the first European artist to do so, though after going through many transitions the idea eventually proved crucial in the evolution of modern art. Runciman epitomised his understanding of the ideal of primitive art in the *Origin of Painting*[2] in 1771, which was a subject subsequently treated by many artists as symbolising the original simplicity and therefore the imaginative and moral purity of art in man's primitive state.

In the drawing of Ossian, or 'the Bard', Runciman laid great stress – through the manner of drawing, the setting, and the image of the wind blowing in trees, cloak and hair – on the bard's union with nature. The bard is both inspired by nature and part of it:

> Amang the trees where humming bees
> At buds and flowers were hinging, O,
> Auld Caledon drew out her drone
> And to her pipe was singing, O.

Burns' lines, with minor adaptations, could describe Runciman's picture. Runciman himself was influenced by MacPherson and by Hugh Blair writing on Ossian,[3] but probably most importantly by one of his closest friends, David Herd, collector of ballads. Herd had published his first collection of ballads, *Scots Songs*, in 1769 and in the preface he wrote about the connection between the landscape and the way of life of the people and the poetry they produced. The idea passed into history through the myth of Burns the ploughman-poet and is referred to directly in the portrait of Burns against the Ayrshire landscape by Nasmith, in Raeburn's portrait of Scott among ruins and mountains at Bowhill, and in Wilkie's portrait of Scott and his family in rural dress which is discussed below.

Although MacPherson's Ossian and the Scottish ballads may now seem very different from each other, to a late eighteenth-century enthusiast they were directly comparable. Both appeared to be associated with the living traditions of an ancient and indigenous culture with which, because it was Scottish, people could legitimately identify. The culture of Highland Scotland, as that of the pastoral lowlands, could be claimed to be innocent and untouched by European high culture which seemed so corrupt. Their poetry and music could be regarded as partaking of the simplicity, directness and intensity of Rousseau's ideal as Runciman attempted to capture it in his paintings. There were, therefore, compelling reasons for high art to endeavour to identify itself with popular culture, as Wordsworth and Coleridge attempted to do in 1798, in the *Lyrical Ballads,* but in Scotland this identification seems to have cost no effort.

Runciman and Herd had a close mutual friend in the poet Robert Fergusson. All three were members of the Cape Club, a drinking club that drew its members from the small business and artisan class of Edinburgh which included actors, poets, musicians and painters. Significantly they drank porter not the fashionable drink, claret. Music, poetry, and song were a regular part of their entertainment. They would sing familiar songs or compose new ones to old tunes. The musicians, after a formal concert at the theatre or St Cecilia's Hall, would repair to the Cape for more congenial entertainment, at times composing music themselves for special occasions. Some of their songs survive in manuscript. There is even one by Runciman. Fergusson was a sophisticated poet with a European consciousness, yet he clearly was expressing feelings that he shared with his fellow club members when he wrote, in 'On the Death of Scots Music':

> Now foreign sonnets bear the gree,
> And crabbit queer variety

> Of sounds fresh sprung from Italy,
>   A bastard breed!
> Unlike that saft tongu'd melody
>   Which now lies dead ...
> O Scotland! that could yence afford
> To bang the pith of Koman sword,
> Winna your sons, wi' joint accord,
>   To battle speed?
> And fight till music be restored,
>   That now lies dead.

Even more directly he wrote in 'The Daft Days':

> Fiddlers, your pins in temper fix,
> And roset weel your fiddle-sticks,
> But banish vile Italian tricks
>   From out your quorum
> Nor fortes wi' pianos mix,
>   Gie's Tullochgorum.

Finally he returned to the theme much more elaborately in 'Hame Content' where towards the end he invites Fancy to come and

> ... a' your springs delightfu' lowse
> On Tweeda's bank or Cowdenknowes,
> That ta'en wi' thy enchanting sang,
> Our Scottish lads may round yethrang,
> Sae pleas'd, they'll never fash again
> To court you on Italian plain;
> Soon will they guess ye only wear
> The simple garb o' Nature here;
> Mair comely far an' fair to sight
> Whan in her easy clothing dight,
> Than in disguise ye was before
> On Tibur's or on Arno's shore.

These sentiments may seem chauvinistic to the delicate sensibility of modern high culture but to Fergusson and his friends what was at issue was not a mere matter of musical taste. Nature, which lies at the centre of his argument, was not an excuse for elegant sentimentalis-

127

ing, but, three years before the American Declaration of Independence, the key to remaking the world from those first principles to which they believed the survival of a genuine folk tradition of music and poetry gave them access.

Fergusson could therefore draw strength for his central beliefs as a poet from popular traditions in music and poetry, just as Burns did after him. It was much more difficult for a visual artist to do this. The ideal simplicity of the *Origin of Painting* was an abstraction, and even in Runciman's Ossian pictures identification with the 'naturalness' of the oral tradition was indirect. The problem was solved by the painters turning directly to living Scots poetry and away from the dominant classical (or Italian) visual tradition, back to the Dutch achievement of the seventeenth century to which Scotland had originally been so close. The first painter to do this was Runciman's contemporary, David Allan. He had aspired to success in the current international style but in 1787 he brought what had seemed to be an amusing sideline into the centre of his art. He had always done genre drawings but in that year he undertook a series of illustrations to Allan Ramsay's *Gentle Shepherd*, which were published in an edition of the play by the Foulis brothers.[4] He defended the transition from conventional high art in an ingenious preface.

> In the humbler walk of Painting, which consists in the just representation of ordinary Life (by which, it is believed, the best moral effects may be often produced), there can be no better models than what Nature, in this country, daily presents to our view. Without descending to mean and low objects, it is possible, by a strict adherence to truth and nature, to produce compositions which, though not so striking as the sublimer efforts of the pencil, are yet capable both of pleasing and instructing, in a very high degree.
>
> This consideration has incited me to present the public with a series of designs illustrating the different scenes of a justly admired Pastoral, the 'Gentle Shepherd' of Allan Ramsay. This piece, it is well known, he composed in the neighbourhood of Pentland Hills, a few miles from Edinburgh, where the shepherds to this day sing his songs, and the old people remember him reciting his own verses. I have studied the same characters on the same spot, and I find that he has drawn faithfully, and

with taste, from Nature. This, likewise, has been my model of imitation, and while I attempted in these sketches to express the ideas of the Poet, I have endeavoured to preserve the costume as nearly as possible, by an exact delineation of such scenes and persons as he actually had in his eye.

Thus his main defence makes essentially the same point as Runciman makes through his Ossian pictures. It is to stress the naturalness of the manners and way of life of the people he represents and their relationship to the landscape in which they live, but also significantly he stresses the truth of his representation. For all the seeming artificiality of his images he claims to be dealing with the real world.

Allan came into more direct contact with the popular tradition than he could with the *Gentle Shepherd* when on the instigation of the poet's publisher, George Thomson, he undertook a series of twenty etched illustrations to Burns's collection of Scots songs. These illustrations were never properly published[5] but they are of the greatest importance in demonstrating a connection between the attempt at direct and unsentimental depiction of ordinary life and the tradition of popular song.

Scenes of music-making and dance appear quite frequently in Allan's drawings throughout his life. One of the earliest of his works is a drawing of his father playing the flute. In Italy he depicted dancers, and Calabrian Shepherds playing the bagpipes. Back in Scotland it was he who, in 1780, introduced the theme of the Penny Wedding to Scottish art. It became central to the iconography of the depiction of folk music, treated by David Deuchar, directly after Allan's composition, Alexander Carse, William Lizars, and David Wilkie. As late as 1870 it inspired in literature the climactic scene of William Alexander's *Johnny Gibb of Gushetneuk*. Allan's inspiration may have lain partly in Hogarth but his image derived more directly from the *Country Wedding* of Jacob de Witte at Penicuik House. A highland piper stands at the centre of this picture. Painted by a Dutch artist in Scotland in the late seventeenth century, it provided an essential link between the contemporary depiction of popular life with music at its heart and the directness of the Dutch style. The example of the poets enabled Allan to turn this pedigree and claim that his representations of popular life should be taken seriously as art and not be seen as just an amusing sideline. There was of course genre painting elsewhere, but nowhere did it share these objectives, and at this point for two generations Scottish art parted company with the art of the rest of Europe.

Allan's own talent was slender enough and had the matter rested with him this aspect of Scottish art might have been an interesting but minor episode. However, the real potential of the conjunction of painting and the traditions of folk music was declared not by him, but in a single picture by an artist of far greater power, Raeburn, in his portrait of Neil Gow. This was painted in 1806. As a portrait the only rivals it has from its own time are in the work of Goya and David. It shows the fiddler seated, dressed in his customary check trews and absorbed in his music. The strength, simplicity and direct-ness of the image, and the painting of it, are not only a just comment on the man, but also on his music. Here there are no Italian tricks, and in place of artificiality, which was the dominant characteristic of contemporary portraiture elsewhere, the image is utterly concrete. Its dignity derives from the artist's respect for the individuality of his sitter. Through Neil Gow, Raeburn has given visible form to the qualities in the popular tradition from which Fergusson and Burns drew strength. Beside this portrait his nearly contemporary portrait of Scott seems strangely ambivalent.

The portrait of Neil Gow is exceptional in its theme in Raeburn's art though its qualities are not. It was Wilkie who developed this aspect of Scottish painting and who, for the first time since Hogarth, painted people as naturally dignified in ordinary life no matter what their class or occupation. From Wilkie this tradition passed into European art as a whole. He acknowledged a debt to Raeburn in his own early self-portrait (National Gallery of Scotland), but the influ-ence on him of the older artist was more far-reaching than its appear-ance in this one image might suggest. Raeburn's example enabled Wilkie to bring a new kind of directness to David Allan's subject matter. In keeping with this, from his first major picture, *Pitlessie Fair* of 1804, all his best pictures describe a world that he knew. Pitlessie in Fife was his own village and though the picture is indebted to Hogarth and to Dutch and Flemish painters the image is convinc-ingly first-hand. Though there is an element of drollery in this and other early pictures, the humour is without mockery, and reflects a wholly sympathetic response to a familiar world.

Pitlessie Fair celebrates popular life. The artist is part of the scene that he depicts. (He is not there in person, but his signature on a wheelbarrow is being peed on by a dog.) Musicians are out in force. There is a piper from a highland regiment emphatically blowing his nose, not his pipes, reflecting Wilkie's opinion of the quality of military pipe music, no doubt. There is a blind fiddler in the background competing with the general cacophony, and prominent in the foreground is a group of boys listening in rapt attention to one of their number performing on the Jew's harp. Another boy competing on a tin trumpet is being vigorously hushed by one of the listeners. This vignette seems to be a comment on the nature of folk music. The children, the simplicity of the instrument and their serious response to it reflecting the original ideal simplicity from which the folk tradition was believed to spring. Wilkie here adumbrates an important idea of the nature of childish sensibility that he does not himself pursue, but which re-emerges a little later applied directly to visual art in the work of Walter Geikie (see below).

The blind fiddler, the Jew's harp and the highland piper all provided Wilkie with separate subjects, the first two shortly after his move to London. The *Blind Fiddler* of 1807 was in fact one of the pictures whose success established his reputation there. He also treated a number of other musical themes. The most elaborate was his *Penny Wedding* of 1818 in which he included as musicians Neil and Donald Gow. The picture went into the Royal Collection. It should therefore be the high point of the story of how Wilkie successfully made high art from music, dance and popular custom, but the seeds of alienation were already sown. The fact that the custom of the Penny Wedding was supposed to be already extinct should not matter as the subject had by this time such an important place in the iconography of Scottish art, but even by including Neil Gow, who died in 1808, Wilkie was setting his scene in the past. In spite of its rusticity, he has, too, made the occasion distinctly elegant through his treatment of pose and gesture. He has carefully edited out all sign of the lively excesses which would be natural to such an event and which appear in William Lizars' version of the subject painted a few years earlier. Royalty could safely buy Wilkie's picture, and in fact it was painted to redeem his reputation, in just such quarters, from the tricky situation in which his last major picture had left him. This was *Distraining for Rent*.

There is nothing musical about *Distraining for Rent*, but it was the picture in which Wilkie proved himself the heir to the concreteness of Raeburn's *Neil Gow*. In it, too, he shows how he had seen, as Burns had seen, that this leads inevitably to confronting in some way social injustice . The subject of his picture is the distraint upon the goods of a tenant farmer in the agrarian distress of 1814. In the war-time boom, rents had risen with prices. Prices collapsed, but rents stayed high. Distraint and dispossession were the result. The injustice was plain but Wilkie was made to understand very clearly that this kind of truth was not the business of the artist, and he never took the risk again .

The extent to which Wilkie was fundamentally out of sympathy with his English public was again vividly illustrated in 1818 when he exhibited the small group portrait of Scott with his family and friends now in the Scottish National Portrait Gallery. The picture is unpretentious and, whether or not truthfully, shows the sitters as a rural, though not rustic group. The critical response was remarkable: 'Really, had not Mr Wilkie informed us who this vulgar group represent, we would have been at a loss to have guessed it to have been the representation of the elegant poet and his family. Even with this information we can perceive nothing refined or poetical, not even rustic or pastoral, but rather a common clodpole, and his rude associates and family' *(Annals of the Fine Arts)*.[6]

Elsewhere the picture was attacked as 'violating decency and good taste'.[7] It is ironic that Scott of all people should have helped to provoke such a critical outburst, but certainly the idea of poetic or artistic identification with ordinary life, however artificial it may have been, was unacceptable to contemporary critical taste in England. The Scottish response was strikingly different. The critic of the *Edinburgh Evening Courant* wrote: 'We have seen no painting which places the individual in his everyday feelings so completely before in public.'[8] Wilkie's difficulties seem to have arisen from a direct collision of standards. The tension was eventually fatal to his art. He painted one great and appropriate valedictory masterpiece, the *Cottar's Saturday Night* (Glasgow Art Gallery), a subject previously painted by David Allan for Robert Burns, but otherwise, in the later part of his life his painting was vitiated, literally, by Italian tricks. In the earlier part of his career he had unsuccessfully attempted to adapt his Scottish idiom to specifically English subjects. Ironically the only such picture to have a musical theme shows the parish beadle locking up itinerant musicians as unlicensed beggars. Perhaps it was symbolic. Wilkie was expected to entertain, but decorously, strictly within his license, and with due respect for the social order.

In Scotland, however, the tradition of what was best in Wilkie's art was carried on by Walter Geikie. He was, like Wilkie, a pupil of John Graham at the Trustees Academy – Graham was himself most probably a pupil of Runciman. Although he was the last artist to do so, Geikie identified himself most wholeheartedly with the popular tradition. He was deaf and dumb and it has been customary (as well as convenient) to relegate him to the status of a naïve artist. He was clearly aware of this happening in his own time for one of his etchings shows a group of fashionably dressed artists, no doubt masters of Italian tricks, laughing uproariously at the efforts of a humble artist visible at work in his studio across the street. In contrast to their superior sarcasm an attentive child stands at his elbow. This strikingly anticipates Courbet's picture of himself in the *Painter's Studio* of 1855. He is seen sitting at his easel likewise watched by a child. There is also a child drawing on the floor. Their presence represents the idea of naïvety, or simplicity of response which was central to Courbet's art theory, and which he shared with Baudelaire. Geikie also treated child art directly and in a version of the *Origin of Painting* makes clear his intention in doing so. The participants in the scene are children in contemporary dress and an ordinary environment, instead of adults in a remote and ideal past. They are watched by admiring adults. Their interest makes it clear that this childish activity is something from which older generations can learn.

Geikie treats children drawing, or showing off their pictures, on a number of other occasions. His children are real and their activities as important and dignified as those of any other class of humanity. Their art is part of their daily life in the same way as other kinds of play including music. Through his imagery of child art he describes the transfer into his own art of the values ascribed to folk music. In his transfer he made one vital modification. Not only his children, but all his subjects exist in the contemporary world and in most cases their environment is identifiably urban. He dispelled the myth of pastoral simplicity and replaced it by spontaneous directness to the world of contemporary urban reality. The simple dignity that he gave to ordinary casual scenes of daily life is without parallel in the nineteenth century before 1848 and the development of radical French art. The only exceptions are the lithographs of Géricault and he, like Geikie, was touched by the influence of Wilkie.

Geikie treated music-making directly in a number of pictures. A painting of highland pipers was destroyed in a fire at Hopetoun House a few years ago. One of his grandest compositions is an unfinished engraving of a piper and his boy. The piper is seated and so Geikie pays fitting homage to Raeburn's *Neil Gow*. An etching of Burns' *Jolly Beggars* clearly reveals the direction of his thought and one source of his inspiration. So too does one of his most comic musical compositions, the etching *Tullochgorum*. It shows a man carried away by the music of a fiddle, cavorting wildly before an astonished crowd in Edinburgh's Grassmarket. The picture surely invokes not just the reel *Tullochgorum*, which is its title, but Fergusson's poem, the 'Daft Days', in which it figures so memorably. After invoking *Tullochgorum* in the verse quoted above. Fergusson continues:

> For naught can cheer the heart sae weel
> As can a canty Highland reel,
> It even vivifies the heel
>> To skip and dance:
> Lifeless is he wha canna feel
>> Its influence.

Then he concludes:

> And thou, great god of *Aqua Vitae*!
> Wha sways the empire of this city,
> When fou we're sometimes capernoity,
>> Be thou prepar'd
> To hedge us frae that black banditti,
>> The City Guard.

Fergusson's closing lines remind us forcibly that the world he is describing, in which music has such prominence, is real and immediate. Geikie was true to Fergusson's inspiration, and so, at either end of a period of sixty years, poet and artist identify, and pay homage, to the central role of popular music in their image of a vigorous and unified national culture.

After Geikie's death in 1840, informal music-making effectively disappeared as a subject from Scottish art. If it does appear, as in John Philip's *La Gloria*, it is safely detached from contemporary reality, in this case set in Spain. Scottish painting continued at its best to subscribe to values of real visual truth and, doing so, later in the century found common ground with progressive painting in Holland and in France; but in some way it was emasculated. After D. O. Hill's pioneer adoption of photography to record the Disruption Assembly of 1843, for all its real qualities the internal logic of Scottish art seems never again to have led it to confront any fundamental questions of value. In 1843 the attempt to create a unified culture based on the dignity of the individual seems finally to have failed. In the march of class alienation through the nineteenth century, visual art was forced on to the side of the established order. This happened in England and it was only the revolutionary tradition resurgent in 1848 and 1870 that prevented it happening in France. The Scottish artists struggled against the process from a very early date and did so in the name of a national culture epitomised by the popular musical tradition. Considering the forces ranged against it the attempt was inevitably doomed to failure. The fate of Wilkie clearly revealed that there was no room for reconciliation and those who, like Geikie, made no attempt to compromise, were soon dealt with by posterity. The otherwise admirable Robert Brydall wrote of Geikie in 1889: '. . . as too often happens in the case of mutes, he failed to develop any of the higher qualities that are necessary to constitute an artist'.[8]

Chambers Biographical Dictionary of Eminent Scotsmen in the 1870 edition was indirectly just as damning of Neil Gow. It devotes several pages to Gow, though not much space to his music. The tone of the articles can be judged from the following extracts:

> We have already said that he (Neil Gow) lived on terms of great familiarity with his superiors, in whose presence he spoke his mind and cracked his jokes unawed by either their rank or wealth – indeed they generally delighted in drawing out his homely, forcible, and humorous observations ... (for example).

> Being one day at Dunkeld House, Lady Charlotte Drummond sat down to the pianoforte, when Neil said to the Duchess, 'That lassie o' yours, me leddie, has a good ear.' A gentleman present said, 'I thought, Neil, you had more manners than to call her grace's daughter a lassie.' To which our musician replied, 'What wud I ca' her? I never heard she was a laddie'; which, while it more astonished the gentleman, highly amused the noble parties themselves.[9]

Neil Gow, who provided Raeburn with the occasion for his most heroic statement on the nature of human dignity, is reduced to the status of a clown. In just the same way the inhabitants of Wilkie's pictures, having been granted the privilege of moving in the noble company of high art, had to be careful to remember that it was their business to amuse. His picture of a ruined tenant farmer was simply in bad taste. Scottish culture has to be kept in its proper place and above all the pursuit of a unified sensibility has to be discouraged. It could be dangerous; and so we are left with two halves of a dismembered culture; the tradition of folksy entertainment on the one hand and the emasculated art of the Royal Scottish Academy on the other.

NOTES

1 Private collection reproduced pl. 56 in J. D. Macmillan, 'Truly National Designs, Runciman's subject at Penicuik', *Art History* I.l. 1978.

2 Collection Sir James Clerk of Penicuik, reproduced in Robert Rosenblum, 'The Origin of Painting', *Art Bulletin,* Dec. 1957.

3 Hugh Blair, *A Critical Dissertation on the Poems of Ossian son of Fingal,* 1763.

4 Allan Ramsay, *The Gentle Shepherd,* Edinburgh, 1787.

5 Thomson himself only published two of these in *Scottish Airs,* Edinburgh 1818. A number of the etchings to the songs were published by Alexander Campbell in *Songs of the Lowlands of Scotland,* 1798. Allan also painted for Burns *The Cottar's Saturday Night* at Thomson's instigation.

6 *Annals of the Fine Arts* III, 1818, p. 295, quoted by Arthur Marks, 'The Paintings of Wilkie to 1825', Courtauld Institute of Art, PhD 1968.

7 *The Monthly Mirror* quoted by W. T. Whitley, *Art in England 1800-1820,* p. 284.

8 11 Dec. 1817, quoted by Marks, p. 402 note 122.

9 *Chambers Biographical Dictionary of Eminent Scotsmen,* London, 1870.

(i)

Neil Gow, by Raeburn, 1806.

Penny Wedding, by David Allan, 1818.

Children Drawing, by Geikie.

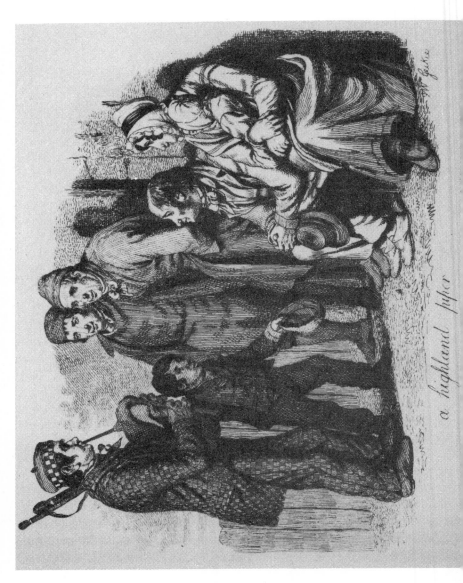

Highland Piper, by Geikie.

An engraving by George Mabon of the town piper and drummer
in Haddington.

Hog Bagpiper.

Pig playing bagpipe; carved in stone; Melrose Abbey, 14th century.

An engraving of Sir David Wilkie's *The Bagpiper*.

The Pipes and Folk Music

HUGH CHEAPE

The pipes and folk music are both part and parcel of Scotland's cultural tradition but, in the opinion of some, they have been considered as occupying distinct camps. The history of the pipes and piping shows that they are as much the music of the folk as any other aspect of our musical heritage, but they have developed features which have tended to set them apart.

If pipe music seems to stand apart, it may be fairer to attribute this not to characteristics of the music but rather to its following and practitioners. Nevertheless, it may initially be useful to review some of the characteristics of piping in order to understand where it stands in relation to folk music. It is not untypical of an art form or tradition, whose history is obscure and patchy, to sustain a host of myths and controversies. This is typically so in the case of a tradition which constitutes an important part of our national make-up. We can here select for examination from the hoary myths such subjects as the origins of piping, piping in the Lowlands, the different types of bagpipe and the origins of piping in the Highlands. Consideration of these must lead to the conclusion that the pipes and folk music are intimately bound up with each other.

The history of the pipes is a long one, but should not be considered in isolation either from the general historical trend of events or from literature, art and other aspects of cultural life. There has been and often still is a tendency for the piping enthusiast and even the scholar to consider their subject in isolation, to know little and care less about the influences that have borne on the development of the instrument and its music.

If there is a hint of exclusiveness among pipers it may have grown out of this long history. While some elements of Scotland's musical life have declined and disappeared, changing fortunes have brought the three-drone great Highland bagpipe to the forefront of the stage in the last two hundred years. This simple fact of survival has not been without its repeated crises, but the success story of the pipes is such that few might have foreseen, four centuries ago when the pipes were so familiar all over Europe, that they would survive in such a vigorous and definite form on Europe's north-west Atlantic seaboard.

Ceòl Mór and competitions are two features of piping which tend to set it apart. Pipe music has two modes, a classical and popular. The Highland bagpipe, as compared with other types of bagpipe, is unique in possessing a form of music peculiar to itself, *ceòl mór*, or *piobaireachd* as it is now generally called. *Piobaireachd* is the Gaelic word meaning simply piping, pipe music or the art of playing on the bagpipe. The word has for some time been adopted to denote *ceòl mór* or great music, the classical music of the pipes. The word anglicised in the form *pibroch* is often attributed to Scott but probably pre-dates him. In Gaelic, of course, this music is still called *ceòl mór*, as distinct from *ceòl beag* or light music. *Ceòl mór* has seemed a remote and rarified, almost an abstract art, understood and played by only a few. The shortage of exponents of *ceòl mór* last century inspired the foundation of the Piobaireachd Society in 1902 which has since done so much to support this esoteric art.[1]

Piping has become fiercely competitive with both band and solo competitions. For most of the piping world, competition is the essence and life-blood of the art and all recognise that standards and presentation are always rising and that the audiences are becoming more and more critical. In fact, the better the piper and the greater his reputation, the more fiercely critical his audience will be. However distasteful this might seem, it can be seen as a measure of the success and vigour of the pipes.

If such keen competition and all its rituals has not appealed to the folk musician, performer and evangelist rather than competitor, he might be forgiven for regarding piping as a whole as far removed from folk music. He might consider that pipe music has been filtered through too many refining non-traditional influences. It is of course a highly published tradition, and the transmission of piping now depends very largely on books and sheet music.

'Folk music' itself is a label which defies definition; it can be all things to all men but it can also be as muddled a concept, however strenuously defended, as the layman's concept of piping. 'Folk' has been used in a pejorative sense, suggesting perhaps the antithesis of intelligentsia. This is invidious and it is unfortunate that the English usage does not have the catholic and collective overtones of *das volk*. Even if there is a clear-cut folk-professional dichotomy, and the professionals have to look down on folk-opera and similar presentations in order to preserve their self-esteem, there will be a popular definition of 'folk music' which is inadmissible for the *forscher von überlieferungen*. Some may say simply that folk music includes any songs or melodies, vaguely recognised as old, perhaps with an ancestry no more venerable than the Edwardian music-hall, sung to guitar accompaniment by exponents known to their audiences through broadcasting, records or television.

One realises that folk music ought to be old to be respectable, that is, set to the old modes, perhaps verse repeating, transmitted verbally from generation to generation, and therefore unaccompanied by script and the composers unknown, presumably or preferably themselves unlettered; and the milieu in which this music is longest preserved has been the rural one. But in fact most of the pieces which we might loosely describe as 'folk music' will contradict some, if not all, of these conditions. It cannot be claimed for example that folk music stops at 1800. The bothy ballads form a significant corpus of traditional music and song whose most creative period falls within the last hundred years.[2] Many well-known songs are of known authorship and literary creations from the pen of Robert Burns, Allan Ramsay, William Thomson, James Hogg, Sir Walter Scott and others. Some may be forgeries, however well intentioned, such as some of the ballads published by historian John Pinkerton in 1783.[3]

Although these new texts might be suitably balanced and tidied, few were creations *ex nihilo,* and most preserved older if often fragmentary ballad texts. Many of these songs were set to pre-existing tunes, the old song and dance airs which survived comparatively vigorously in Scotland.

In the 'sang schules' and musical foundations of the religious houses in Scotland, sophisticated music for several instruments and voices had come into favour in the later medieval period. In the seventeenth century, the air and dance songs of oral tradition more than held their own, and in fact polyphonic works lost ground. The early manuscript collections that have survived, such as the Skene MS and the Guthrie MS of the first half of the seventeenth century, include a surprising admixture of folk music with 'fine music' – surprising perhaps in that these manuscripts must reflect the tastes of those in the upper echelons of society, the landed and monied classes.

The first half of the eighteenth century saw a number of publications which revived old songs and melodies for an enthusiastic and receptive Scottish audience. Notable are James Watson's *Choice Collection* (1706-11), Allan Ramsay's *Evergreen* (1724) and *Tea-Table Miscellany* (1724-37) and William Thomson's *Orpheus Caledonius* (1725 and 1733). Many old folk airs survived therefore to be adopted by David Herd, Robert Burns and others. Of course, it is impossible to estimate how much of the old songs did not survive.

Finally, it goes without saying that much of what might loosely be termed folk music may in reality be highly aristocratic in theme and origin. Kinship with noble families or clan chiefs was a valuable asset if generally a diminishing one. But although families were depressed in the social scale, they inherited the values of their forefathers and perpetuated them in their song tradition, and this is particularly striking in Gaelic poetry and song.

In spite of respective mild prejudices of piping and folk music, changing fashions have done much to bring the parties together in a positive way in the last decade. Many of the folk bands and groups sport a piper of some description. One of the most popular bagpipes in this advance has been the Irish pipes, the *Union or Uillean* pipes. There has been a surge of interest in this instrument in recent years. At the end of the last century there were few players, few instruments and no following. After the protracted battles in Ireland over national independence and the land question, and the violence of the Fenian movement in the 1860s, many turned to cultural ideals which might cater for the intellectual needs of a besieged nation. Yeats and the Anglo-Irish literary revival were replaced by the Gaelic League founded by Douglas Hyde and Eóin MacNéill in 1893. In a climate of new interest for things Irish, several pipers' clubs were founded and the early enthusiasm has helped to preserve the art of the Irish pipes into our own day.

The so-called *organ-pipes* of Ireland, with their keyed chanters and regulators, have moved on beyond the melodic range of the Highland pipes and may have thus earned themselves the disapproval of their more traditional cousins. Players of the Highland pipes, raised on a stricter rubric, find it hard to accept that pipers can introduce elaboration into their music almost at their whim and, depending on individual skill therefore, more or less spontaneous elaboration becomes the hallmark of the individual player. Even today, the exponents of the Irish pipes seem to be a comparatively small band. They and folk musicians may rightly regard themselves as the vanguard of a revival, rescuing traditional music from vulgarisation, attrition and destruction, broadcasting it to as wide an audience as possible and enlisting more instruments and techniques to do so. A recent arrival on the scene in the bands is the Lowland or Border bellows bagpipe, the *caul-wind pipes*. Twenty years ago, this instrument seemed to have been declared extinct. But even then, there were some able performers on the Lowland pipes about whom most of the piping fraternity in Scotland were quite ignorant.

The embryogenic obsession with origins is a popular and topical subject, but it might fairly be said to be a futile exercise to investigate the origins of the bagpipe. It is, however, a subject which attracts much speculation, both of a casual and of a committed kind. Pipes and bagpipes have existed in many and varied forms in most areas of Europe and the East for as long as recorded history. Francis Collinson, in his thorough survey of the bagpipe's development, has suggested from archaeological evidence that the instrument's history stretches back over about 5,000 years.[4] Like many features of European life, they emerge in written history in classical sources, but here the problem is one of interpretation. We have no clear idea of the form of the pipes mentioned by different writers. Many of them were probably the foundation element of all bagpipes, simply a reed pipe with a blade cut in the cane itself. This prototype of course still exists as the reed or bourtree whistle and also the single beating reed, the drone reed of the bagpipe. At least from the classical literature of Greece and Rome it emerges that the pipes were popular, and it is probably significant that the great god Pan of Greek mythology, who made and played on reed pipes, was so influential and symbolic, standing for a universal god.

The origin of the pipes in Scotland may have to remain an eternal puzzle although different theories have been given an airing. One that never fails to raise interest is that the Romans marched into Scotland to the sound of the bagpipes – their own that is, rather than those of their oppressed foes. The Romans, an urbane people, introduced such essentials of Scottish life as Christianity and hens and it seems possible, if not highly credible, that they also introduced the bagpipe. The hide bag, used as a reservoir of air to sustain the flow of air through the reeds, may have been attached to pipes at a comparatively early date. Even the drones, which we tend to think of as a medieval addition, had existed in principle at a much earlier date in the double or triple chanters fixed together, pitched to harmonise or sounding a continuous note. There are one or two representations in carvings on stone in Scotland of this sort of instrument which fall within the first millennium AD.

Any theory suggesting that one of our great national possessions was introduced by an imperialistic Mediterranean power may be unacceptable. To counter this, it might be claimed that the pipes in some form or another, the *shepherd's pipe*, existed here already and like many other features of civilised man's life developed spontaneously and independently wherever man was settled. This idea belongs to theories of the origin of music and is a subject beyond scope here. Music is a fundamental aspect of the intellect but it is tempting to minimise the influence of the shepherd's pipe, the solace of the solitary man in the wilderness. The bagpipe has rarely been a solitary instrument in that sense and there must have been more dynamic forces behind its development. If the Romans did indeed bring the pipes to Scotland, it would inspire first fear, then admiration, then imitation. Another reason for giving prominence to the urbane invaders of Scotland is that the spread of the bagpipes in Europe is not a 'rustic' phenomenon but rather an urban one.

Although it is nowhere specifically stated, the real spread of the bagpipe and its development into the universal musical instrument of medieval Europe must belong to the period known to historians as the 'Twelfth-Century Renaissance'. Representations of pipes and pipers appear with the proliferation of illuminated manuscripts and of church building and adornment after the twelfth century. The pipes, both droneless bagpipe, the *chorus,* and later the pipe with drones, appear in English sources from the thirteenth century and slightly later in Scotland. Our earliest evidence for the instrument in a readily recognisable form is in the carving on medieval church buildings. Carvings at Melrose Abbey and Roslin Chapel show the bagpipes with a single drone. Strong visual images were an essential element of medieval art and sculpture; these instruments have been put in the hands of such diverse beings as angels and pigs; we cannot therefore read moral strictures into these representations. Kirk censure, though generally overplayed by the historian, belonged to a later era.

The social history of the pipes in the Middle Ages was closely linked to the general cultural changes of the day, a link that further research might rewardingly establish. The growth of towns was one of the most significant movements of the period before the fourteenth century, and this occurred most dramatically in northern France and Flanders, very much in the centre of western Christendom. This was also a vigorous period in church life following the foundation and spread of the new monastic orders and it may have been in this period that Scotland came to know the old church modes and develop its own balladry and songs in the modal system.

In Scotland, the founders par excellence of the towns and burghs are the twelfth and thirteenth centuries' kings, David I and William the Lion. These settlements were the points where southern influence and the English tongue made their most significant advances in the old Gaelic kingdom. From the point of view of the founders of the burghs, the crown primarily, but also the church and later nobles, some of the most popular of the settlers were Flemings, famous in Europe as merchants and traders. The prime attraction of burghs was that they were free of many of the burdens and commitments of feudal society; they became gradually self-governing and later Scottish kings safeguarded their economic position and privileges by statute.[5]

Scotland must have shared in the musical heritage of Europe through the burghs and also through the court. One or two early references show that the kings of the Scots enjoyed their music in the thirteenth century. We know, for example, that Alexander III had a harper who was rewarded with a holding of land.[6] The tradition of rewarding the families of poets and musicians with rent-free holdings survived longest in the Highlands and Islands and is well attested in the later period. Late seventeenth-century rentals of MacLean lands in Mull for example include the harper and two hereditary piping families holding land in return for their services.[7] In the fragmentary Scottish records, the first references to pipers indicate crown patronage. In the fourteenth century, it appears that there were court pipers in the payment of David II;[8] James I was himself a piper of some repute and we can believe this of the author of *Peblis to the Play*. In the fifteenth century, we have a clearer picture of crown patronage of music and poetry, especially with the Treasurer's Accounts which are extant from the latter years of James III's reign, giving James IV (1488-1513) an historical advantage over his predecessors. We find the King making frequent payments to pipers, some of them from England.[9] Piping in England may have enjoyed a high reputation in this period because there were salaried pipers at the English court and some had been sent abroad to schools of minstrelsy.[10]

The art of the bagpipe in the Middle Ages was certainly a renaissance one and also an urban one and we soon learn of official pipers in the burghs. The second half of the fifteenth century in Scotland saw the expansion of the burghs in a period of prosperity, the material evidence of which is still with us in the form of fine stone buildings such as collegiate and burgh churches. The *common good*, the property, funds and goods belonging to the burghs, became a source for the enrichment of burgh life, including the provision of minstrels and musicians. Scott in *Old Mortality* describes the duties and emoluments of Niel Blane, town piper and landlord of the Howff, a sinecure which must have been typical of Lowland burghs by the seventeenth century. He possessed:

> the Piper's Croft, as it is still called, a field of about an acre in extent, five merks, and a new livery-coat of the town's colours yearly; some hopes of a dollar upon the day of the election of magistrates, providing the Provost were able and willing to afford such a gratuity; and the privilege of paying, at all the

respectable houses in the neighbourhood, an annual visit at springtime to rejoice their hearts with his music, to comfort his own with their ale and brandy, and to beg from each a modicum of seed-corn.[11]

A house was also part of the reward of the town pipers, and in Jedburgh for example, the Piper's House can still be seen, with a stone statuette of a piper set on the gable. This was the dwelling of the Hasties, the piping family who had held office heritably by tradition from the fifteenth century into the nineteenth.

During the eighteenth and early nineteenth centuries, the setts of the burghs and their self-perpetuating oligarchies came increasingly under criticism. It is no surprise to find the demise of the burgh minstrels roughly coinciding with the Burgh Reform Act of 1833 and the consequent changes in burgh organisation of that period. The governing bodies had to be answerable to their more numerous electors, and in a utilitarian age they were forced to abandon their patronage of simple entertainment for the more mundane responsibilities of policing, cleansing, lighting and transport.

One of the most renowned of Scottish pipers is Habbie Simpson, the early seventeenth-century Town Piper of Kilbarchan in Renfrewshire, whose life and reputation are celebrated in an elegy by the laird-poet Robert Semple of Beltrees. This poem makes mention of the piper's repertoire; besides our knowledge of the pipers themselves, we thirst to know of course what they played in the street and on the burgh muir. Robert Semple mentions *Trixie* and *The Maiden Trace* which seem to be dance airs; he mentions *The Day it Daws* and *Hunt's Up*, both mentioned by other poets such as William Dunbar.[12]

Many tunes are alluded to in the sixteenth-century Bannatyne Manuscript, notably in the long list of song titles in *Colkelbie's Sow*, but we only have half the story because no melodies are given.[13] Many of the melodies are still with us under the guise of a different key or time signature or usually a different name. The classic example of a tune that has undergone these changes and is representative of many more is *Hey Tuttie Tattie*; this was a popular song tune, played by burgh pipers and traditionally the marching song of the Scots at Bannockburn.[14] This melody in common with many others was adopted by Burns and survives today in the song *Scots Wha Hae*, and also in the popular pipe reel *The Wind That Shakes the Barley*. Other tunes of the burgh pipers have a less complicated history. *Dumbarton's Drums* is a tune that has survived probably in its original state, because it was adopted as the March Past of the Royal Scots. These seem to be the only isolated examples of which we have any real knowledge; others such as *Go to Berwick, Jonnie*, and *Dalkeith has got a rare thing*, which are mentioned in contemporary sources, seem to be unknown today, at least under these names.[15] The changes and fashions of the last two hundred years may distract us into the illusion of strict divisions between pipe music and folk music. As we can see from the usage of those old melodies which are reasonably documented, this is artificial. The process of discovery, rewriting, resetting and renaming which went on in the eighteenth and nineteenth centuries has masked the fact that a great pool of music, of song and dance airs, existed as the common stock of both the vocal and the instrumental traditions.

It may be difficult to visualise the pipes in any form other than that which is familiar to us today. But the Highland bagpipe with its strongly established characteristics is a relatively recent arrival in the history of the instrument. The Highland pipes were being made in their present form from the late eighteenth century. In its period of vigorous development in the later Middle Ages, the bagpipe took many forms in Scotland and in Europe as a whole. The wide variety of forms and types common between the fourteenth and seventeenth centuries suggests that this was the busy period of bagpipe history and in Scotland itself, a surprisingly wide variety survived until recent times; for example, the so-called Lowland pipes, the Scottish small pipes, the Scottish 'union' pipe, examples of which are preserved in museum collections.[16]

Another survival, at least until the end of the eighteenth century, was the curiosity known to us as the Stock-and-Horn of which a fine example is preserved in the National Museum of Antiquities of Scotland.[17] This is a hornpipe, one of the more primitive reedpipes, distinguished by the feature of a bell of horn at its mouth. Burns was keen to find an example and wrote to his friend George Thomson, the music editor, in November 1794:

'. . . I have, *at last*, gotten one, but it is a very rude instrument.

– It is composed of three parts; the stock, which is the hinder thigh-bone of a sheep, such as you see in a mutton ham; the horn, which is a common Highland cow's horn, cut off at the smaller end, untill the aperture be large enough to admit the 'stock' to be pushed up through the horn, untill it be held by the thicker or hip-end of the thigh-bone; and lastly, an oaten reed exactly cut and notched like that which you see every shepherd boy have when the corn-stems are green and fullgrown ... This of mine was made by a man from the braes of Athole, and is exactly what the shepherds wont to use in that country ...'[18]

Towards the end of this busy period of European bagpipe history, there are some very striking illustrations of the instrument in use. The engravings and paintings of Dürer and Brueghel provide a vivid impression of the playing of the bagpipe in northern Europe in the sixteenth century. The pipes in the paintings of Pieter Brueghel the Elder, for instance, are two-drone pipes and there is a noteworthy consistency in the way in which they are depicted. The technical detail and similarity of the instruments suggests that a competent wood-turning trade existed in sixteenth-century Flanders, making bagpipes in the fashionable and conventional form of the day. Brueghel, it must be remembered, was depicting the excesses of an indulgent peasantry and for moral example, an element of scorn and opprobrium may have attached itself to the bagpipe. It was in fact beginning to lose ground in Europe as new instruments of high, medium and low ranges were being developed. During the fifteenth and later centuries, and especially in the so-called Baroque era, new classes of instruments were created for flutes, recorders and viols, to include the ranges through soprano, alto, tenor, bass and doublebass. With the decline of the natural scale and the rise to prominence of Bach's 48 Preludes and Fugues, some instruments simply went out of fashion. Other instruments were adapted by the addition of keys and valves. Even the bagpipe, in the form of the French *Musette*, made some concessions to these changes and enjoyed considerable popularity in the reigns of Louis XIV and Louis XV, when the enthusiasm for pastoral operas was at its height in France.

It is important not to set popular or folk music and art or classical music at opposite poles. Many composers have drawn on the idioms and the melodies of folk song and dance such as most notably the

147

F

English Elizabethan keyboard composers, Haydn, Grieg, Dvořák and Vaughan Williams; even the great Bach did not ignore the pipes. His French Suite No. 5 in G, a slow dance movement in 6/4 time, was written for bagpipe accompaniment. But the success or failure of an instrument over time need not necessarily be decided by whether it increases its range by the addition of keys or not, and the most successful of the bagpipes has consistently and obstinately turned its face against such adapatations. What injects an instrument or a musical tradition with the energy to survive and to flourish is patronage – particularly monied patronage – and this fact has been demonstrated time and again, whether it is in Central Europe, Lowland Scotland or the Outer Hebrides.

Research is only just beginning to lay bare some of the circumstances of the society in which the bagpipe took root to flourish so vigorously and with which it is identified so strongly. Highland communities presumably had a well-developed musical tradition both instrumental and in song when the bagpipe was adopted. Some of the strength of such a tradition may be accounted for by the Lordship of the Isles. The descendants of Somerled, and especially the four Lords, John, Donald, Alexander and John, whose suzerainty covered 150 years from the mid-fourteenth century, were responsible for patronage of the arts of which we still have material evidence. Apart from their administrative officials, council and judges, the Lordship had hereditary poets, the MacMhuirichs, *seanchaidhs* and harpers. The tradition of the MacArthurs, pipers to the MacDonalds of Sleat, claimed that they had been pipers to the Lords of the Isles and that their home had been in Islay which was at the heart of the Lordship.

The professional and learned orders, it must be remembered, flourished both in Scotland and in Ireland and the very fragmentary evidence from both countries suggests that pipers were customarily included in the retinues of king, noble and chieftain. The decline of the learned orders was swifter in Ireland than in Scotland, and even after the elimination of the Lordship of the Isles in the sixteenth century, some of the aristocratic Gaelic households maintained their patronage for poets and musicians into the eighteenth century. The MacLeods of Dunvegan, of course, spring to mind with their famous harper, Roderick Morison, *An Clarsair Dall*, and their more famous dynasty of pipers, the MacCrimmons, who had their piping school at Boreraig in Duirinish.[19] The shift of power to the House of Argyll in the sixteenth century and their destruction of the vestigial power of the Lordship tend to make the Campbells the devil of the piece, but they also maintained patronage for learning and music in their household. In the early sixteenth century Book of the Dean of Lismore, *Mac Cailein's* critical ability is recognised, and one of the most notable of the *Aos-dàna* or poet families, the MacEwans, was maintained by the Argyll household.[20] The sixteenth and seventeenth centuries in the Highlands and Islands form the period in which piping developed most strikingly. The events and personalities might be usefully documented from the point of view of musical history to illustrate the political, social and economic matrix in which *ceòl mór* was composed.

Many theorists have discussed the origins of *ceòl mór* and of the piping dynasties, especially the MacCrimmons. We begin to learn of them in the later sixteenth century and the last of the family in a direct line died in the first half of the nineteenth century. A rare glimpse of the family at the end of their era is given us by Alexander Campbell of *Albyn's Anthology* fame. He has left a manuscript account of a visit to Donald Ruadh MacCrimmon at Glenelg in 1814 when the master and his pupil, Alexander Bruce, performed for their visitor.[21] Curiosity about the MacCrimmons has spawned a series of accounts of their origins. An exotic tradition of their migration from Cremona in Italy to Skye can hardly have much foundation in fact. But its proponents have even ignored the possible factual truth behind such an account; that a MacCrimmon ancestor might have joined in with crusaders from Scotland on their journey to and from the Mediterranean and Holy Land. Their own traditions include Islay, like the MacArthurs, and are credible as being within the Lordship of the Isles, and also Ireland which is a distinct possibility. On the other hand, they may have originated in Skye itself or in Harris, being one of the lesser families which came under the sway of the MacLeods as the predominant kin of that area, and which came to perform the service of piping heritably for them.[22]

The origins of *piobaireachd* or *ceòl mór* are similarly obscure. One or two of the tunes, by their names, might be dated to the fifteenth century, such as *Black Donald's March,* and one even to the fourteenth

149

century, *The Battle of the North Inch of Perth* of 1396; but these may be later compositions in the form in which we have them now, with commemorative titles given to them at a later date. Certainly the conventions of *piobaireachd* place it firmly in the Gaelic learned tradition of Scotland and Ireland. We have record of members of the MacCrimmon family travelling to Ireland as part of their training which was considered essential in these arts, as with poetry and the practice of the formal literary language. In 1703, Martin Martin described the high-caste *filidh* whose province was the *dàn* or syllabic verse as composing in the dark with a plaid about their heads and a stone on their bellies, and similar accounts survive of the bardic schools in Ireland.[23] The late Angus MacPherson told how the MacCrimmon pipers subjected themselves to similar rigours while composing their tunes.[24]

The instrumentalists in the professional hierarchy, primarily the harpers, composed in stressed metre as opposed to syllabic verse in which the musical rhythms and stress can change. The form of song metre used by the instrumentalists was *òran* or *àmhran*, that is stressed metre, with a stanza of fixed form and symmetrical in shape, usually with four phrases and a fixed number of regular stresses in each phrase. The origins of this form of metre and composition are not specifically Gaelic; it is an international tradition belonging to medieval Europe. It was not acceptable in the period of classical Gaelic and in composition of panegyric verse by the high-class poets before the seventeenth century. With the decline of the bardic orders, *òran* came to be used for eulogy and elegy and it is at exactly this same period that *ceòl mór* emerges, well developed, in tunes formally composed as in the panegyric verse tradition and of known authorship.

The popularity of the pipes in this period also must owe something to the social changes that were taking place. After a period of internal tensions and struggles, known to tradition as *Linn nan Creach*, the Age of Forays, the Highlands began to be drawn into the ramifications of British politics, especially in the period from the 1640s to the 1740s. Though there was never united Gaelic or Highland support for the successive political causes, however emotive, in which the Highlanders were involved, nevertheless, the clans began to be recognised as a significant strategic force. They had to find more and more men to put into the field and whereas formerly the harp had been the instrument for inciting the men to battle, later and larger armies such as appeared in the Montrose wars required a more strident instrument. Even the composers of *ceòl mór* were aware of cultural clashes and political causes and we have such titles as *Beloved Scotland, Lament for the Union* and *Lament for Viscount Dundee*.

In describing the characteristics of a musical tradition, there is a tendency to impart a strictness to the poetic or instrumental modes such as *dàn* or *ceòl mór*. In practice the rules and cautels were disregarded. But one of the earliest men to commit information to paper about piping is expansive about rules of composition in *ceòl mór*. Joseph MacDonald was the son of the Rev. Murdoch MacDonald, Durness, the patron of Rob Donn, and the younger brother of the Rev. Patrick MacDonald, the compiler of *A Collection of Highland Vocal Airs* (1784). Joseph MacDonald himself was the author of *A Compleat Theory of the Scots Highland Bagpipe*, written on a voyage to India about 1761 on his way to take up a post with the East India Company.[25] Tragically, he died of fever shortly after his arrival there, taking a great deal of knowledge on the subject with him. His work, which survived in manuscript to be published posthumously, was the first collection of *piobaireachd* written in staff notation. He describes how sixteenth and seventeenth-century pipers regulated the metrical structure of their tunes. Time was measured by the four fingers of the left hand, the conventional unit of measurement known as a *finger*. A tune could be considered regular when the *ùrlar* or ground, what he called the *adagio*, being the tempo indication for slow time, consisted of four quarters, each of which contained two, four or eight fingers.[26] The ground might normally contain sixteen fingers and such a system accord well with the conventions of *òran*.

Joseph MacDonald speaks of pipe music as a relic of the past and like many a collector of the oral tradition, he tended to overstate the crisis facing the material in which he was himself interested, in order to rouse others from their apathy. He was, of course, writing within the period of the Disarming Act which was not repealed until 1782.[27] He writes that the Highland pipes would only be used for pieces of music specially written for them such as *piobaireachd* and jigs; he divides pipe tunes into marches, including gatherings, and 'rural pieces', by which we might understand *ceòl meadhonach or* airs.

Speaking of the eighteenth century therefore, Joseph MacDonald seems to suggest that the pipers' pabulum was *ceòl mór* and that *ceòl beag* was not really considered to be worthy of performance on the Highland bagpipe. This may be difficult to appreciate from our standpoint today but striking corroboration of this tradition was provided by the justly famous late Pipe Major John MacDonald, Inverness, when he recalled his early tuition from Calum Piobair, one of the great exponents of the MacCrimmon tradition:

'I received most of my tuition in *piobaireachd* from Calum MacPherson, at Catlodge, Badenoch. Calum was easily the best player of *piobaireachd* I have ever known. He hardly ever played March, Strathspey and Reel, only *Piobaireachd* and Jigs. Each morning, Calum used to play Jigs on the chanter while breakfast was being got ready ... After breakfast, he would take his barrow to the peat moss, cut a turf, and build up a fire with wet peat for the day. He would then sit down beside me, take away all books and pipe-music, then sing in his own *Canntaireachd* the ground and different variations of the particular *Piobaireachd* he wished me to learn.'[28]

Canntaireachd here referred to by Pipe Major John MacDonald introduces another complex subject and another important aspect of the piping tradition. It is the word used for the set of vocables by which *ceòl mór* can be sung or recited. In general terms, vowels are used for the melody notes and consonants to characterise the grace notes and doublings, which of course are more complex in *ceòl mór*. It is difficult to appreciate, with the passage of time and the decline in its use, the extent to which *canntaireachd* was a set system. Most pipers, however, are accustomed to using a loose form of *canntaireachd* to describe the notes of their music; this has been parodied by non-pipers and satirists as *heedrum-hodrum*, as representing, not inappropriately, the pipers' art.

It is difficult to assess the extent to which the proscriptive legislation of the eighteenth century militated against the piping tradition. The Highland pipes are not specifically included among the weapons of war. The more insidious threat to piping came from the failure of the patronage of the Gaelic aristocracy and the breakdown of the old social order in the eighteenth century. This is why the piping families and their schools declined. At the end of the century, the old patronage was superseded by the new patronage of Highland Societies in London and Edinburgh and by the growing demands of the army for martial music.

The tradition of piping in the army goes back in some cases to the raising of the earliest regiments. The Scots Guards for example had pipers in the seventeenth century. Our early references to professional bagpipe makers coincides with the raising of Highland regiments during the Seven Years War and American War of Independence, and also of numerous Highland fencible regiments during the second half of the eighteenth century.[29] A custom of employing one or more pipers in each company, usually maintained by the largesse of company commanders, was unofficial until the principle of employing pipers in the British Army was recognised in 1856.

In conclusion, though the strutting uniformed piper seems to be the very antithesis of a folk musician, it should be recognised that the British Army and the nineteenth century imperial wars did much to preserve and perpetuate piping; the legacy is with us still in the form of the huge repertoire of *ceòl beag*, of marches, strathspeys, reels, jigs and hornpipes, and the vast numbers of sets of pipes that were made to supply the demand. As we have seen, the development of the pipes has been a long and complicated process which is by no means static now. They marched in step with European renaissance and medieval society but then faltered in some areas, never to recover, as new systems of music developed. In Scotland, they thrived on the sixteenth and seventeenth-century interest in folk song and melody, both of the revival and of the new compositions in the folk style. The pipes were of course one of the vehicles by which folk melodies were transmitted and this is still patently true today. If the pipes seem to stand apart from folk music, it is in the *ceòl mór* tradition which itself has such a long and stable history linking us with the cultural milieu of Gaelic medieval society. Piping is standing in the wings while the compatibility of traditional music and newer styles is investigated. If folk music experiments with new techniques and new styles, it will increase the responsibility of the pipes to see that the best of our musical traditions, the best of folk music, is preserved and transmitted to future generations.

NOTES

1 Apart from organising teaching and the major competitions, they have published 12 volumes of *piobaireachd*.
2 See, for example, Gavin Greig, *Folk-song in Buchan and Folk-Song of the North-East*, Hatboro (Pennsylvania, 1963); and John Ord, *The Bothy Songs and Ballads of Aberdeen, Banff and Moray, Angus and the Mearns* (Paisley, 1930).
3 John Pinkerton (ed.), *Scottish Tragic Ballads* (London, 1781-83).
4 Francis Collinson, *The Bagpipe* (London, 1975), pp. 9-10.
5 For a summary of early burgh development, see A. A. M. Duncan, *Scotland: The Making of the Kingdom*, The Edinburgh History of Scotland, Vol. I (Edinburgh, 1975), chapter 18. See also W. Mackay Mackenzie, *The Scottish Burghs* (Edinburgh, 1949).
6 Joseph Bain (ed.), *Calendar of Documents Relating to Scotland, Vol. 2, 1272-1307* (Edinburgh, 1884), p. 224.
7 J. R. N. MacPhail (ed.), *Highland Papers Vol. 1*, Scottish History Society (Edinburgh, 1914), pp. 280, 312, 314.
8 Collinson, *op cit*, pp. 87-8.
9 Thomas Dickson (ed.), *Accounts of the Lord High Treasurer of Scotland, Vol. 1, 1473-1498* (Edinburgh, 1877), cclix-cclx, pp. 115, 180.
10 Collinson, *op cit, p. 90*.
11 Walter Scott, *Old Mortality*, Border Edition 1893, p. 37.
12 Tom Scott (ed.), *The Penguin Book of Scottish Verse* (Harmondsworth, 1970), pp. 233-36.
13 W. Tod Ritchie (ed.), *The Bannatyne Manuscript Vol. 4*, Scottish Text Society (Edinburgh, 1930), pp. 279-308.
14 Francis Collinson. *The Traditional and National Music of Scotland* (London, 1966), p. 2.
15 John Kay, *Original Portraits*, Vol. 2 (Edinburgh, 1838), p. 138.
16 Good examples are preserved in the National Museum of Antiquities of Scotland, the Royal Scottish Museum, the Keep and Bagpipe Museums, Newcastle-upon-Tyne, Inverness Museum and Art Gallery and the Highland Folk Museum, Kingussie.
17 LT 12, given by James Drummond, 1877.
18 J. De L. Ferguson (ed.), *The Letters of Robert Burns, Vol 2, 1790-6* (Oxford, 1931), p. 278.
19 William Matheson, *The Blind Harper. The Songs of Roderick Monson and his Music*, Scottish Gaelic Texts Society, Vol. 12 (Edinburgh, 1970); I. F. Grant, *The MacLeods* (London, 1959).
20 W. J. Watson (ed.), *Scottish Verse from the Book of the Dean of Lismore*, Scottish Gaelic Texts Society, Vol. I (Edinburgh, 1937), p. 3; Angus

Matheson, Bishop Carsewell, *Transactions of the Gaelic Society of Inverness,* Vol. 42 (1953-59), pp. 182, 205.

21 Quoted verbatim in Collinson, *The Bagpipe, op cit,* pp. 195-96.

22 Grant, op cit, p. 27.

23 Martin Martin, A *Description of the Western Islands of Scotland,* ed. D. J. MacLeod (Stirling, 1934), pp. 176-77.

24 Angus MacPherson, A *Highlander Looks Back* (Oban, n.d.), pp. 63-4.

25 Edinburgh University Library, Laing MSS, La. III, p. 804.

26 Discussed by R. L. C. Lorimer, Studies in Pibroch, *Scottish Studies,* Vol. 6 (1962), pp. 1-30.

27 A. H. Millar, Notes on the Proclamation for Disarming of the Highlands in 1746, *Proceedings of the Society of Antiquaries of Scotland,* Vol. 30 (1895-96), pp. 210-24.

28 MacPherson, *op cit,* p. 66.

29 Hugh Cheape, 'The Making of Bagpipes in Scotland', in D. V. Clarke and A. O'Connor (eds.), *From the Stone Age to the Forty Five. Essays Presented to R. B. K. Stevenson* (Edinburgh).

Folk and Protest

NORMAN BUCHAN

I want here both to ruminate on the Folk Song Revival in its relation to popular protest and to try to link this up with the other contributions to this book.

The seventeenth century, of course, was the great age of the political squib and lampoon, mirroring the continuous polemics of the times, often highly sophisticated, sometimes indeed, in Latin, but frequently also popular, analogous to the street snatches of folk rhymes of our times. Maidment's *Book of Scottish Pasquils* is the great source for many of these. For example, 'Ane prophesie concerning the Prayer Book against the Whigges' starts off:

> Filthie leachers
> False teachers
> Cursing preachers
> Never calme;
> Be hook or crook
> Ye'll never brook
> The Service Book
> In this realme.

Or consider the street chant on the Lord Advocate Stewart, who had incurred the wrath of both Whigs and Jacobites as a 'trimmer' (there is a moral here somewhere):

> Sir James Stewart thou'lt hing
> in a string
> Sir James Stewart, knave

and a rogue thou art
For thou ne're had a true heart
to God or the King
Sir James Stewart thou'lt hing
in a string.

And the eighteenth century, whatever the politics of the question, also saw a great popular flowering in the Jacobite songs.

One of the greatest errors we can make is to think that history, especially the history of the common people, ever stands still. It doesn't happen like that. Yet we sometimes get the notion that in the history of our popular culture all things stopped as a result of the industrial revolution and the explosive expansion of our cities. It is, of course, a nonsense. People's cultural life continued when they were surrounded by brick walls of the city ghettoes and not the green hedges that they had left two or three years before. And they took with them into the cities as part of their mental furniture the same kind of cultural background. It is true that they reshaped it, just as their own events shaped them; but they had initially the same rich tradition of song and folklore that people who continued to live in the countryside had. So there was a continuity, however vitiated, but which could often create a kind of mis-relation between their social surroundings and events and the mode and content of cultural expression.

I recognise there is a kind of mystery here, similar to that which Kenneth Logue talks about elsewhere in this book: a century of popular protest but (excluding the special case of Jacobitism) apparently few specific songs surviving in relation to it. Of course, if you are going down a street looking for a likely dyer's or barber's pole to hang Porteous from, you're probably not writing a song – it's more important to hang Porteous. Porteous thereafter passes into a kind of history which may or may not be kept orally alive, but in any case may not necessarily be the kind of stuff which of itself generated songs – though I suspect it would have done. The truth is that there is no balancing point between the number of spectacular events in history and the number of songs that have either been created about these particular events – or have survived.

There are all sorts of reasons why particular songs – which may

157

have been in large circulation at one time – have disappeared. Take Porteous again. If later popular attitudes to that event were to change, then people might not continue to sing about it. And if songs are no longer in common oral use people just don't remember to keep them. If you don't believe me – think of fag photos. At one time every kid in Britain had hundreds, many had thousands, of these. Now they're collector's items – precisely because they were so common that no one apparently needed to bother to preserve them. That can happen to songs too. And the point about the Industrial Revolution is hot that people did not take their background of history along with them in their new way of life, but that the circumstances which continued the re-creation of that background had altered.

The second point I want to make in relation to Kenneth Logue's essay is perhaps best exemplified if we look at Burns's 'Scots Wha Hae'. This was not written about Bruce and Bannockburn at all; it was written precisely and specifically about much more dangerous events, 'struggles', in Burns' words, 'not quite so ancient'. He was referring of course to the trials of the Friends of the People, of Thomas Muir, Palmer, Gerraed, Skirving and Margarot. So the second conclusion we draw is this: that very often songs have to employ, in Lenin's words, 'Aesopian' language – the language of fable – to make their point in safety. I remember Hamish Henderson talking about a Gaelic song on a girl called Morag who was loved from one end of Argyllshire to the other; and, of course, it wasn't Morag – it was the Stuarts that the song was about. Sometimes, in other words, the retention of a protest song brings its own risks. They may disappear, or disappear into fable. Who, at enthusiastic Caledonian Society suppers, knows they are hymning enemies of the state, transported for treason?

There were certain periods in more recent times (the Easter Rising in 1916, for example) when singing certain songs – and you could only remember them by singing – could, of course, get you in jail.

Finally, there was coming through well into the nineteenth century the long urban tradition of broadsheets and chapbooks. This too had a tradition of protest.

So in the cities, the people still had singing. But they also had a problem. Their own culture was largely bucolic. It is easier to copy than to create afresh – indeed, copying is essential to the whole folk process. The tendency, in other words, was not to say 'let us find a new means of expression', but a reinforcing of the nostalgic in content as it copied the known and inherited forms of largely rural song. Almost on a *prima facie* basis we could say that this would happen. But we have other evidence too. Whether in prose – from Walter Scott right up to the appalling *Window in Thrums* – or in poetry – Tannahill, or the *Whistlebinkie* school coming from, of all places, Glasgow – our nineteenth-century middle and high-brow literature virtually ignored our cities and our industries. The influence of Scott and Burns was so great – and the traumatic effect of the Industrial Revolution had so weakened the strong popular tradition on which these two had fed – that the nostalgic, the bucolic and the imitative ruled.

Now, if that is true in poetry, clearly it was even more difficult for a folk art, of which a major ingredient is initiation, tradition and continuity, to burst through into becoming a significant reflecter of an urban folk reality. Difficult, but not impossible. And there were other factors.

Urban folk had another cultural need, the need to develop their own kind of social organisation – and that *is* a cultural as much as a political matter. And while there was a massive break from the eighteenth to the nineteenth century, nonetheless there was a link. And that was in the continuation, during the first three decades, of perhaps the most literate, certainly the most radical and articulate, section of the people – the weavers. They engineered the carry-over from the independent yeoman radical tradition of the countryside and villages – of which Burns' career was a kind of swan song – into the new radical social organisations that were necessary and were therefore being developed. We see this in weaver poets like Alexander Wilson and the strong politically radical tradition around him among the weavers of Renfrewshire.

I have so far tried to list four elements which combine to give working-class expression in the nineteenth century its particular form:
1. The continuity of folk song (albeit rural).
2. A continuing link through the weavers (and, to a lesser extent, the socially isolated coal miners) with a longer 'protest' tradition.
3. The creation of new working-class social organisations.
4. An indigenous urban folk tradition – based on chapbooks,

broadsheets and broadside ballads.

This last element should not be underestimated. If not properly 'folk' they were essentially embodiments of popular attitudes. They disseminated and kept alive folk ballads. I am lucky enough to possess the collection of broadsheet ballads that David Laing put together for his own use in early nineteenth-century Edinburgh. They run to more than 900 different entries. From the Parker ballads in seventeenth-century London onwards they circulated literally in hundreds of thousands. [Incidentally, time after time, they are testimony to the strength and endurance of the oral folk tradition. The chorus of a Parker version of 'The Old Maid in the Garret' is very different from most recently recorded Scottish versions but is identical, to a minute degree, with versions found this century in the Appalachian Mountains.]

We know that an early nineteenth-century (approximately 1820) broadsheet ballad, 'Jamie Raeburn', sold a hundred thousand copies! An almost unbelievable circulation even for such a fine song. So there is now this further connection between the written page (not literary page; but recording on paper) and the street and itinerant singers.

Incidentally the normal sign of a bad song is that it calls Scotland 'Caledonia'. 'Jamie Raeburn' is the exception that proves the rule!

My name is Jamie Raeburn, frae Glasgow toon I came;
My place and habitation I'm forced tae leave wi' shame;
From my place and habitation I now maun gang awa',
Far frae the bonnie hills and dales o' Caledonia.

It was early one morning, just by the break of day,
We were 'wakened by the turnkey, who unto us did say –
'Arise, ye hapless convicts, arise ye ane and a',
This is the day ye are to stray from Caledonia.'

We all arose, put on our clothes, our hearts were full of grief,
Our friends who a' stood round the coach, could grant us no relief;
Our parents, wives, and sweethearts, their hearts were broke in twa,
To see us leave the hills and dales o' Caledonia.

Farewell, my aged mother, I'm vexed for what I've done,
I hope none will cast up to you the face that I have run;

I hope God will protect you when I am far awa,
Far from the bonnie hills and dales of Caledonia.

Farewell, my honest father, you are the best of men,
And likewise my own sweetheart, it's Catherine is her name,
Nae mair we'll walk by Clyde's clear stream or by the Broomielaw,
For I must leave the hills and dales of Caledonia.

And this illustrates something else. The real Jamie Raeburn was widely believed to be innocent. Now, songs of protest don't usually stop and say: 'What is the nature of the contemporary political struggle? How shall we advance that struggle?' Most often protest is mobilised to the individual and the individual case. What moved people into action on Polaris was as much an individual disgust and revulsion as it was a political analysis. So with Jamie Raeburn; it is taken at the time as a song, not just about Jamie Raeburn, but against injustice. But the more specifically political injustices – the executions of Baird and Hardie or of Pearly Wilson – did not circulate on broadsheets in this way, except possibly for the usual hack dying confessions. If they existed they circulated orally and could not compete with the broadsheet – and they were too dangerous to print.

So the kind of protest that the new urban working class were finding around them was not just political in the abstract sense. It was, as we have seen, personal and individual. But how better to personalise politics than through anti-Royalist forms? (And the real nerve of many of these suggests they were in fact less dangerous than support for the organised political radicals like Thomas Muir.)

Some of these productions would certainly not get published in the popular equivalents of our own day – not even on page 3! This kind of thing:

Come all you bold Britons, and list for awhile,
And I will sing you a song that will make you smile,
A young Prince of Wales is come to town,
The pride of all the nation, and heir to the crown,
On the ninth of November, 'tis true 'pon my life,
All Buckingham Palace was bustle and strife,
The nurses stared at each other with joy,
Bawling, our queen she has got a most beautiful boy.

161

Then Albert he stepped in with a face full of glee,
And danced and he dandled his son on his knee,
When all in an instant his countenance fell,
And he cried, 'Don't I see a most terrible smell!'
'Mine Cot,' says Al., 'oh Lord what a mess!
He has completely spoilt my new morning dress,
Be quick go fetch me some napkins or towels,
For my son, the young Prince, is relaxed in his bowels.'

That scurrilous piece of irreverancy is published on the same side of a penny broadsheet as another one with the same title – 'A New Song on the Birth of the Prince of Wales '. But the point of the companion piece is that it specifically attacks the cost of the business:

Now to get these little niceties the taxes must be rose
For the little Prince of Wales wants so many suits of clothes,
So they must tax the frying pan, the windows and the doors,
The bedsteads and the tables, kitchen-pokers and the floors.

Protest is not, of course, always and inevitably on the side of the 'noble'. There is always a great chauvinism lying dormant and not always very dormant – in the British working class. It combined nicely with the fact that Albert was a German:

I am a German just arrived
   With you for to be mingling
My passage it was paid
   From Germany to England;
To wed your blooming Queen;
   For better or worse I take her
My father is a duke
   And I'm a sausage maker.

You Englishmen are rich
   Or I am much mistaken
You have good bread and beer
   With mutton, beef and bacon
While father's folks at home
   Live all the week on cabbage
And on a Sunday they will dine
   On sour crout and cabbage.

162

So there was a conscious protest thread of anti-royalty, and therefore anti-establishment in general. At the same time there was the continuing folk tradition I have described (via weavers and miners) which provided a form for some kind of industrial folk material to develop. One of the earliest and one of the best songs is 'John O' Grinfelt':

(First verse and last)

I'm a poor cotton weaver as many one knows,
I've nowt to eat i'the house an I've worn out my cloas,
You'd hardly give sixpence for all I have on,
My clugs they are brossen and stockings I've none,
You'd think it wur hard to be sent into th' world,
    To clem and do th' best ot you con.

Our Margit declared if hoo'd cloas to put on,
Hoo'd go up to Lundun an see the big mon
An if things didn't alter when hoo had been,
Hoo swears hoo'd feight blood up toth e'en,
Hoo's nought again th' Queen but likes a fair thing,
    An hoo says hoo can tell when hoo's hurt.

I think that's a marvellous last line. They did not know who hurt and how they were hurt, so that they were continuing and sharpening a line of protest which had yet to be tapped by the developing working class political organisations.

I suppose we can conveniently mark the beginnings of conscious working-class political development in any significant way as coming from the Chartists. Earlier there were, of course, demonstrations, campaigning, strikes – the weavers in Glasgow, for example. But we can see a clear line now developing through the Chartists, the First International, and so on to the beginnings of a Labour movement associated with the ideology of socialism. The earlier movement – and the mining or weaving songs of protest were either limited to precise and sectional conditions or associated with the Liberté, Egalité, Fraternité of the French Revolution – was the great bourgeois, liberal democratic tradition, rather than a class tradition and socialist ideology. This earlier movement was perhaps best exemplified in poetry and song by Burns, Shelley and Byron.

The new movement had a problem in seeking a popular expression. Its proponents saw the richness of the bourgeois world around them and its values. They saw the degradation of the cities and the hardness of industry. Therefore their aim was to conquer this richness, to assimilate and possess these values rather than to develop their own. Paradoxically therefore, even as there was a growing consciousness and confidence in themselves as a class, it was to the elite cultural expression that they aspired. Instead of using and exploiting a folk tradition therefore, they sought to enhance their own dignity by absorbing and using the cultural forms of the opposing class. Hence their songs of protest in the political movement were, say, Blake's 'Jerusalem' or 'England Arise' by Edward Carpenter. They were marching to new horizons and using hymn-like aspirational songs to do it.

Now the aspirational songs were important, but in their exclusiveness they deserted a major weapon – the humorous polemics of the folk tradition, the sharp scurrility seen in the anti-royalist broadsheet ballads. To cock a snook at authority was as important as to paint the vision glorious.

This weakness meant that they themselves created a kind of break in the developing working-class culture. We didn't find the confidence to use that weapon fully in Britain till after the Second World War.

In America it came earlier, but even the Wobblies still used the noble hymn tunes though injecting them with a parodic sharpness – like the Messianic tune to 'Solidarity Forever':

When the Union's inspiration through the workers'
blood shall run
There can be no power greater anywhere beneath the sun
Yet what force on earth is weaker than the feeble strength of one,
But the Union makes us strong.

Chorus:

Solidarity for ever!
Solidarity for ever!
Solidarity for ever!
For the Union makes us strong.

In our hands is placed a power greater than their hoarded gold,
Greater than the might of armies magnified a thousand fold,
We can break their haughty power, gain our freedom when
                                    we learn
That the Union makes us strong.

Chorus: Solidarity for ever!
                         Etc.

From America therefore began the synthesis between the nobility
of the hymn background and the need to use that to weld a unity
around and through the Union. (Why let all the good tunes go to the
devil?)

Now when incidents happen, people are involved. As strikes take
place it is no longer a matter only for the ideologues, it is on a popular
level, a folk level, and the natural folk expression occurs. Thus in the
great strike of 1890 for the 'Dockers' Tanner' we see precisely this
happening:

At the docks there is a strike that the company don't like
A tanner on the hour they'll have to pay:
Like slaves they'd have us work far more than any Turk
And make us sweat our lives out every day.

Chorus:
Strike, boys, strike for better wages!
Strike, boys, strike for better pay!
Go on fighting at the docks,
Stick it out like fighting cocks
Go on fighting till the bosses they give way!

Every morning there are flocks for employment at the docks,
Hard working men who scarce can get a meal;
With wives and children dear, it would make you shed a tear
If you only knew the hardship that they feel.

Chorus:
If it's slavery that you seek, for about a quid a week,
They'll take you on as soon as you come near,
Sweat your guts out with a will, or they'll try your job to fill,
But that won't wash with working men, that's clear.

Chorus

We'll stand up for our rights and the company we will fight,
Supported by our brothers everywhere,
For we have friends galore – the good old stevedores,
And the seamen and the firemen they are there.

Chorus

Starvation, 'tis they bids to a man with seven kids,
When he brings home only fifteen pence a day,
For what can you get to eat on seven-and-six a week,
When it often takes it all the rent to pay?

Chorus

Here's a health to Mr Burns, he's done us all a turn,
Ben Tillet, Mann and Mr Toomey too:
We won't give in a bit, for we've got 'em in a fit,
And we've put the old dock-company in a stew.

Chorus

Of course people who wrote things like 'England Arise' or 'These
Things Shall Be' couldn't have written a song like that. A lack of grace
was necessary. They had been so involved earlier with their noble
aspirations that they often forgot they were sometimes in a dirty
fight. When they realised this, more of a street style of expression
began to be used and not merely the borrowing of songs from
ideologues. Protest was using an older folk tradition again – as in
'The Dirty Black Miners':

> It's in the even' after dark,
> When the black-leg miner creeps to work,
> Wi' his moleskin pants and dorty shart,
> There goes the black-leg miners.
>
> They take their picks and down they go
> To hew the coal that lies below;
> But there's not a woman in this town's row
> Will look at a black-leg miner.
>
> O, Deleval is a terrible place;
> They rub wet clay in the black-leg's face,

And around the heap they run a foot race
To catch the black-leg miner.

And divvent gan near the Seghill mine,
Across the Way they stretch a line
To catch the throat and break the spine
Of the dirty black-leg miners.

They'll take your tools and duds as well,
And hoy them doon the pit of hell;
Doon ye goe and fare y' well,
Ye dorty black-leg miners.

So join the Union while ye may,
Don't wait til your dyin' day –
'Cause that may not be far away
Ye dorty black-leg miners.

Parody also played its part. The popular songs of the day were a ready quarry for songs of protest as with children's songs or football songs. Here is rather a nice one – from the Wobblies – to the tune of 'After the Ball was Over':

Once a pretty maiden
Climbed on an old man's knee,
Asked for a story:
'Papa, tell me
Why are you lonely?
Why are you sad?
Why do your shop-mates
Call you a scab?'

And the chorus goes:

After the strike is over
After the men have won
After the shops have opened
After the notice is down,
Many the heart is aching
though the hope seems bright
That many a scale will vanish
After the strike!

In America they made this breakthrough quicker than in Britain, surprisingly, I think. And perhaps because they hadn't quite the same European-based ideologues that the British movement had, they went for the noble rather than fighting the class struggle with all the weapons the working class had more readily to hand. And of course the Wobblies were the great masters of humour and parody, with their organiser-bard, Joe Hill, and his songs like 'It's a Long Way Down to the Soupline, It's a Long Way to Go' or 'Pie in the Sky':

> Long-haired preachers come out every night
> Try to tell us what's wrong and what's right;
> But when asked how 'bout something to eat,
> They will answer with voices so sweet:

> *Chorus:* You will eat bye and bye
> In that glorious land above the sky.
> Work and pray, live on hay,
> You'll get pie in the sky when you die.

[You will find all these brought together in a magnificent anthology of Wobbly songs, poems, cartoons, called *Rebel Voices*, edited by Joyce Kornbluh and published by the University of Michigan Press. We have no such book in Scotland or Britain. Yet we have a notable expert in the field of industrial song, A. L. Lloyd, who produced *Come All Ye Bold Miners*. Yet the trade union movement have never yet commissioned someone like Lloyd to compile a comparable songbook of the British trade union movement.]

So this is how the thing was developing, with the two strands, the 'noble' and then the folk idiom, coming through, usually in the form of parody or satire. And only slowly was the latter beginning to be used also for the 'aspirational' song. (Though, at moments of heightened political consciousness, and mass involvement, this emphasis dramatically changed: notably so in the events following the Easter Rising in Dublin.) In Britain as a whole the emphasis still tended to be on the respectable – the Orpheus Choir under the socialist Hugh Robertson being a notable example.

I remember asking the conductor of a Communist choir shortly after the Second World War: 'Why don't you sing British political

songs?' And got the reply: 'There are no good British political songs.'
This was just on the eve of the folk song revival in this country, when
we were still singing things like 'Sovietland so dear to every toiler' or,
on the Red Air Force, 'And every propeller is roaring, Defending the
USSR'.

On the other hand parody lampoons were making some headway
in the thirties and forties – for example in Unity Theatre or in the
student movement – songs like 'Pity the Downtrodden Landlord' or
'The Man Who Waters the Workers' Beer'. The parodies on the whole
were never very good but they did help to break down the uptight,
stiff-necked, Calvinist, respectable incubus laid upon us by the fear
of being thought irresponsible and irreverent. So they did pave the
way for an acceptance of precisely those two qualities when the folk
revival came.

Here are a couple of these products from the 1930s, from a little
booklet called *People's Parodies:*

(Tune: 'Lillibulero')
Oh, Brother Smith have you heard the decree?
Hore-Belisha, bludgeons and blood.
Government wants you to join A.R.P.
  Hore-Belisha, Cooper and Wood.
Brown and Butler, Inskip and Simon,
  Chamberlain waits for the sickening thud
Clear out Parliament, National Government
Labour unite – and to hell with the brood.

Or, in an attack on Nancy Astor and the Cliveden set:

'Where have you been all the day
  Neville boy, Neville boy?
Having fun down Cliveden way,
  Me Neville boy?'

'Yes, I stayed for lunch and tea,
For they think a lot of me,
And me Nancy tickled me fancy,
  Oh me charming Neville boy.'

All a bit forced, slightly too clever, much too 'in' and lacking in gutsiness. Things like this tend to be parodies for the page, though they could work in revue or pantomime, and we did use them in that way.

The real breakthrough in this direction came when we learned from the young American political singers and song writers like Earl Robertson, Lee Hays and, above all, Woody Guthrie, Cisco Houston and Pete Seeger. The last three along with Lee Hays formed the Almanac Singers, the forerunners of The Weavers.

The marvellous thing about Woody was that he could say to people: 'Look, that thing you're doing you can sing about. That dam you're building is worth singing about; that boat you're sailing in is worth singing about; that union you belong to is worth singing about.' Nothing very new about that; it's what the folk tradition exists of. Woody just did it – and showed it still worked. So he was a tremendous catalyst in song, not just in deceptive simplicity but in hoicking back into song a whole colossal range of material. The Lomaxes were collecting – cowboy and frontier songs, especially. And the young Pete Seeger was learning from his father, a distinguished musicologist. Pete says that when he first heard his father playing some of the old country songs he said: 'Where did you discover these?' And his father replied: 'Discover, son? They were never lost!'

The Weavers were smashed for a period by McCarthyism, banned individually and collectively from many concert halls and radio during that 'scoundrel time'. Few now remember that during much of that period one of the rare liberal influences in the college campus was Pete Seeger. Many will remember the explosive effect of the first reunion of The Weavers in New York's Carnegie Hall in 1955, signalling the beginning of the end for McCarthyism. The two records of that concert had an enormously fertilising effect on the Revival here – helping to create a natural alliance between protest and folk song. It also helped to sanctify the use of the guitar. It was the instrument of the young; it was portable; it followed rather than controlled the feel of a song.

Now, there have been frequent arguments about the relationship of protest and folk song throughout the Revival. There were those – usually circulating around the fringe of Cecil Sharp House – who felt that folk music was being exploited by the politically minded. But, of course, the relationship is much deeper than that. It is organic. In a class society, any expression of a submerged group to be considered, or to express itself, has elements of protest. Protest and folk song are mutually stimulating.

And I want to illustrate this through two specific Scottish-based movements and four Scottish writers – Hamish Henderson, Ewan MacColl, Matt McGinn and Morris Blythman. If there was any starting-point for the Scottish Folk Revival it was in the People's Festival Ceilidh of 1951 organised by Hamish Henderson. This was not an event sponsored by the official Festival, but by the Labour Festival Committee, a body composed of the organisations of protest – Labour Party, Communist Party, trade unions, Trades Councils. So right from the beginning there was this strong and direct involvement. It is a nonsense to talk about who was exploiting whom. Song and protest went together, as Burns said about whisky and freedom.

I had known Hamish for some years. Every now and again he would mutter about collecting songs, seeing the travelling folk and so on. I had heard songs. People played pianos and sang to them. I knew what song was – but I didn't know what Hamish was on about! True, he wrote a song for the historic John MacLean Rally of 1948 – 'The MacLean March'. And I thought that was fine – a good noble song ...

But it required something more. We had to be confronted with the material and the traditional singers themselves. And that was what Hamish did at that extraordinary event in 1951. Singers like Jimmy MacBeath, Jessie Murray (who gave us that night that most fragile of tunes, 'Skippin' Barfit Through the Heather'), John Strachan, Flora McNeil, young Arthur Argo, grandson of Gavin Greig. And we were like Pete Seeger: 'Where did you discover these? ' and Hamish and the singers were saying back: 'Brother, they were never lost!'.

Now, also participating in that People's Festival was Theatre Workshop, whose resident playwright was Ewan MacColl. And he, blessed with a marvellous voice, was experimenting with song in drama – for example, the ballad opera, *Johnny Noble*. In Ewan, too, we see the impossibility of separating folk song and protest. He used song directly, polemically: on strikes, on peace, to defend the rights of ramblers on the moors of Northern England, on apartheid:

> I support the boycott, and here's the reason why,

For I can smell apartheid in an Outspan lemon pie.

But he also, above all the singers throughout the folk clubs of Britain, was the one who continually emphasised the importance of hanging on to the great tradition and refused to compromise or allow clubs to degenerate into mere sing-song howffs. He also recognised, like Woody, the importance of giving confidence to working people, encouraging a pride and, indeed, boastfulness about their work and about their life, like the early 'Champion at Keepin' 'em Rolling' about the long-distance lorry driver. This got its fullest expression in his radio documentary ballads. These did three things. Firstly, they were sound equivalents of the best of film documentary, drawing on the actual speech of working people, and weaving around this a pattern of song and music, in order to tell a simple truth. Secondly, they built up the kind of confidence that would make effective the protest contained within them. And thirdly, they left the young and developing folk movement with a number of fine new songs, like 'I'm a Free Born Man' about the travelling folk, or 'Shoals of Herring' from *Singing the Fishing*.

Irreverence had its own bard in Matt McGinn. Like the nineteenth-century broadsheets he cocked a snook with a vengeance. And the period in which he developed, the decaying world of the late fifties and early sixties, was made for him. He was the most prolific song-writer since Burns. Children's songs like 'Wee Kirkcudbright Centipede' or 'The Red Yo-Yo' or 'Coorie Doon' were matched by continual sardonic commentary on the seamier side of high politics. I think particularly of songs like the one on the Christine Keeler and John Profumo scandal:

> For here was a Tory and a ryebuck Red
> Fighting oot the Cold War in Christine's bed.

Or, when Home emerged as Prime Minister:

> We'll dress him up as a kiltie
> We'll gie him a tammy and sword,
> And while we're aw noddin'
> We'll no' think o' Flodden
> And how they first made him a Lord.

172

Matt had one other immense advantage; he wrote from within.
Where others could only write about the nobility of the workers, Matt
– as with some of the Wobblies' parodies – could say, 'Hi, we're not
all that noble. Sometimes we do a bit too much bloody overtime for
the good of the rest of us ...'. A song like 'Three Nights and a Sunday'
was only possible from someone like Matt:

> There's a fella doon the road that I avoid,
> He's wan o' them they call the unemployed.
> He says it's all because of me,
> He canny get a job and I've got three.
> Three nights and a Sunday double time.
>
> *Chorus:*
> Three nights and a Sunday double time,
> Three nights and a Sunday double time.
> I work aw day and I work aw night,
> Tae hell wi' you Jack, I'm all right;
> Three nights and a Sunday double time.
>
> The wife came tae the work the ither day.
> Says she 'We've anither wee one on the way.'
> Says I 'No wonder you can laugh,
> I've no' been hame for a year and a half.'
> Three nights and a Sunday double time.
>
> *Chorus*
>
> I never miss the pub on a Friday night.
> And there you'll always find me gay and bright.
> You'll see me down at the Old Bay Horse,
> I'm a weekend waiter there of course.
> Three nights and a Sunday double time.
>
> *Chorus*
>
> There's some will head for heaven when they die,
> Tae find a Dunlopillo in the sky.
> But I'll be going to the ither place,
> For an idle life I couldny face.
> Three nights and a Sunday double time.

Chorus

He understood and helped to show others the link between children's songs and songs of protest. There was plenty to draw upon. this from the hungry thirties for example:

> I'm no' the factor nor the gas-man
> Napoleon nor Ronald Colman.
> When you hear me rat-tat-tat upon your door
> Have your money in the bank, or money in the store.
> You'd better look oot or else I'll get ye,
> Try an' catch me if ye can,
> For I'm neither Santa Claus nor Doug-el-las Fairbanks,
> – I am the Means Test Man
> (Ta-ra-ra-ra-ra-ra ...)

And this connection was made too, within the two specific movements I want to refer to. One was Scottish Republicanism.

The first returning to the streets tradition of anti-royalty and anti-establishment sentiments was being led by Morris Blythman, the poet 'Thurso Berwick'. He had been turning increasingly to simple political balladry using the popular tunes of the streets, as well as the older tunes like 'Harlaw' that we were beginning to learn again. Two incidents helped him. One was the stealing of the Stone of Destiny. (He once said to me: 'You can't write songs until something happens.' In other words abstractions, however noble, are not enough.) This incident brought about a booklet, *Songs o' the Stane*, to which Morris persuaded a number of leading poets to contribute anonymously: T. S. Law, Sidney Goodsir Smith, Norman McCaig, Morris himself. But it was symptomatically a singer (Johnny McEvoy), not a poet, who contributed the most lasting song about the Stone, 'The Wee Magic Stane', with its fine comic idea about a multitude of stones being turned off on a production line so that, in the confusion, the 'real yin got bunged in alang wi' the rest':

> So if ever ye come on a stane wi' a ring
> Jist sit yersel doon an appoint yersel King,
> For there's nane wud be able tae challenge yer claim
> That ye'd croont yersel King on the Destiny Stane.

This incident captured the imagination – and sense of humour – of Scotland. And of course this is necessary if a protest song is to succeed. There must be a popular response around the incident, talk, chatter, jokes, anecdotes; there was around this. For example, the story went that one suspect was hauled in for questioning. After hours of fierce examination under a bright light he at last said wearily:

> 'All right, all right. Turn that thing off and I'll tell you who stole it.'
> The leaned forward eagerly. 'Right, who stole it?'
> 'Edward the First!' he replied.

Morris was right therefore in emphasising the hard actuality of incident as opposed to abstraction as the way forward in song protest. He illustrated precisely this in his own 'Scottish Breakaway', a nationalist and republican song, using as its moral the English attitude towards Scotland as epitomised by calling the Queen the 'Second' instead of the first Elizabeth of a United Kingdom, and as its 'incident' the popular interest in the refusal of the Palace to allow Princess Margaret to marry Captain Townsend. It uses a highly popular (even hated!) tune, 'The Sash'. It is a useful model for successful protest song making!

> Oh, Scotland hisnae got a King
> An she hisnae got a Queen.
> Hoo can ye hae the Second Liz
> When the first wan's never been?
>
> *Chorus:*
> Nae Liz the Wan, nae Lilibet the Twa,
> Nae Liz will ever dae.
> For we'll mak oor land Republican
> In a Scottish breakaway.
>
> Her man's cried the Duke o' Edinburgh
> He's wan o' the kiltie Greeks.
> 'But dinny blaw ma kilts awa'
> For it's Lizzie wears the breeks!'

Chorus

Noo her sister Meg's got a bonny pair o' legs
But she didny want a German or a Greek.
Peter Townshend was her choice, but he didny suit the boys,
So they sellt him up the creek

Chorus

Ah, but Meg was fly, an' she beat them by an' by,
Wi' Tony hyphenated Armstrong.
But the question o' the day, behind the Royal display,
Wis: 'Who did Suzie Wong?'.

Chorus

Sae, here's tae the lion, tae the bonny rampant lion,
An' a lang streetch tae his paw.
Gie a Hampden roar, an' it's oot the door,
Ta ta tae Cherlie's maw.

And the other movement which so stimulated the rise of protest song was, of course, the Campaign for Nuclear Disarmament, Aldermaston and, for us in Scotland especially, the anti-Polaris campaign. We marched, we protested, we sang; and we brought all the strands together. Writers like Hamish and Morris were, like the singers themselves, writing jingles and snatches, like 'Oor een are on the Target', as well as the fuller songs, comic and apocalyptic alike.

But there was a distinction, to me quite noticeable at the time, between the English and the Scottish response. At Aldermaston, the 'noble ' strand tended to dominate (leavened of course by American songs like 'We Shall Not Be Moved'). The songs were 'The H-Bomb's Thunder' with its hymn-like quality, or the aspirational 'Family of Man' by Karl Dallas. But in Scotland, almost instinctively, it was the irreverent that dominated: 'Ding Dong Dollar' with its chorus 'Naw, ye canny spend a dollar when ye're deid', and nice comic verses like:

Oh, the Yanks hiv jist drapped anchor at Dunoon,
An' they've got a civic welcome fae the toon
As they came up the measured mile, Bonny Mary o' Argyle
Was wearing spangled drawers below her goon.

And I think that the difference was that in Scotland we had always been closer to the basic folk material. The revival came truer in Scotland, and less precious than in England, and so too with our songs of protest. We were closer to the earlier Wobblies than to the comparable English song movement at that time. Perhaps this is best illustrated by an example of each. First a snatch of 'The H-Bomb's Thunder':

> Don't you hear the H-Bomb's thunder,
> Echo like the crack of doom?
> While the rend the skies asunder
> Fallout makes the world a tomb. .
>
> *Chorus:*
> Men and women, stand together
> Do not heed the men of war;
> Make you minds up, now or never,
> Ban the bomb for evermore.

But at Dunoon we sang:

> The USA are gien' subs away
> Giein' sub away,
> Giein' subs away-ay-ay-ay
> The USA are giein' subs away,
> But we dinna want Polaris.
>
> Ye can tell the Yanks tae drap them doon the stanks
> Drap the doon the stanks,
> Drap them doon the sta-a-a-anks
> (Etc.)

So the songs of protest had enlarged and been emancipated. Their irreverence was not an immaturity but a sign of confidence. It was no longer a case of trying to imitate or outdo their betters. There was an awareness, implicit, of their own popular culture, which also had its own nobility. There was an ease in the use of folk tunes that was miles away from the earlier parodies.

In all this and at all points, Hamish Henderson has been a central figure. Collector and catalyst he also happened to be poet and song writer. And a protester *sans pareil!*

I knew his work long before I knew he existed. For I, too, was in the Eighth Army in Italy and sang 'D-Day Dodgers' with the rest of them. Who had written it, I didn't enquire. I must have thought it had sprung fully formed from the bloodstained soil around Monte Cassino. And in a sense it had. It exactly expressed the popular mood of the men at the time. But the point is that the mood required form and substance and point. It required, in other words, a makar. And Hamish was the makar.

The folk process is a strange thing. Hamish wrote a song of protest against the imprisonment of Nelson Mandela in South Africa. He used a Spanish Republican song for his tune, 'Viva la Quice Brigata'. From Spain to Scotland to South Africa. For the song was taken up by the Africans and absorbed:

> They have sentenced the men of Rivonia
> Ubugwala, ubugwala
> The comrades of Nelson Mandela
> Ubugwala, ubugwala
> He is buried alive in an island
> Free Mandela, free Mandela, free Mandela.

And then, the 'top and hem of our story', he has produced the great anthem of protest in our Scottish folk revival: 'The Freedom Come All Ye'. In it the noble, the 'aspirational', the folk are properly and appropriately fused together:

> Roch the wind in the clear day's daw-in',
>   Blaws the cloods heelster gowdy ow'r the bay.
> But there's mair nor a roch wind blawin'
>   Through the great glen o' the warld the day.
> It's a thocht that will gar oot rottans –
>   A' they rogues that gang gallus fresh and gay –
> Tak' the road an' seek ither loanins
>   For their ill ploys tae sport an' play.

> Nae mair will the bonnie callants
>   Mairch tae war, when oor braggarts crousely craw,
> Nor wee weans frae pit-heid an' clachan
>   Mourn the ships sailin' doon the Broomielaw.

Broken families in lands we've herriet
  Will curse Scotland the Brave nae mair, nae mair;
Black an' white, ane til ither mairriet
  Mak' the vile barracks o' their maisters bare.

O come all ye at hame wi' freedom,
  Never heed whit the hoodies croak for doom;
In your hoose a' the bairns o' Adam
  Can find breid, barley bree an' painted room.
When Maclean meets wi's freens in Springburn
  A' the roses an' geans will turn tae bloom,
And a black boy frae yont Nyanga
  Dings the fell gallows o' the burghers doon.

I have to thank Miss Ann Neilson for undertaking the difficult task of preparing the transcript of the tape recording of what was very much an unscripted lecture.

G

The Folksong Revival in Scotland

ADAM MacNAUGHTON

The questions I would like to take as my starting-point are: Why was there a folksong revival? Why was a revival necessary? Why did we not grow up singing the songs that have since been revived? The simple and simplistic answer is industrialisation. The nineteenth century, first-generation city dweller may have passed on his songs to his children, but their children, born in the city, seeing little relevance in the old ballads, rejected them; a generation or so later, having acquired the city-dweller's more aggressive, high-paced sense of humour, they rejected also the gentle fun of the country songs. Then the young music industry, with an eye on the newly literate market, catered for urban tastes with music-hall songs and refined drawing-room ballads, which found their way into rural repertoires and often caused the old songs to be hidden away. It has been the task of the revival to unearth these old songs, preserved by rural singers in spite of the twentieth-century onslaught of Denmark Street and Tin Pan Alley.

Yet even before the nineteenth century there had been revivals of interest in folksongs, for example, with the growth of Literary Romanticism. Herd, Ramsay, Pinkerton, Thomson, Johnson, Burns and Cunningham in the eighteenth century, and Motherwell, Kinloch, Buchan, Scott, Kirkpatrick Sharpe and Jameson in the early nineteenth century, all published collections of songs. They were, for the most part, city men and scholars, looking on the singers and reciters as the last of their line, and the songs largely as museum pieces – unless we are to regard such clubs as the Cape Club, to which David Herd belonged, as the forerunners of the folksong clubs. No, the songs were collected for the interest of the antiquarians and gentry, as a glance at the subscribers' lists for such works as the *Orpheus Caledonius* (1733) will show. Collections were often published in very small editions, like the thirty copies of Charles Kirkpatrick Sharpe's *A Ballad Book* (1823), the preface of which may serve to illustrate the attitude of the collectors:[1]]

> I was anxious after this fashion to preserve a few Songs that afforded me much delight in my early youth, and are not to be found at all, or complete, or in the same shape in other Collections. These have been mostly gathered from the mouths of nurses, wet and dry, singing to their babes and sucklings, dairy-maids pursuing their vocations in the cowhouse, and tenants' daughters, while giving the Lady a spinning day, whilom an anniversary tribute in Annandale ... Though I am sensible that none of these Ballads are of much merit, I regret that my memory doth not now serve me to as many more ...

If that was the antiquarians' revival, the one at the turn of the century might be called the religious revival, not just because so many of the collectors (Baring-Gould, J. B. Duncan) were clergymen but because there was something of the crusader about their attitude to the songs. Again there was the belief that this was a last-ditch rescue operation. 'In less than a decade,' wrote Cecil Sharp in 1907, 'English folksinging will be extinct.' Sharp, however, was a revivalist. He saw folksong as the basis for an English school in classical music. Moreover, he saw an important role for folksong in education:[2]

> Folk music is clearly the best and most natural basis upon which to found a musical education. If the songs are carefully graded, beginning with traditional nursery rhymes and advancing by slow degrees to the more difficult folk songs, no other musical pabulum will be needed until the child has reached the age of ten or eleven years. By that time folk music will have served its purpose, and the child will be prepared to make a wider excursion into the realms of art music.

Similar attitudes obviously prevailed in Scottish educational circles and have done in school music departments to the present day. This is why the early revival was largely academic, and why in the

1950s we needed a folksong revival in which the people, and particularly young people, did not feel that 'culture' was being forced upon them from above.

Various attempts have been made to explain why the revival happened in the 1950s. The period since 1950 can certainly be seen as similar to the Romantic period of the first revival in a number of ways: the rising interest in nationalism, the swing in arts, and especially poetry, from obscurity to simplicity, from the critical standpoint of 'A poem is a poem is a poem' to that of 'a poet is a man writing for men'. One influence often suggested is the bomb, as it was suggested as a cause for most ills and most moods of the fifties and sixties; young people felt threatened and disillusioned by the legacy which the older generation had left them. They were seeking an escape in the music of a bygone age. Or, if you prefer, they were the first generation of 'Kinsey Kids', unsupported by parental, religious or educational authority, and they were seeking their roots, seeking something stable in a world of change. Or perhaps these young people were simply tired of the banality of popular songs about unspecified handsome men and vague dream girls, and seized eagerly on the skiffle songs about real railwaymen, cotton-pickers or outlaws, and on the cheap, easy-to-play instrument which was to transform popular music, the guitar. Jazz clubs and skiffle groups were to provide the musical education for the early revival singers.

And the hour brought forth the man! Hamish Henderson. He worked with Alan Lomax on the collecting tours when so many of the traditional singers who were to become household names were discovered. With the late Calum Mclean he was one of the first apostles of the School of Scottish Studies. He wrote the revival's finest songs. And in 1951 and the following years, he arranged the seminal People's Festival Ceilidhs, in which the best of our native traditions, Lowland and Gaelic, were revealed to young city-dwellers. It was at these ceilidhs that the singing of Jimmy MacBeath and Jeannie Robertson made its impact on the people who were to be responsible for the start of the revival proper, on Ewan MacColl, on Arthur Argo, who was later to start the Aberdeen Folk Club, and on Norman Buchan and Morris Blythman, both of whom actively promoted folk-music in Glasgow schools and were closely involved in the beginnings of the Glasgow Folk Song Club.

The first thing that distinguishes this revival from its predecessors, if we accept the People's Festivals as a starting-point, is the motivation of its begetters; the People 's Festivals were conceived as a counterweight to the Edinburgh International Festival with its influx of tourists and culture-vultures when, in the words of Norman Buchan:

> Aw Princes Street was in a rout
> An' plagued by every kind o' tout.
> The rich hae tickets but we're without –
> They're ower dear at the Festal-o.

Like the Romantic antiquarians, the collectors this time saw themselves as rescuers, but they did not see the songs as museum pieces. Like Cecil Sharpe, they wished the songs to live. However, far from being mere stepping-stones to an appreciation of classical music, the songs were seen as an important part of our culture, as great art, different from the Italian/German art music of the official Festival but perhaps of greater worth to the real people of Edinburgh, Glasgow, Buckie, Moffat or Kirkwall. It is hardly surprising that folksong in Scottish schools has tended to be the preserve of the English Department rather than the Music Department.

Another difference is that the technical side of collecting has altered greatly. The tape-recorder has replaced the notebook and pencil. The commercial publication of recordings of traditional singers means that many more people can experience something that the printed page cannot convey – the style in which the songs are sung. One shudders to think what happened to the songs in the earlier revivals before they reached the ears of the public:[3]

> 'As the Scottish songs are the flights of genius, devoid of art, they bid defiance to artificial graces and affected cadences. A Scots song can only be sung in taste by a Scottish voice ... We sometimes, however, find a foreign master, who, with a genius for the pathetic, and a knowledge of the subject and words, has afforded very high pleasure in a Scottish song. Who could hear with insensibility, or without being moved in the greatest degree, Tenducci sing 'I'll never leave thee'; or 'The braes of Ballendine'; or 'will ye go to the ewe-bughts, Marion?' sung by Signora Corri?'

183

Since the beginning of the revival there has been a growth in the productions of these recordings. In the early fifties H.M.V. published a number of Kennedy-Lomax pieces, but the American 'Folkways' series showed that there was a place for specialist folksong labels. Collectors Records in the fifties and early sixties produced EPs of singers as diverse as Guy Carawan and Jeannie Robertson, Blind Lemon Jefferson and Jimmy MacBeath. They also recorded young singers such as Robin Hall. But the company which has contributed most to the revival is undoubtedly Topic, who began back in the days of 78s, issuing records of Ewan MacColl, and who have built a list over the years of both traditional and revival singers which is unsurpassed even by Folkways. Yet the pride of that list is perhaps the reissued series of ten LPs, 'Folksongs of Britain', edited by Peter Kennedy and Alan Lomax, and originally issued by Caedmon Records. Much of the credit for Topic's expanded recording policy during the sixties is due to Bill Leader, who later formed his own record company, Leader Records, also featuring traditional singers but giving more space to revival performers. The established companies contributed too; in particular, Argo, a subsidiary of Decca, published much of Ewan MacColl's work from the late sixties, including that *tour de force* of comparative scholarship, 'The Long Harvest'.

Both radio and television played their part in the early revival, radio providing an introduction to traditional singers in Peter Kennedy's 'As I Roved Out' programmes, and television making use of folk music while it was fashionable with Robin Hall and Jimmy McGregor on BBC's 'Tonight' and The Reivers (Josh Macrae, Enoch Kent and Rena Swankie) on STV's 'Jigtime', a series which lasted 40 weeks in 1958. Since then the television ration has been meagre and we can only regret that so little of Jeannie Robertson, Jimmy MacBeath, Davie Stewart and the rest remains on film, since they were all very much visual performers. Of the current BBC radio programmes, 'Folkweave' gives good coverage of the British revival, with very few contributions from traditional singers, while Radio Scotland's 'Haven't Heard a Horse Sing' has so far been rather tentative in its approach to the North-East tradition. On the commercial stations Radio Forth has one hour per week and Radio Clyde rejected its original programme in which Drew Moyes presented a

wide range of folk music on record, in favour of two pop-folk programmes whose appeal is perhaps wider but not so deep.

One cannot, in referring to radio, omit to mention the Radio
Ballads of Ewan MacColl and Charles Parker. This was a new concept in documentary broadcasting. Hundreds of hours of interview
and actual speech were reduced to a tightly constructed programme
on a group of people, usually people of a disappearing breed –
boxers, steam railwaymen, travellers, herring-fishers – linked with
traditional music and with songs created out of the hundreds of
hours of talk, including some of the best songs of the revival, like
'Freeborn Man', 'Shoals of Herring' or 'Schooldays Over'.

Ours being a literate society, the printed media have also been
important. Before records were so readily available the songbooks
were indispensable to young singers eager to build up a repertoire
quickly. In his essay, Norman Buchan refers to the songs associated
with the anti-Polaris campaign and with the removal of the Stone of
Destiny. The spread of these songs was greatly accelerated by slim
(and cheap) volumes like *Songs o the Stane, Ding Dong Dollar,* and the
Rebels' Ceilidh Songbooks. Of particular importance was Norman
Buchan's own *101 Scottish Songs* which appeared first in 1962, perhaps the time of greatest demand for words and music, with folksong
clubs recently opened in Dunfermline, Kirkcaldy, Aberdeen and
Perth. One should also mention Ewan MacColl's collections, *The
Shuttle and the Cage, Personal Choice* and *The Singing Island,* and the
earlier *Scotland Sings,* which was already a rarity by 1960. Another
publishing event which altered the repertoires of singers throughout
Britain was Dover Books' reprinting of F. J. Child's *English and Scottish Popular Ballads,* at about £1 per volume.

The first magazine of the revival was initiated by the London
Youth Choir. *Sing,* based to some extent on the American *Sing Out,*
started in 1954 with Eric Winter as editor, and in its first year included songs by Ewan MacColl, Norman Buchan and Morris
Blythman. Scottish magazines have been less durable. In Glasgow,
Andrew Moyes has made three attempts, each running to two issues:
two series of *Scottish Folknotes* and one called *Folkwest.* The best folk
club magazine was without doubt *Chapbook,* which existed from
1964-69, growing out of an Aberdeen club newsletter. It was edited
by Arthur Argo, Ian Philip and Carl MacDougall, three folk-music

enthusiasts with experience in journalism but not, unfortunately, in business management, and debt brought *Chapbook* to an end. It is perhaps with this lesson in mind that *Sandy Bell's Broadsheet* has remained a newsletter, not aspiring to become a magazine. It does carry articles on folksong from time to time but its main function is to inform its readers of what is happening in clubs, on the air and on record. The only regular newspaper feature was Norman Buchan's song-a-week column in the *Weekly Scotsman*, which, however, at no time evoked the sort of response which Gavin Greig achieved with his 'Buchany' articles in the earlier revival.

Since the advent of Professor McQueen to the School of Scottish Studies and with the end to the School's first phase of desperate collecting – and the recent deaths of so many contributors show how right this policy was – more time has been devoted to publication, to 'feedback', with the excellent *Tocher* supplementing the established academic journal, *Scottish Studies*, and making available to a wider readership the School's archive material. In addition the School has co-operated with Tangent Records to produce the magnificent *Scottish Tradition* series of albums featuring both Gaelic and Scots, vocal and instrumental, treasures from all periods of the School's recording.

Otherwise at university level there is little evidence of a folksong revival. Only two universities feature folklore in any form as an academic subject. In Edinburgh, again at the School of Scottish Studies, two undergraduate courses are offered. The first is in Oral Literature and Popular Tradition, and the second, rather more advanced, a course on the Oral Traditional Culture of Scotland. Only at Stirling, however, under David Buchan, author of *The Ballad and the Folk*, the only critical work on Scottish folksong to take account of modern folklore studies, can one take folklore to degree level, with a degree in English and Folklife Studies.[5] The other universities offer nothing beyond extra-mural courses.

At school level the story is different. The recent SED document on Scottish Literature in the Secondary School was little short of fulsome in its recommendation of folksong for all age groups and abilities. Scottish schools broadcasts, with producers such as David Campbell and Isla MacLean, make wide use of folk material, particularly that of the children's own traditions. Every new poetry anthology includes some folksongs, and some, such as *Poetry and Song* or the Penguin

Voices series, have accompanying records with singers like the Critics Group, Ewan MacColl, Peggy Seeger and Tom Paley.

From the outset of the revival, schoolteachers have shown an interest. They have started clubs in schools and, also in the classroom, they have tried to pass on a knowledge and love of the traditional culture of Scotland. Morris Blythman at Allan Glen's and Norman Buchan at Rutherglen Academy were the pioneers, both of them also involved from the start in the Glasgow Folksong Club. But Fife Education Authority showed itself to be the most folksong-conscious in Scotland by employing Josh Macrae and Archie Fisher to teach folk-guitar in schools. The man responsible for these developments was the late Jack Stewart, headmaster at Temple Hall School and a founder-member of the Kirkcaldy Folk Club in 1962.

It is outside the schools, however, that the development most characteristic of the revival has taken place, the spread of interest among young people in folksong clubs. And what's their history? One is tempted to reply with viola, 'None, my Lord,' because there has been little basic change in folksong clubs in the twenty-two years since the Glasgow club was founded in the Corner House Cafeteria in Trongate. The history is one, not of organic development, of progress, but of a following of fashions, of changing programmes influenced from outside Scotland.

The People's Festival Ceilidhs sparked an interest in folk music in several people but it was initially a private, informal interest, to be followed up in one's own home. In the meantime, young people in the Scottish cities went to jazz clubs and jazz dances to hear music played by young Scots in the bands of Ian Menzies, George Penman and numerous others. From 1952 onwards they might have heard some members of the band, the rhythm section, play and sing something which they called skiffle. Before long, the interval spots at jazz clubs were being filled by independent skiffle groups, playing and singing American folksongs, using the guitar and other cheap, often improvised, rhythm instruments like the washboard and tea chest bass. In 1954 a reviewer could write of a 'Ballads and Blues' concert at the Festival Hall:[6]

> But the best Jazz numbers were those in which the folksingers took a hand. When Mr Lloyd sang the 'Ghost Soldier Blues' and

Mr MacColl sang 'Another Man Done Gone', both with Mr Colyer's band, nobody in the vast audience doubted the connection between ballads and blues.

That London audience, however, also heard MacColl sing ballads like 'Eppie Morrie' and they heard traditional musicians like Margaret Barry and Michael Gorman. The Scottish jazz clubs had not come as far as that.

Nonetheless, the skiffle groups were soon including Scottish songs in their repertoires. Then they began to call themselves folk groups, and solo singers began to appear in the jazz club spots. The peak of skiffle's poularity in Scotland was probably 1957 when the All Scotland Skiffle Championships attracted over one hundred entries.

By that time, though, the first Scottish folksong clubs had been formed by people who had attended the original ceilidhs – Hamish Henderson in Edinburgh (*The Crown* is distinguished by being the oldest club in continuous existence to the present day) and Norman Buchan and Morris Blythman in Glasgow.[7] In 1959 a second Edinburgh club, *The Howff*, grew out of a Festival-time organisation called 'The Sporranslitters', and by 1962 there were clubs in Kirkcaldy, Perth, Dunfermline, St Andrews, Falkirk and Aberdeen. At the jazz clubs people had danced to the music, and in the folksong clubs the audiences were still eager to participate. Even people who would never sing before an audience learned the words of each new song they liked. The singers learned and sang everything, from Huddie Leadbetter's blues to Jeannie Robertson's ballads like 'Harlaw' or to the two Gaelic songs which were printed in *The Rebels' Ceilidh Songbook*. And there were singers! There were so many regular floor singers at the Glasgow club that you had to establish yourself by doing one song per week over several months before you were promoted to the two-song rank. It proved an excellent way for young singers to gain confidence and build a repertoire.

None of the clubs had an exclusive musical policy with regard to guests. Good singers were welcome from anywhere, traditional or revival. In most places local traditional singers were in short supply but the Aberdeen club could call on such as Jeannie Robertson, Jimmy MacBeath, Rob Watt and John McDonald. They also had as guests Ewan MacColl and Peggy Seeger, Pete Seeger, Doc Watson, Cyril Tawney and others. They welcomed, too, young Scottish singers like Norman Kennedy, The Gaugers, Danny Cooper (all local), and Josh Macrae, Ray and Archie Fisher, Hamish Imlach and Owen Hand. The club policy of booking local traditional singers was not necessarily a reflection of audience taste. Two hundred members would turn out to hear Ray and Archie Fisher or Pete Seeger but when the great Jeannie Robertson was the guest the attendance might be under forty.

For those who have not visited a folk club, the proceedings generally are as follows: in a three-hour programme the guest will sing an hour to an hour-and-a-half, and the rest of the proceedings will be sung by local and casual visiting singers, doing ten to twenty minutes each. This pattern, in most Scottish clubs, has survived virtually unchanged since the beginnings.

The club programmes, on the other hand, are affected by changing trends, by influences from furth of Scotland, though Aberdeen, with its strong local tradition, was less subject to this. In the early post-skiffle era, the influence was still American – Leadbelly, folk bluesmen like Muddy Waters, Woody Guthrie and, above all, the Weavers and Pete Seeger. The Scottish folk club attitude to the music was Seeger's – folksong should unite (working-class) peoples, music is an international language. The ideal song was one which was all chorus, like the American Negro spirituals which were sung without irony by young radicals who might then sing an anti-American CND song. And to prove just how international it was, Seeger would teach an audience to sing one of several African or Hebrew choruses which he had in his repertoire. Each succeeding trend would leave a layer of disciples who are still singing in the clubs today, and the Seeger trend is no exception. There are at least two solo banjo-players singing the club circuit who owe to Seeger their attitudes and their style of accompaniment.

From the days of skiffle, there had been Scottish songs sung but they paled into insignificance at one's first experience of Jeannie Robertson or Jimmy MacBeath, both of whom made several visits to the clubs in Glasgow and Edinburgh. Other traditional singers who were 'revived' include the Stewart family of Blairgowrie, Willie Scott, a border shepherd for long a resident singer at *The Howff* in Dunfermline, or Davey Stewart, who could be heard plying his trade in the streets of Glasgow. The performances gave so much that one could not get from a record, because all of these singers had (or have) presence, whether it be the raucous honesty of Jimmy MacBeath, the controlled power of Jeannie Robertson, or the quieter dignity of Willie Scott. Their visits, backed by the work of Ewan MacColl, a more frequent guest in the sixties than he is now, formed the most important influence of all. It changed the emphasis of the revival from internationalism to a cultural nationalism, leading to the formation of clubs in which a deliberate Scottish-songs-for-Scottish-singers policy was followed, and to the division of clubs into sheep and goats, or 'ethnic' and 'commercial', a division that is still with us, though some of the acrimony has gone out of the discussion.

The American influences, however, were not finished. Now came the American song-writing invasion, spearheaded by Bob Dylan. He experimented with verbal and musical form, and he spawned several local imitators, some of whom continue to set to music vague symbolism in the manner of 'A Hard Rain's Agonna Fall'.

Then came the Clancy Brothers. Irish songs and Aran sweaters were the order of the day. Their imitation gusto and orchestrated enthusiasm are still with us. This style is the mark of the semi-professional folk groups who sing at clubs in hotels throughout the country, clubs which subsist with a whole programme of guest singers and no local enthusiasts.

The influences that followed were English. Nineteen sixty-five saw the first records of the Watersons and Martin Carthy. The Watersons introduced an element which we had learned to regard as foreign to folksong – harmony. They perhaps took as their starting point the singing of the Copper family but quickly established their own eminently inimitable (and often imitated) style. Their importance lay in the encouragement they gave to unaccompanied singers by showing what four strong voices were capable of. Martin Carthy also sang unaccompanied on occasion but it was his guitar playing and choice of song which has had the lasting influence, an influence matched only by Archie Fisher among the Scottish revival singers.

In the 1970s the most striking growth has been on the instrumental side. The guitar may still be the most common instrument but the native instruments (fiddle, pipes, concertina) have become familiar in all Scottish clubs. Lone fiddlers there had been from the beginning, among them Bobby Campbell in Glasgow and Dave Swarbrick making influential recordings with the Ian Campbell Folk Group from the late fifties. Among the first Scottish groups to use the fiddle and concertina were The Gaugers in Aberdeen and The Clutha in Glasgow. But the instrumental breakthrough of the seventies has been the music of the Chieftains and, later, other Irish groups like the Bothy Band and Na Fili. Their effect on the young Scottish groups can be clearly heard in instrumentation, in repertoire and in style with bands like Silly Wizard, Ossian, Battlefield and others. And some might argue that the Gaelic-speaking areas of the Isles and Ireland were one musical community in days past.

Another phenomenon which should be mentioned is the development of the 'folk comedian'. In the clubs where the audience came merely to be entertained, and not to learn or to participate, there was no interest in informed introductions to the songs. This led to singers to indulge in comic introductions which often evoked more, or more audible, audience response than the songs. Seduced by this the singers talked more and sang less. This was the school of Alex Campbell, Billy Connolly, Bill Barclay and many a minor comic.

There have been several Scottish bands of note in the world of 'Electric Folk', among them the J.S.D. Band, Five Hand Reel and the Tannahill Weavers, but this has had little effect on the clubs, which usually meet in small rooms where the amplified sound becomes overpowering. Nor could the clubs afford the fees charged by these groups to cover their electricity bills.

What then would one find in a Scottish folk club today? One would expect a high percentage of Scottish material, and there are several clubs where it is the organisers' policy to encourage this. Yet when I recently visited a club in Glasgow where the guest was singing mainly English traditional material to a Carthy-influenced guitar accompaniment, the floor-singing programme, all by local singers too young to remember the trends of the sixties, included only eight Scottish songs (three of them traceable to recordings by Ewan MacColl), an unaccompanied sea-shanty, an Irish song of the '98 rebellion, 'Goodbye Booze' sung very much in the Clancy style, and songs by Lightning Hopkins, Woody Guthrie, Bob Dylan, John Denver, and Simon and Garfunkel. And I believe there are as many

Scottish clubs where this would be typical as there are clubs where it would never happen.

Has there been no change since 1966, when *Chapbook* in successive editorials bemoaned the state of the Scottish clubs in the following terms?

> Where has the Scottish folksong movement gone wrong? Why does a country with such a wonderfully rich heritage of tradition allow so many tartan cowboys and thinly-disguised pop groups to dominate the revival?[8]

> Advancement of knowledge is progress, exploring your own and other cultures is progress, getting social history into perspective is progress – but turning up week after week merely to be entertained (perhaps with the sop of joining in a few chorus songs) is not.[9]

One form of action to try to change the situation here criticised has been the attempt to form a federation of clubs which might exert some influence on programmes. One major obstacle has been the short life of so many clubs. Many fail to last two years, sometimes because of commercial pressures by the owner of the premises, sometimes because when the members become more informed, the club fare is no longer satisfactory and they prefer to deepen their interest on their own. In the sixties Glasgow and the West saw a one-man attempt by Drew Moyes to organise folksong clubs on a full-time basis. At the height of his activity in 'Folk Song Clyde Valley', he had clubs running in the Glasgow area and as far out as Helensburgh and Aberfoyle on six nights of the week, in addition to craft classes, topical workshops and instrumental tuition. He was, however, torn between his own interest in traditional music and the need to make money to live on by presenting artists attractive to a wide public, with the result that the organisation failed. Two attempts at committee-run Scottish federations were also shortlived. One can only wish better success to the current attempt to forge inter-club links.

A highly significant event in the revival was the formation in 1965 of the Traditional Music and Song Association and with it the traditional music festival at Blairgowrie, where instead of trying to get traditional singers to go to revival clubs in the cities, the revival enthusiasts were brought to the traditional musicians. So successful was this that there are now three such festivals annually in Scotland, at Kinross, Newcastleton and Keith.

That is one point of hope for the Scottish revival. Another about which I shall say little since Norman Buchan has dealt with it in his paper, is the body of song that the last twenty years has produced, from the political squibs of Thurso Berwick and Jim McLean to the characterisations of Eric Bogle, from Matt McGinn's amalgam of folksong and Glasgow music-hall to Hamish Henderson's poetry borne on pipe-tunes. Another lies in the young groups which are now beginning to 'dominate the revival', the post-Chieftains bands. They seem to be musically superior to and better informed than many of their predecessors – a far cry from the 'tartan cowboys'.

NOTES

1 Sharp's *A Ballad Book* forms the first part of *Choice Old Scottish Ballads*, (ed.) T. G. Stevenson (Edinburgh, 1976).

2 Cecil J. Sharp, *English Folk Song: Some Conclusions* (London, 1965).

3 'Dissertation on the Scottish Music' by William Tytler, Esq., cited in Ritson's *Scottish Songs* (Edinburgh, 1794).

4 In the original talk I mistakenly credited the Workers' Music Association with the foundation of *Sing*. I am indebted to Mr Karl Dallas for the correct information. He also took me to task in the short time for discussion because, in my review of the major trends, I failed to mention the influence on guitar playing of Davey Graham, Bert Jansch and John Renbourn.

5 Since this paper was delivered Scottish Folk studies have suffered a further blow. David Buchan has departed to Newfoundland.

6 *Sing*, Vol. 1, No. 3.

7 For the information about the Edinburgh clubs I must thank Mrs Ailie Munro, who allowed me to read the relevant chapter of her forthcoming book on the folksong revival. Arthur Argo, John Watt and Norman Buchan gave me information about Aberdeen, Dunfermline and Glasgow respectively.

8 *Chapbook*, Vol. 3, No. 2.

9 *Chapbook*, Vol. 3, No. 3.

Folk Now

JOHN BARROW

The final contribution to this series of essays is intended as a contemporary view of folk music, with the philosophy that 'folk' is to be found in any nation or group of people based on a common root or ancestry. As soon as people congregate, folk exists; the analysts to quantify or qualify the manifestation follow later. Folk is the cultural foundation stone of any people. Without an indigenous culture reflecting or transmitting the feelings of the people society would be anaemic with little or no idea of its own significance. Hence the strength of feeling expressed through the medium of folk by, for example, exiles from Chile where the current political ideology is very anti-people.

A second approach to constructing a philosophy of folk is that without an indigenous culture there can be no so-called higher art forms. Here, by implication, the author will risk the scorn of many arty high-heid yins by considering folk as an art form. What can be conveyed through this idea is that if there is a literature, a drama, a visual art and so on, it has to be founded on the bedrock of the nation's expressed culture or exist *in vacuo*. If such higher art forms are imported they have a reduced validity in the context of the nation to which they are brought unless they strike some popular chord. Thus a preoccupation with, for instance, Scottish ballet in its own right is fine, but in a Scottish context it has to be related to the indigenous culture of the nation and should reflect or transmit that, rather than stay comfortably within the traditional offerings associated with such an art form, important though they may be.

How then are these ideas made manifest in Scotland and elsewhere today? One observation could be made by anyone who lives in Scotland and keeps his ears even half-open. There is a clear understanding at a very basic level, throughout the population, of what a folk song or tune sounds like or could sound like. This applies equally to people who go to folk clubs, concerts or festivals, or to those who listen to the overtly tartan antics of certain disc jockeys, or to those who are members of fiddle and accordion clubs, and to followers of all the other forms of music one can associate with Scotland. It applies also to those who express a dislike of folk music, because in order to dislike something one has to make a value judgement, which implies knowledge, however limited, rudimentary or erroneous.

One might imagine from such an observation that the whole country should be singing and playing folk music. That this is not the case is evident and it is probably a good thing too that the hills are not alive with music. It would become extremely wearing to have nothing but folk music and might well be dangerous to the health of the culture if no other stimulus was available to ginger the happy complacency such a state could engender. The main problem is that the people who have this sort of instinctive idea of folk very often treat it as unimportant and often subjugate it in favour of the great god of classical music or Tin Pan Alley, almost in a forelock-tugging way. I think that outdated educational attitudes are largely responsible for this, but fortunately the anglicisation of Scotland is not as prevalent as in the past, when certain standards were abstracted at the expense of Scotland.

Today, one of the best-known public fronts for folk music is the folk club. There are other manifestations of course through the fiddle and accordion clubs, the Strathspey and reel societies and piping organisations, but the folk club is the one which deals mostly with song, although not necessarily exclusively. Folk clubs, in fact, have the broadest approach and are used as platforms by a large variety of performers, from singers of traditional ballads to poets, budding country and western singers, songwriters singing their own quite often appalling material, and any others who find that what they are trying to do does not fit in anywhere else. I must say that I find this approach at once the most satisfactory and probably the greatest weakness in the folk clubs. Most satisfactory, because I am basically egalitarian in outlook as far as one can be without becoming an anarchist, and weak, because all sorts of oddballs and rotten performers get time to inflict themselves on the audience.

One of the more common criticisms against folk clubs is that they can become a parade ground for the organisers' egos. While true in many cases, I think the deeper and more sinister reality behind this remark is that the organisers become, more or less by definition, the arbiters of taste in their part of the folk world. This I find positively dangerous if we accept either the maintenance of an indigenous culture, or its development into something new but distinguishably related as being as important and worthwhile. The audiences who go to a given folk club are thus exposed to what the organiser(s) think is good folk music or to what seems to keep bringing the audience back. How many folk club organisers actually sit down and think about what they are embarking on before the club's first night (or, just as importantly, after the voyage has started)? Some may say that such navel-contemplation is not important, that the music is there to be enjoyed – take it at its face value. I go along with that, but if you don't nurture the plant and care for its roots it will become prey to disease and fungi, wither and die. The commercial entrepreneurs find it easy to move in to make a parasitic buck here and there either through folk clubs or through tours or concerts – anywhere that an audience can be persuaded to part with some cash. And the entrepreneur has little time or thought for the arguments being expounded here.

Folk clubs should automatically be one manifestation of an indigenous culture. Strictly, of course, the folk club should be one of the tips of the iceberg carved from the omnipresent glacier of music and lore in the community. In the city, 'community' becomes a less useful term and the folk club can tend to be a museum of traditional rural song (I do not mention instrumental music here since that has fewer borders to negotiate). For example, one year at Newcastleton Folk Festival the singing competition entrants were mostly non-local, young, and from an urban background. About three out of the field of twenty or so were local, older, and from a rural background. There are different ways of interpreting this. It may be that the local young folk simply do not want to take part in competitions or don't sing, or don't take an active part in the old traditions. The winner that year was from an urban background singing a traditional song associated with rural matters, as were most of the songs that were sung. It could be argued that it was a competition where it might be expected that the entrants would perform traditional rural songs since that was the ambience of the set-up. The singers were not at all ill-at-ease or out of their depth with these old songs about times and events they had little or no ken about.

In rural areas in Scotland there is a significant lack of folk clubs, as there is in the north-west Gaelic country. Does this mean that music and song are in such a healthy state that they do not need the arbitrary crutch of a club? Maybe, but the counter to that would be that these are the areas where there has been an explosion of interest in fiddle and accordion music in the seventies, so that now there are more fiddle and accordion clubs in most rural areas than folk clubs, while few of the cities have fiddle and accordion clubs, though many folk clubs.

Not only do fiddle and accordion clubs outnumber folk clubs in Scotland, but very often they present their guests to much larger audiences than the average folk club. This is probably because they tend to meet monthly in comparison to most folk clubs who meet weekly; and the fiddle and accordion 'season' lasts only from October to May against the folk clubs' year-round involvement. There is evidently a financial element at work here since it must be cheaper to go out once a month than once a week or perhaps every fortnight. This must dictate the operation of the folk clubs to a large degree and is responsible, in part, for the large regular audiences at the fiddle and accordion clubs, apart from the obvious fact that folk go there because they enjoy the music. The average members' admission price in folk clubs in Scotland is probably around 60p, which brings in over a fifty-week period £30 per member (if they are all good members and attend every week). The average-size club room can hold around eighty people, perhaps a little less, so the income from a full house is £50 if the room is filled with members (unlikely, and this sum would be increased with non-members' admissions). After deducting the club's expenses, the guest artist would be lucky to take away £40 for his night's work – and that is based on the assumption of a full house, which is not guaranteed. If, however, the club met in larger premises, say, around 120 capacity, charged £1.50 for admission and met once a month, the cost to the audience would be £18 per head per year, which is a considerable reduction on the weekly meetings, even at more than double the price. In addition, the revenue from the door each night on a full house would be £180 which, even on a 60 per cent turn-out would provide a fair amount of money for fees and expenses. This could ensure consistently larger audiences and larger fees for artists who, by today's standards, are ludicrously underpaid – assuming of course that artists can be found who are 'worth ' this kind of money. Many are, but many audiences are less than open-minded about their club's menu, which means that some excellent artists do not get the chance to perform. (Here we return to the earlier discussion of the influence of club organisers and simultaneously remember the halcyon days when it seemed that club audiences were loyal to their clubs, turning up each night no matter who was booked.)

As Adam MacNaughton says, the folk club today is more or less an exact copy of the earliest days of the late fifties when folk clubs were taking their first tentative and exciting steps. A monthly meeting does work in some places – there is an excellent folk club in Melrose which is currently running on these lines (though not charging as much as £1.50) – but one of the worries expressed is that this kind of approach reduces the feeling of belonging to a club. Once a month means that a high intensity has to be injected to ensure the audience return after the fallow four weeks since the previous meeting, although it could be said that meeting weekly requires a greater commitment on the part of the audience. Melrose seems, at the moment anyway, to be running extremely successfully.

In recent years an oft-made criticism of the organisation of a typical folk club night has been that the guest artist rarely does enough to really earn his money. Typically, the guest might be expected to do between thirty and forty-five minutes in each of two halves of the evening, while the rest of the two and a half hours is filled by organisers, poets, country and western singers and, occasionally, some good performances from the 'floor'. The reasons for this formula appear to have become obscured, but it is now established as the standard way to run a folk club. Clubs in Europe and in North America, however, have reversed this by expecting performers to do up to three spots in a night, each lasting perhaps forty-five to sixty minutes.

There are two broad schools of thought on how to run a folk club night. One says book the best and reduce the chancers and comic singers to a minimum, if not less; the other claims the folk club to be the forcing ground of new talent and if the folk scene as it is known today is to survive it is essential to promote tomorrow's 'stars' or, perhaps less emotively, professionals. The two schools can peacefully co-exist, however, using a folky version of Parkinson's Law. That is, if the number of floor performers expands to fill the time available, run a workshop night at some other time during the week, or month, to allow them to overflow. This then allows the club to maintain a booking policy featuring high quality talent and/or big names (not necessarily the same thing) as well as having the nursery bringing the fresh talent on. Such an arrangement takes time and people to organise but it does happen that some clubs run workshops in addition to their weekly meetings. It depends on the time the organisers feel they can devote to the club and still retain the semblance of a social life.

Since 1973 there has been a decline in the number of Scottish folk clubs from approximately seventy-five to just over thirty. This is a startling statistic. The most rapid reduction occurred through 1974-75 but it appears now that a stable level has been reached. According to the Scottish Folk Directory – as good a source for this information as any – about thirty clubs or regular folk venues disappeared in the two years up to the end of 1975, with a less rapid decline after this period to just over thirty. It is important to know why this occurred, bearing in mind that the same sort of thing happened south of the border over roughly the same period. No one has yet produced the answer – although none seem sufficiently concerned to actively pursue the question.

If some assessment of this phenomenon could be made then the information could be of use to the folk club scene as a whole, at least in Scotland. The blame or reasons for this national decline have been laid almost exclusively at the door of the Exchequer. The period of decline coincides almost exactly with motor fuel price rises and inflation at a time when the country as a whole seemed incapable of accepting the way things seemed to be going. It seemed impossible at that time that a pint of beer could ever cost over 30p or that a gallon of petrol could rise to cost more than 75p, but inexorably the prices

199

rose and the number of clubs declined. This was not the only reason for the evident decline in numbers. It would be a brave man who said there has been no connection at all. It is more likely that at that time people decided that what they were being offered in the folk clubs, or at least some of them, just wasn't worth the effort. Even those clubs still running today and considering themselves to be marginally successful, would say that audiences generally are not as reliably big as in days past. So, as soon as the folk-going public felt the pound in its pocket not stretching quite as far as it did once, a certain lack of idealism crept in to what had once been a scene full of idealists, and the practical problems of the next month's rent loomed larger on the budget. There did not appear to be any particularly noticeable drop in people going out to enjoy themselves generally, so where did the folk audience go and why? They certainly appeared to desert the folk clubs (although not the folk festivals perhaps) and presumably either stayed at home to save what money they had or decided to look for better value for their money elsewhere.

As prices rose then naturally the performers' fees had to rise to allow them to keep to their chosen profession. Clubs were very reluctant at first to increase their admission prices and membership rates, although every other form of entertainment that depended on its box office was confronting the public with a fact of life at every performance (except some of the larger outfits which depended on government, i.e. Arts Council, support to cushion them against the rate of inflation). Eventually, however, they capitulated. In many cases performers simply had to double their fees between 1973-1976 to stay alive. Some of the higher-paid couldn't double their fees because that would have priced them out of the market, as the clubs' increased admission charges and the public's image of the value of the 'pound' – a dubious yardstick at the best of times – meant that fees reaching £50 – £60 or more were hard to justify in the folk club world.

Scotland suffered in one particular way because of her population distribution. Most of the folk clubs are in the central belt. North of Perth in Aberdeen, Inverness, Ullapool, Thurso, Orkney, Stornoway (and at one time Wick) there are folk clubs, but not all are easily accessible, being dependent on the weather and, for the performer who uses public transport, are nearly out of the question as a profit-making venture. The galling thing is that nearly all these northern clubs are considered good to play by artists either because of the receptive audiences or because of the hospitality or both.

During the seventies the Scottish folk clubs made a bad error of judgement in not approaching other sources of finance to help keep them going and indeed improve their situation by keeping admission prices down while paying performers what they were worth. The Scottish Arts Council, while admitting their ignorance of folk music and the folk scene, indicated that they would be prepared to look at applications for assistance from folk clubs in the way in which they treated all the other requests for help from similar bodies. To my knowledge one folk club (Edinburgh) and two folk festivals have applied to the Arts Council for help with specific projects since then and received money. One remark passed by those not applying was that it was thought that the Arts Council exercised some form of censorship with the allocation of money, and that was not on. 'We don't want to be controlled by the Arts Council!' That this remark had been based on surmise (and is, as far as I know, a folk tale) without anyone finding out about it, shows the extent of the folk clubs' concern with the way things were developing. The opportunity still exists for the clubs to take this offer of support. (Apart from the irony of the supposedly indigenous and spontaneous culture receiving grants from the government to keep it going in one form, I would never advocate Arts Council backing as a full-time measure, but surely any non-censorial helping hand is to be grasped in such times as these.)

These last have been rather gloomy paragraphs. It's time to redress the balance with some more positive aspects of recent years.

Through the sixties the major influence in folk music, outside America, was Ireland, with most notably the Clancy Brothers and Tommy Makem and, slightly later, the Dubliners. Wild mimicking folkies with beer mugs, Aran sweaters and furiously flailed guitars probably did more harm to what the general public thought of as folk music than anyone before or since – damage we are still not clear of today! Adam MacNaughton mentions this phenomenon but fails to connect convincingly its once omnipresent influence via later Irish groups (of which the Chieftains are perhaps the best-known example) with the current resurgence of interest in Scottish instrumental music. In fact, the new Scottish musical nationalism is but one facet of a musical nationalism that has moved through Europe and North America since the early seventies and which I believe is tied in closely with Irish origins.

Rod Stradling, the talented young English melodeon player, described the trend to me at Loughborough Folk Festival in 1976 by pointing out that a lot of folk in England, especially the south, had got fed up with Irish music and song. Not that there was anything wrong with the songs and tunes themselves; the problem was simply the degree of overkill. People seemed to think there must be some way to find 'new' traditional music and turned to the music of their own country or area. Now, in some parts of England, the ceilidh dance clubs are as popular as the folk clubs, with their presentations of English country dance music.

The extent of the Irish influence can be gauged by the fact that there were, and maybe still are, several folk groups on the Continent performing Irish, and sometimes Scottish, music and songs. One group I heard of from Copenhagen, called 'Paddy Doyle's', was comprised entirely of Danes with Aran sweaters who sang with lusty Irish accents. Germany has experienced this kind of thing more than other non-English-speaking countries in that she has a largely English-speaking army of occupation with a chain of messes and NAAFIs or PXs bringing in English-speaking acts. Because of the extremely bad taste left by the Hitler Youths ' misuse of German folk music there was a generation gap in the continuance of traditional German music and song which was easily filled by British and American imports. Also, because the fees across the North Sea were better than at home in the British Isles, many artists probably could not now exist as professionals without making trips to the Continent to keep them going. Over the latter half of the seventies, however. there has been a steady and, in Germany's case, courageous, move throughout the western continental countries to find their own music and song. One notable example of this is Alan Stivell, the major guest at the Edinburgh Folk Festival and a native of Brittany; and there are many other examples throughout Europe now.

Scotland has not been an exception in this reawakening of interest in home-grown music. Song has always been a strong factor in the Scots tradition, but since the revival of interest in folk music in the mid-fifties, instrumental music has not played such a noticeable part until recent years. Particularly obvious is the booming interest in fiddle and accordion clubs and Highland reel and Strathspey societies. Young musicians appear to be less aware of, or perhaps less keen to observe, the boundaries that existed between the traditional music of the pipes and other instruments, with the result that multi-instrumental groups like Silly Wizard, Battlefield (in their previous incarnation when they did not have a piper) and Ossian have all used pipe tunes set for other instruments to great effect. In a footnote in the May 1978 edition of the magazine *International Piper* the editor remarks: 'Both the Battlefield and Whistlebinkies use the bagpipe to excellent effect and what is more, the pipers are of a very professional standard. They also showed that it was quite unnecessary to venture out of the Scottish idiom to combine successfully with other instruments. Their renditions of Strathspeys, reels and jigs were first class.' (I reckon that just about says it all.)

Another aspect of the Scottish and UK folk scene is the continuing popularity of the folk festivals. Scotland now boasts over a dozen which, in relation to the number of folk clubs (as a guide to the size of potential audience), is a considerable number. Most of the Scots festivals are well established, having run for over four or five years, with Edinburgh, Glenfarg and Carrbridge as the babies. But why should festivals have retained their popularity in a scene that seems to be suffering a recession currently? Perhaps it is to do with the freewheeling atmosphere of the festivals – do what you want, when you want to do it – from which the informal sessions so vital to any folk festival spring, and added to which the official bill of fare is a bonus. The clubs' more regimented approach, with its lack of opportunity for a good crack without the audience disappearing to the bar, may be helping here – if we assume that all festival-goers are also club-goers. (I do not subscribe to the idea of an apparent club-festival dichotomy which one correspondent to *Folk News* in 1978 talked about. I think most folk would just accept that clubs and festivals are different in concept, leave it at that and get on and enjoy them while they can.)

The great physicist and philosopher, Heisenberg, propounded his well-known 'Uncertainty Principle' to show that in the atomic domain at least, the closer one tried to look at its tiny constituents, the

more difficult it became to pinpoint them. A broad everyday interpretation of this might be the phrase, 'What you gain on the
roundabouts, you lose on the swings' or, more simply, 'You can't win
them all'. Alternatively, what Heisenberg was saying was that the
observer must inevitably interact with the observed, which is more
succinct and less obvious. The ecologist might extend this to include
man's depredation of his surroundings. Whenever we interact with
the environment something has to give or change because of that
interaction.

This may seem distant from the subject of folk music, but we
should all, who are 'involved', be aware of our interference with
traditions whenever we 'do' something with them. The natural way
of things stopped when the moguls of Tin Pan Alley saw that they
could make a couple of bob out of this reawakened interest in folk
music. Money is a great leveller and might be termed a sibling to the
mother of invention. On the one hand there are careful academics
attempting to observe and preserve that which was and might not be
again, while on the other there are folk who shift the focal point from
the discreet intervention of the academic to the more public presentation of what has been academically recorded. The whole folk scene,
particularly the very public festivals and clubs, comes within that
latter category and should be aware of its role and sensitive to the
delicate nature of the web in which it finds itself. It should be
particularly aware of its own self-propagating nature inasmuch as
clubs spawn clubs in the image of themselves and so, like bureaucra-
cies, come to believe in themselves and forget what they are there to
serve.

The arbitrary nature of the folk scene today started off and spread
without help from big business in any form. Today, some twenty
years on, big business is not entirely exempt from blame. We have
crass commercial exploitation by entrepreneurs and others of the so
called tartan/white heather image of Scotland, and the media have to
carry their share of the blame for this. The amount of time devoted to
what most folk would call good folk music, song, dance, stories and
lore in general on our mass communication networks, is pathetically
small. Instead, we are bombarded with pap from all sides. It appears
that the only time STV come close to presenting arts programmes is
when the charter is up for scrutiny and renewal and they want to be

seen to be adhering to its terms. It is easy to sympathise to an extent with the commercial pressures under which the ITV networks exist – but not with 'Thingummyjig', that terrible piece of trash put out by STV (and described by one of the company's chiefs as 'an ethnic hooley'!) – and not with the BBC, the one lynchpin of communication one might hope would be above commercial pressure. As a non-profit organisation, for the BBC to attempt to compete with commercial stations is simply illogical. The BBC should be allowed to make good programmes without fear or favour. (I think it was Lord Reith who remarked that when the BBC entered the ratings game, it would have failed in its purpose.) A glimmer of hope was extended with the advent of Radio Scotland in 1978. John Pickles, the head of the new station, said in an interview on 'Spinning Wheel' (one of the old BBC programmes) that he wanted to get away from the above-mentioned tartan/white heather image with which the BBC had for long been associated. What happened next? Radio Forth's puerile purveyor of tartan trash was hired to work for the new station! And they wonder why people hold their hands up in despair.

* * * * *

I make no apology for dealing primarily with folk clubs and other manifestations of the folk world today. This is what I know best and I do believe it is important that the clubs should be aware of where it's at with regard to their role in the overall fabric of our culture. This form of presentation of folk music, dance and song may have been largely alien twenty years ago, but now that it is here to stay I think better use should be made of the infrastructure which exists (in an unwritten form) amongst the various organisations, to allow them to become more effective in their work of presenting the nation's culture to as broad an audience as possible. Particularly during the present economic unrest should not the clubs, as the first line in the public eye, be thinking hard about exactly what their role is and how best to achieve this role? I think so.

POSTSCRIPT

Glasclune and Drumlochy

HAMISH HENDERSON

[This poem is a product of the folk revival – it grew and developed as spoken (and sung) poetry at Edinburgh Festival readings in the mid-sixties. These took place mainly at the original Traverse Theatre building in the Lawnmarket, and in the Crown Bar (now demolished) in Lothian Street, where the E.U. Folksong Society held its reunions.

Right from the earliest period of the 'People's Festivals' in Edinburgh (1951, 1952, 1953) poetry readings were an integral part of the growing 'folk scene'. The first of these were organised by the late Alan Riddell, founder of *Lines Review*. Excerpts from Hugh MacDiarmid's 'A Drunk Man Looks at the Thistle' were given at the 1951 People's Festival ceilidh, between the rumbustious ballad singing of John Strachan and the vivacious piping sprees of John Burgess. Young poets were encouraged to contribute to these sessions. Much of the work of Alan Jackson and Tom Leonard has its ultimate origin in this particular creative blend of oral poetry and traditional Scottish song. Matt McGinn's work was also to a considerable extent inspired by it.

(Alan Jackson's version of 'The Minister to his Flock', an ancient orally transmitted joke which can be found in Richard M. Dorson's *Folk-Tales Told Around the World*, page 43, was given by him at one of the Traverse ceilidhs in 1963.

> Aye, ye're enjoyin' yoursels noo wi' your drinkin' and your women and your nights oot at the pictures, and never a thought given to the Word of God, and his great and terrible laws.

206

> But ye'll change your tune when ye're doon below in the fiery
> pit, and ye're burnin' and ye're sufferin', and ye'll cry: 'O Lord,
> Lord, we didna ken, we didna ken.' And the Lord in his infinite
> mercy will bend doon frae Heaven and say: 'Well, ye ken noo.'

This joke, which epitomises the barbaric black humour of Calvinist
Scotland, was energetically applauded by a predominantly English
youthful audience which assumed that it was by Alan himself – and
indeed it fell naturally into place between such poems as 'Knox' and
'Lord Save us, it's the Minister'. It appears – attributed to anon – in
Alan's collection *Well, Ye Ken Noo,* produced in Bristol with the aid of
the CND duplicator in 1963.)

'Glasclune and Drumlochy' is based on an historical tale which I
heard in Glenshee, Perthshire, when I was a child. The subject matter
is clearly blood-brother to many tales of Appallachian feuds. As
children we naturally believed the story to be true, and indeed it may
well be founded on fact.

The ruins of the castle of Glasclune are about three miles north-
west of Blairgowrie, home of the 'Stewarts of Blair'. Glasclune is
described in the *Ordnance Gazeteer of Scotland* (Edinburgh, 1884) as
'an ancient baronial fortalice on the border of Kinloch parish,
Perthshire, crowning the steep bank of a ravine at the boundary with
Blairgowrie parish. The stronghold of *the powerful family of Blair,* it
was once a place of considerable strength, both natural and artificial,
and is now represented by somewhat imposing ruins. ' The ruins
were decidedly less imposing when we played around them – and in
them – as children in the 1920s, and since then decay has proceeded
apace. Indeed, Glasclune has gradually become for me a symbol like
the mill which Hugh MacDiarmid apostrophises in 'Depth and the
Chthonian Image' (a long poem which is subtitled 'On looking at a
ruined mill and thinking of the greatest'):

> The mills o' God grind sma', but they
> In you maun crumble imperceptibly tae.

However, Glasclune is still there: the keep of Drumlochy, which bore
the brunt of cannon fire, had disappeared off the face of the earth.
(The Mains of Drumlochy is a farm.)

Glasclune appears once – and dramatically – in medieval Scottish history. It was the scene of a battle in 1392, when one of the sons of Alexander Stewart – son of Robert II, and well known to history as 'The Wolf of Badenoch' – made an incursion into Stormont and the Braes of Angus. This foray was a kind of curtain-raiser to the more famous Highland invasion of 1411, when Donald of the Isles, leading a large army of 'Katherans', was fought to a standstill at Harlaw. In Wynton's *Original Cronykil of Scotland* (Book IX, Chapter XIV) there is a graphic account in verse of the battle of Glasclune, including an episode in which a knight from Dundee called Sir Davy de Lyndesay speared a Highlander, and was himself wounded by the dying cateran who writhed up the spear-shaft and cut Lyndesay's boot and stirrup leather and his leg to the bone.

> Sua, on his hors he sittand than,
> Throw the body he strayk a man
> Wytht his spere down to the erde:
> That man hald fast his awyn swerd
> In tyl his neve, and wp thrawand
> He pressit hym, nocht agayn standand.
> That he wes pressit to the erd,
> And wylh a swake thare off his swerd
> The sterap lethire and the bute
> Thre ply or foure, abone the fute
> He straik the Lyndesay to the bane.
> That man na straike gave bot that ane
> For thare he deit: yeit nevirtheles
> That gude Lord thare wondil wes,
> And had deit thare that day,
> Had nochl his men had hym away
> Agane his wil out of that pres.

Wynton locates the battle at 'Gaskclune', but this is certainly the Glasclune of my childhood, for it is referred to as being in the Stermond (Stormont); furthermore Bower, in the *Scotichronicon*, locates the conflict in 'Glenbrereth', probably glen Brerachan, which is the same general area. Bower informs us that Walter Ogilvy, Sheriff of Angus, was slain *per Cateranos quorum caput fuit Duncanus Stewart filius don-ini Alexandri comitis de Buchan* (by caterans whose leader was Duncan Stewart, son of the lord Alexander, Earl of Buchan).

(It is interesting to note that it was a brother of this same Duncan, leader of the 'caterans', who as Earl of Mar led the Aberdeenshire army against Donald of the Isles at Harlaw. So much for the over-simplified view of these conflicts as being simply and solely between 'Highlands' and 'Lowlands'.)

My poem is, as it were, an echo of this old warfare, as it still remotely pulsates in the folk memory. The 'clannish confine' lies in jagged outline across Scottish history. I was thinking also, of course, of the millennial internecine conflict of humankind, which in our century bids fair to write *finis* to the 'haill clanjamfrie'. – The sung part of the poem is the ballad pastiche, and is in italics. The tune is a variant of 'Cam ye by Atholl'.]

From the summit of Cnoc-mahar
  I look on the laigh ...
On fat Strathmore, and its braw
  largesse of lochs;
Black Loch and White Loch, Fengus, Marlee, Clunie
  where the bolstered curlers come ...

But back I turn
northward, and stand at nightfall under Glasclune,
by the canyon cleft of the shaggy shabby Lornty
(the shaggy shabby, the dowdy, duddy Lornty)
that marked the clannish confine.

There were two castles,
two battled keeps, Drumlochy and Glasclune,
that kept a bloodfeud bienly on the boil.
They sat on their airse and they girned fell gyte at ither
('I'll paisley your fitt', 'I'll brackley your invereye')
... and atween, the scrogs of the dowdy duddy Lornty.
Drumlochy's laird was a slew-eye dye-blue bloodhound
who fought, as his sires had fought, with steel (cold steel!)
and said the other mugger couldn't take it.
But Glasclune knew six of that: he was progressive,
and to be in tune with the times was all his rage.

Now, one day he went out and bought a cannon
(a quare old toy unknown to the lad next door):
with this he gave Drumlochy a thorough pasting –
dang doon his wall, gave his stately pile the shakes:
in fact, blockbust him quite.

'The moral of this,' said Glasclune, with 'ill-concealed'
hidalgo satisfaction, 'is that Right
 – unready starter in the donnybrook stakes –
must still rise early to possess the field.'

Now wae's me Glasclune
  Glasclune and Drumlochy
They bashed ither blue
  By the back side o' Knockie.

Drumlochy focht fair,
  But Glasclune the deceiver
Made free wi' a firewark
  Tae blaw up his neebor.

Then shame, black shame, ay, shame on the bluidy Blairs!
  Shame on the Blairs, an' sic wuddifu races.
They think nae sin
  when they put the boot in
In the eyes of all ceevilized folk tae disgrace us.

Ochone Drumlochy
  Glasclune and Drumlochy –
Twa herts on ae shiv

  An' a shitten larach.